Grace to ALL

By Paul Gray
and the Grace to ALL team

Grace to ALL

By Paul Gray
and the Grace to ALL team

Printed and Electronic Versions
ISBN 978-1-956353-18-1
ISBN Ebook 978-1-956353-19-8
(Paul Gray/Motivation Champs)

The book was printed
in the United States of America.

Special discount may apply on bulk quantities.
Please contact Paul Gray to order.
gracetoallwithpaulgray@gmail.com

WARMUP ACT

Most every weekend, for eight years, Paul Gray provided his audience with a buffet of great jazz musicians and their music. At Paul Gray's Jazz Place, you would be inspired by toe-tapping rhythms, melodies, and harmonies that would lift your vibes and put a smile on your face.

People would leave, saying, "I felt like the musicians were on fire, and I was too!"

During a three-hour performance, you'd hear Paul introduce extraordinarily gifted performers, intersperse tidbits about their history, peers, contributions to the world of Jazz and give the audience the opportunity to interact with them in a very personal way. You would experience "oneness" and community with contemporary performers who were carrying on the tradition of a unique and wonderful musical tradition.

These musicians played different styles of Jazz, had individual ways of expressing themselves via improvisation, and uniquely demonstrated the joys and synergy of creating in real-time with a TEAM of peers.

In much the same way, in *Grace to ALL*, you'll hear Paul introduce you to an eclectic group of Spiritual 'improvisors' who will inspire you in a "jazzy" way that's much different than a "staid, rigid, play-by-the-note religious doctrinal system."

In these pages, you'll meet and have the opportunity to connect and interact with contemporary "mystics"—those who personally hear from God—just as YOU can! They each have different styles and ways of expressing themselves via spiritual improvisation, and they uniquely demonstrate the joys and synergy of creating in real-time with a TEAM of peers ... who may eventually include you!

Prepare to join those who have been "set on fire and are glowing with pure light" and be prepared to say, "I AM too!"

INTRODUCTION

What you're about to read in this book will help you THRIVE!

Thrive: grow or develop well or vigorously; flourish; prosper; bloom.

This is not a "religious" book. It's not a "self-help" book. It doesn't contain "5 steps to a better life." It is a book about spirituality ... which many times is quite the opposite of "religion." You're about to meet a Team of people who are on a journey ... just like you. Their lives are all about helping people thrive ... thrive in ways you may never have dreamed possible! Put your checkbook and credit cards away. You won't need them. Your new team is about giving, not taking.

To start with, ask yourself this question: "Do I want things to be better for me and my loved ones?" We all want that, but life has a way of beating some of us down, stealing our dreams, killing our desires, destroying our joy, and even leaving us without hope. That may have happened to you or to someone whom you very much love and care for.

Your team members have all experienced to some degree a life without hope and experienced to a great degree a life filled with real hope, expectation of the best! We're learning that real hope is not wishful thinking; it's confident expectation based on true reality. The reason for that is grace.

You've maybe known someone named Grace, or heard the word at church, or sang Amazing Grace, or said 'Grace' at a meal. The KEY to thriving in every area of your life (spiritual, financial, social, physical, etc.) is to realize that Grace is a real person who already knows you and wants more than anything for you two to thrive in a relationship that is better than you've ever dared imagine is possible!

Grace is the leader of your team! You don't have to say any magic words, jump through any hoops, beg, squall or bawl to make up for your past, take a class or prove your sincerity to know Grace. Grace is closer than the air you breathe. Grace knew you before you were born, has always known you and always will know you, and loves you unconditionally, warts and all!

I've read scores of 'God books.' I've studied and taught the Bible. I was involved in traditional churches since the first week of my life.

I have a closet full of tee shirts that all say "Been there, done that, disappointed." Many of the books I've read have some merit. Scripture certainly has merit—when read through the lens of Truth (another name for Grace). I've known wonderful people in religious settings and had some good experiences. But I never met Grace in any of those.

There are a plethora of names people have for Deity. You've heard them: God, Almighty, Lord, Jehovah, Creator; those are just a few.

Jesus was the first person in recorded history to call God 'Father, and He taught and showed us that Father was nothing like religion portrayed as its version of *god*.

Jesus told us that if we'd seen Him, we'd seen The Father, that He and The Father are exactly alike. And He showed us a person and life like no other … a life that thrived!

The night before religious and political thugs killed Him, Jesus said, "Don't worry, I'm going to send you another one exactly like me … only invisible. One that will live in you, never leave you, has always loved you, is for you, and saves you from whatever obstacles life throws your way."

Jesus kept His word! The One Jesus was talking about is Grace.

Oh, I know you've probably heard all sorts of other names or descriptions of Grace. You may be a little on edge because you're hearing what sounds like a feminine name. Actually, the name Jesus used (he spoke Aramaic) is feminine. Don't let that throw you. Grace is spirit (neither male nor female). A spirit, the Spirit.

Throughout this book, *Grace to ALL*, I use the name Grace intentionally.

My purpose, like the people you're going to read about in the following pages, is to introduce you to someone who has always known you, someone who is closer than a twin brother or twin sister. Someone who is totally good, who has your best interest at heart, who constantly makes your life better, who empowers you to thrive, and who absolutely guarantees you that One Day, All things will be made right for All people, and All people will enjoy Grace forever!

The really Good News is, that Day is now! Most of us just don't know it yet. But you're getting ready to! In these next pages, you will:

Meet the over-the-top extraordinary person: Grace!

Come to know Grace intimately and infinitely!

Partner with Grace in changing your life for the better and see your dreams manifest!

Experience the kind of life you always dreamed about.

Connect with real-life Grace people who will encourage, inspire, motivate, and love you … just like Grace! You will be inspired and encouraged by the *Grace to ALL* Team who, like me and you, are all at different places in their journey.

Those whom you'll read about believe, share, teach, and mentor their small (and ever-expanding) groups the following:

- The Pure Grace of God to ALL people
- God's unconditional Love for ALL people
- Jesus is the Savior of ALL people
- God is Pure Light with no trace of darkness
- God is in ALL people
- God is Pure Goodness and Good to ALL people
- Grace is God's continual expression of Love working ALL things for the good of ALL and bringing about Ultimate Restoration of ALL to our original genesis—made in God's image and likeness.

A helpful acrostic to clarify our current working definition of Grace is:

G — God's

R — Relational

A — Agape (Unconditional Love, inclusion, and acceptance of ALL people)

C — Christ

E — Exact (Christ is the Exact representation of the Father. Anything we see, hear, or read in Scripture or elsewhere that is contrary to Christ's Life and His revelation of God, who is an all-good Father; Unconditionally Loving Father; Pure Light with no trace of darkness, and totally good to ALL people, is a perverted and distorted perception of the Only True God)

The *Grace to ALL* Team you will soon read about each have different backgrounds, different former denominational affiliations, different thoughts about when and how God will bring about the Ultimate

Restoration of ALL. They each have different personalities and ways of sharing and proclaiming God's grace to all.

I have interviewed all of them on my podcast, *Grace to ALL* (found at www.gracetoall.net), and I confidently expect that each of them can be a tremendous blessing to you and your friends as you Grow in Grace. Some of them may live in your city or state! All of them are accessible via the internet.

My confident hope and expectation is that you, your friends, and relatives will "connect" with one or more of them and perhaps become part of the *Grace to ALL* Team! In the information section at the end of the book, you'll find information about their contact info, videos, podcasts, courses, and other materials.

In between each featured story, I've compiled short snippets of "aha" moments where I've become aware of the world's doctrinal system of lies about God, ourselves, and ALL people. I share them with you, not to try to get you to believe what I believe but to set you free from the lies of organized religion.

Before you meet your new teammates, I want to relate a story that's foundational for seeing the power of Grace. Hundreds of years ago, there was a man with a really funny name—Zerubbabel. I don't know how to pronounce that, and I love nicknames—so I just call him "Zeb." Zeb had a ton of obstacles in his life, and try as he might, he couldn't overcome them. His life was like a bad dream. One day, he woke up (literally and spiritually), and an angel showed him a lampstand of gold, with a bowl on the top, and told him that it would yield to him a ceaseless supply of oil (oil was code name for the 'Spirit of God').

The angel said, "God knows you have this great mountain of human obstacles that you can't overcome and you've lost all hope. You've tried with all your might, and you know it's not going to change by your might, nor your power ... but God says it will change by His Spirit!"

Zeb finished that conversation by saying, "Cheer up! God is going to level that mountain of human obstacles and turn it into a mere molehill! And when He's finished, all the people will shout loudly, 'Grace, Grace to it!'"

As a result of what you will see and experience through the people you're about to meet, you, too, will learn to go through your life confidently and excitedly with the attitude of "Grace, Grace to it!"

Contents

Introduction to "Grace I Ams"

Sandwiched between each of the following articles about *Grace to ALL* folks, you will find "Grace I Ams." The purpose of each of these "Grace I Ams" is to help you know, experience, and internalize the truth of what The Creator of the Universe says is true about you.

To start with, it's ALL Good! It's ALL Good now, and it's ALL Good forever!

This process will require an open mind, heart, and spirit because virtually everyone has a false concept of what God thinks about them. We have false concepts about what scripture words actually mean … that alone has distorted and perverted all the Really Good things The Creator says are true about you.

The scripture word translated as "confess" doesn't bring to mind a positive experience, does it? IT SHOULD! The actual word means "To agree with, to say the same thing as."

The Only True God, Jesus, Papa, and Grace want us to let go of our false concepts about ourselves (and other people) and instead embrace, believe, and live from the truth of who we truly are!

While all the Grace I AMs you're going to read about come from Scripture, I'm purposely not giving you the scripture references. The reason is that when most of us start to see them, our spirit goes "Yes!" but our mind says, "Show me where that is in the Bible." Then we read a version that may be poorly translated; we remember what someone else with an agenda said that verse "clearly means," and/or we read the footnotes or commentary that give us what someone else with an agenda thinks it means.

I want you to listen to the Teacher within you—The Spirit of Grace and Truth—the Mind of Christ. Call the Teacher whatever you'd like, and ask, "Is this true? Is God really this good? Am I really who God says I am here?" Then *listen.*

You will come to recognize the Teacher's Voice! Your spirit will resonate with The Spirit in you! The Spirit of Christ will confirm to your spirit the stunning truths about you! Then agree! Take sides with your Creator and begin to really live!

The Grace I AMs are here specifically to help anyone who's ever experienced mountains of human obstacles: hard times, troubles, rejection, fear, hurtful words, anxiety, anger, mild or severe depression, or living seemingly without hope. In other words, most everyone!

Of course, we don't ignore negative situations and circumstances, but it's never helpful to dwell on, repeat, or catastrophize our negative situations. Words have great power! Every time we speak about our negative situation, we experience it again! Our goal is to not only change our minds but also our words, especially our self-talk!

So, to all our human obstacles, we say and apply Grace ... Grace to it! Thank God this is a proven, powerful way to change ... first, our mindset, then our words, then our situation.

Perhaps the most amazing and impactful Grace truth you will ever grasp comes from this statement by Jesus' closest friend, John, who knew Jesus better than anyone:

"So now, with us awakening to our full inclusion in this love union, everything is perfect! Its completeness is not compromised in contradiction. Our confident conversation echoes this fellowship even in the face of crisis; because, as Jesus is, so are we in this world—our lives are mirrored in him. We are as blameless in this life as Jesus is! This perfect love union is the source of our confidence."

As you come to know and believe the love that God/Grace has unveiled within you, you awaken to the full inclusion of your love union, where everything is perfect!

What happens to you, what goes on around you, your circumstances and situation may not seem perfect, but within you—in your Secret Place—you ARE perfect, just like Jesus, the Son of God, God Himself!

Take a few minutes in your secret place with your primary Teammates, Jesus, Papa, and Grace, and say (out loud if you can) several times slowly, "I Am Just Like Jesus Is!"

MUCH MORE!
(You're gonna LOVE this!)

This book, *Grace to ALL*, is about a vision that is MUCH MORE than I ever dreamed about when I started the *Grace to ALL* podcasts and then began to write the book in hopes of connecting people.

Apostle Paul often writes about how "God's Grace will accomplish MUCH MORE than your greatest request, your most unbelievable dream, and exceed your wildest imagination! He will outdo them all, for his miraculous power constantly energizes you."

Here's the MUCH MORE than I initially dreamed or imagined: All profits from the sale of this book are 100% given to solo parents (single Moms and Dads) who need financial help.

The second person featured in this book is Mike Popovich, who founded the "Inspire 100" ministry that helps solo parents and their children. Mike grew up the youngest of seven kids in a single-parent family and knows first-hand what the experience is like.

Our "The Grace Restoration Team" was inspired by "Inspire 100." People from around the United States are now part of this team.

I've found that most of us have a desire to be part of something bigger than ourselves, to be part of a team that works together for a compelling cause. There's something very special about the feeling we get from making a real difference in the lives of people in need. I think that's directly linked to our all being children of God, participating in the Divine Nature!

There is a myriad of worthy causes that help a plethora of people with needs. You may already have one or more that touches your heart. You may also be interested in partnering with us to help Single Moms and their children who are among the most vulnerable in our society.

There are over 14,000,000 single parents in the United States, most of whom are sole providers for the more than 22,000,000 children who are being raised in single-parent homes.

These 36,000,000 single parents and their kids can feel abandoned, rejected, judged, stuck, and without hope. We can't help them all, but we can help some! Our Team provides unconditional Love and Grace in tangible ways: Financial, spiritual, and relational.

My daughter became a single mom in 2009 when her twenty-nine-year-old husband died of cancer, leaving her and her three-year-old son behind. Fortunately, our daughter had loving financial, spiritual, and relational support from her church and both sides of her family.

Sadly, many widows and other single parents don't have much, if any such, support. Many single parents work more than one job to support themselves and their kids, and some have trouble keeping those jobs because they are the only family member who can stay home with a sick child. Needless to say, these parents can be physically, emotionally, spiritually, and financially drained.

We can't help them all, but we can help some!

Our Grace Restoration Team consists of people across the country who provide financial help via tax-deductible donations. Any team member can nominate a single parent for help.

We provide many nominees with immediate financial help. We provide optional, no-strings-attached spiritual help in the form of Unconditional Love, Grace, Inclusion, and Acceptance through online contact, books (*Grace to ALL* and others), podcasts, videos, and online groups that fit their schedules. There is no fee for any of these resources. Whenever possible, we help them connect with groups in their communities.

In the section immediately following the guest profiles you're about to read, we've profiled a few examples of those to whom we've provided thousands of dollars in help in the first few months of partnering with people like you to do MUCH MORE!

DRUM ROLL, PLEASE!

You're about to get to know the *Grace to ALL* Team, and you may possibly team up with some of us! We'd love to get to know you!

Sprinkled between each of the following articles about *Grace to ALL* folks, you will find a variety of short inspirational pieces that will help you know, experience, and internalize the truth of what The Creator of the Universe says is true about you!

DON KEATHLEY
From Religion to Revelation

"IF YOU SIT IN CHURCH TOMORROW, hearing another message of conformational bias, aka the same old boring message you have heard a kazillion times, only with a different title, and you know inside that something is just not adding up, and that there is more to all this, you're right ...

"That's the first step in awakening out of a religious stupor and entering into a life outside the religious box and into the life you have always had in Christ but were asleep to its reality." ~Don Keathley

"Why would we want hell to be true?" Former evangelical pastor Don Keathley has grappled with that all-important question and no longer believes that religious lie. In fact, he teaches and writes about when and where the lie originated!

Don Keathley, President of Global Grace Seminary, was born in Battle Creek, Michigan, and lived there until he graduated from Marshall High School. He is married to his wife, Linda, and they have two married daughters, Janell and Shawn, and four grandchildren. Don has pastored churches in Michigan, Wisconsin, and Florida and is the retired founding pastor of Grace Point Community Church in Houston. Don has experienced many awakenings to the revelation of pure grace and the inclusion of the Father. He sees many people across the globe waking up, and Don has now moved his ministry online to what he calls the Digital Cathedral. Being online has expanded his ability to teach and reach this much wider audience awakening to the revelation of true grace. He also has a Facebook group under the name Don Keathley Ministries, where many like-minded people traveling this same road can gather to share and learn.

Don Keathley was a pastor in what is known as "evangelicalism" for many years. He was educated in the traditions of all the well-known doctrines and has taught and preached on them himself, including one called eternal conscious torment (what is more commonly known as hell, an underground dark afterlife where if you do not love God back or repent of your sin while alive, God's response will be to supernaturally keep you alive and torment you forever).

Over the past several years, Don has been on a journey of discovering truth. All of it is flowing out of the depth of God's love. He says this doctrine of hell is one of the biggest sacred cows in the church, but it runs contrary to the nature of the Father. If you were to go to any mall, you can find people who will know nothing about the love of God, but they will all know about this place called hell. As a pastor, Don has seen the mental health effects that it has caused to good people who have been kept in bondage of fear.

All of this began to change one day when he heard the Spirit of the Father ask him, "Don, how much would your two daughters have to do to you for you to eternally torment them and send them to a place where they would endlessly twist and burn with no hope of ever getting out?"

Don instantly saw that such action is not the nature of the Father! It is not found in Jesus, who is the exact image and representation of the God we do not see. He wanted to know how this false teaching made its way into our church, to begin with.

Don teaches that the hell doctrine has been in the church for a long-enough time but was not there originally. Many have been taught it and never questioned it. Those who do are ostracized and called false teachers. The common response to anyone who does give it actual thought is, "If there is no hell, nobody will serve God," but as Don has learned, the reality is, the opposite happens because it is the goodness of God that leads people to repentance.

The religious system is extraordinarily successful at creating a problem and then becoming the solution. Don calls it the "Problem + Solution = Sale" system. Many in this system will agree that God is love but then quickly follow it up with "He is also just!"

In fact, God's justice flows from His love. Mercy triumphs over Judgement. One question Don believes we should all ask ourselves is, "Why would we want hell to be true?" And from there, begin to contemplate the reality. Ask the questions like "If God is love, and love keeps no record of wrong, how could He then do the opposite and keep a record?" or "How could a God who says 'Love never fails' fail to save every lost person?"

After hearing God ask the question about his daughters and subsequently being motivated by love and the desire for truth, Don began to thoroughly research and debunk the very origin of hell. He asked questions like "Where did the teaching originate? How did the word 'hell' make its way into our English Bible translations?" He found that the more literal translations, like Youngs' Literal Concordance, don't even have the word 'hell' in them. They use four other words—Gehenna, Sheol, Hades, and Tartarus—and they each mean something totally different. He wanted to know how this dark teaching made its way into our churches today.

Dig into "Hell's Illusion," a six-part video series on YouTube, or buy the book of the same name, and you will find most of your questions answered!

Listen to Dr. Don teach Sunday mornings at 10 a.m. Central Time (U.S.) via Done Keathley Ministries on Facebook or YouTube. You'll soon find yourself becoming part of an ever-expanding culture of Grace that is rapidly manifesting around the world!

You can go even deeper on Wednesday evenings at 7 p.m. Central Time (U.S.) and check out Don's "Secret Place" via Don Keathley Ministries on Facebook.

Grace I AM #1

This book and the lives highlighted in it is all about transformation: being transformed from something that wasn't working as we had hoped into something that works better than we ever imagined!

The primary scripture author about hope is a man named Paul. Originally, his name was Saul, and by his own admission, he was the "worst sinner" on the face of the earth. Grace is all about radical changes! Paul became known as the Apostle of Grace and wrote two-thirds of the New Testament!

Paul had the absolute best religious pedigree in a nation that was all about religion. He came from a very religious family, went to private religious schools, studied under the best religious teacher, rose to the top of the religious community, was a leader of religious leaders. He kept all the rules—without fault. And he was an absolute jerk!

He was a religious maniac who was on a mission to persecute, kill, and destroy those who believed differently than he did. He was stubborn, angry, judgmental, mean-spirited, hateful, vindictive, ruthless, and his concept of *god* was just like him!

Then, one day, Grace appeared to Saul, showed him the Light of Truth, and totally changed his life from religious negativity to spiritual positivity. Grace introduced Saul to 'The only True God,' who was a polar opposite of Saul's concept of an angry *god*, and surprise … surprise, who had lived IN Saul from before he was born!

Saul (now named Paul) grasped this personal revelation so well that he immediately changed his life's mission. He went from mean-spirited religious fanatic to sweet-spirited Grace who introduced 'The only True God' to people who started forming little Grace Restoration Teams all over the world! Instead of taking credit for this transformation himself, Paul proclaimed The Truth: "By Grace, I Am what I Am!"

The Only True God personally mentored Paul for some thirteen years in the Arabian desert. As a result of God's revelation to him, Paul began teaching and writing about the greatest spiritual mystery of all time—God has always been in every person. Not separate, not distant, not "out there," not judging and ready to punish the slightest infraction of the law. Just the opposite! Paul told us, "There is a divine mystery—a secret surprise that has been concealed from the world for generations, but now it's being revealed, unfolded, and manifested for ALL to experience. Living within you is the Christ who floods you with the expectation of glory! This mystery of Christ, embedded within us, becomes a heavenly treasure chest of hope filled with the riches of glory for his people, and God wants everyone to know it!

"Christ is our message! We preach to awaken hearts and bring every person into the full understanding of truth. It has become my inspiration and passion in ministry to labor with a tireless intensity, with his power flowing through me, to present to ALL people the revelation of their being perfect in Jesus Christ."

Paul also wrote—drawing on his very personal experience and what Christ told him was true about ALL people: "This is the wonderful message that is being spread everywhere, powerfully changing hearts throughout the earth, just like it has changed you! Every believer of this good news bears the fruit of eternal life as they experience the reality of God's grace.

"And we pray that you would be energized with all his explosive power from the realm of his magnificent glory, filling you with great hope. Your hearts can soar with joyful gratitude when you think of how God made you worthy to receive the glorious inheritance freely given to us by living in the light. He has rescued us completely from the tyrannical rule of darkness and has translated us into the kingdom realm of his beloved Son. For in Christ all our sins are canceled, and we have been set free from our former way of life!"

Like Paul, you are going to become awakened to The Good News about who you really are, always have been, and always will be! You're going to see and love and embrace the real you that you've maybe never met before!

You, the real you, are amazing! God's Amazing Grace—Grace personified—grace in person, in you, has made you perfect! You are embarking on the inexhaustible adventure of knowing who God really is and who you really are!

Take a few minutes in your secret place with your primary Teammates, Jesus, Papa, and Grace, and say (out loud if you can)

several times slowly, "I am who I am by the Grace of God!"

MIKE POPOVICH
Seeing the Impossible Manifest

If you ever have the wonderful experience of spending some time with Mike Popovich, you'll often hear him say, "It's that simple!" Mike experiences and teaches about God freely giving (putting in our hearts) us the desires of our hearts, and then giving (effortlessly bringing them into existence from the unseen to the seen) them to us for our continued enjoyment.

He has always been an entrepreneur and has utilized his technical and business skills to create several successful companies with his wife, Barbara. Mike is a dynamic leader in both business and ministry, who received his B.S. in Aeronautical Engineering from the United States Air Force Academy and subsequently served as an AF Officer for five years. He has spent his entire life studying the magnificence of the human design and how scientific principles are supported by Scripture. He has a great gift of showing people how Quantum Science is also Quantum Spirituality.

As the founder of Freedom Ministries, Mike has spoken to tens of thousands of people around the world in business and ministry settings, blending science and Scripture. His practical teachings help people accomplish things they never thought possible, heal their minds and bodies, and live in loving relationships.

Mike experienced life in a single-parent home from his early grade school years. He and his siblings learned first-hand the dynamics of having a hard-working, dedicated mom who provided for her family on her own. As a result of his childhood experiences and learning of countless similar situations, Mike and Barb started "Inspire 100," initially including 100 individuals who contributed $100 a month for the specific purpose of helping single moms. "Inspire 100" has grown exponentially, including serving single parents and children all over the world.

At the beginning of most of Mike's weekly online messages, he relates stories of solo parents and their families whom they have blessed financially, emotionally, physically, and spiritually that week! Here's a sample of Mike's awareness and teaching: "I AM is the Cry of Victory.

"From the very beginning of Scripture, we see the journey of the firstborn, which is our flesh, to realizing our true identity, a child of God.

"From the beginning, you were God's idea. Starting in Genesis 1, in the beginning, God created Elohim—One God descending into many parts. God dispersed himself into all of us, the many parts of the body of Christ. The writers of Scripture did not see 'the fall' as man guilty of something. They saw it as God's divine plan. God descended into our limited flesh and body of death, God incarnated man, so that we can learn to become God. We experienced the weakness of flesh, we thought we were limited in power, but we come into the full realization of the unlimited power and love of God within us. The last enemy that will be destroyed is death. We will even conquer death itself, which is the ultimate triumph and victory. All Scripture describes this journey from flesh to the unlimited love and power of the Spirit of God within us.

"When we experience limitation, doubt, and all the experiences of man, we ultimately have revelation that the love and unlimited power of God within gives us victory in every situation. When you find yourself in a situation you don't enjoy, there is no adverse judgment or guilt you should feel. Love keeps no record of wrong.

"Christ, the very love and creative power of God, is within you. When you think on things that are not lovely, you are using your imagination, the very wisdom and power of God, in the wrong way. When we say there is no guilt in Christ, it does not mean to just ignore what you have done. What I am saying is, use the saving love and power within you to redeem and restore the situation. Use the unlimited power of the saving anointing within you to bring the situation to victory.

"You can envision life exactly how you would like the situation to turn out, a win-win for all the parties. Jesus Christ, which means 'I AM within that saves,' will burn up the current situation, and all of creation will bend and shape and form to what you are imagining within. There are no limits to what you envision and experience within, which is I AM. All the militaries of the world and governments of the world cannot stop God. You can trust God within to bring you right into what you are experiencing within in your imagination.

"Most our thoughts and emotions are on autopilot. Ninety-five percent of what people think and feel are just rehearsals of past thoughts and emotions. We are instructed to renew our minds daily. Have the mind of Christ. If you find yourself in a situation you no longer desire to experience, I don't care how impossible it may seem, have the mind of Christ. See yourself and life exactly how you would like it to be. Experience it as if it is real right now; this is I AM—the cry of victory in every situation. You will find that all of creation responds to what you are imagining within. Every knee and everything will bow to the creative power within you.

"I AM is the cry of victory. When you see life exactly how you would like it to be within, this is the unlimited love and creative power of God. Nothing can stop it! You can trust it. You can work out your salvation with fear and trembling, which means you will experience the willpower and glory of God within with awe-struck wonder and amazement."

Grace I AM #2

Once we know we're just like Jesus (don't worry if you're not quite there yet; Grace will reveal and confirm it to you!), then it's imperative that we know what Jesus is really like!

Jesus told all the people of His day (especially religious people), "Not a single one of you know my Father or me!"

To my great embarrassment, after twenty years of being a pastor, I found out that was true about me! I knew some things I thought were true about God, but not only did I not know God, most of the things I thought were true about God weren't true at all! I've been ecstatic ever since to see that the negative ideas I had about *god* of religion were polar opposites of what The Only True God is like! Whew!

So, where do we start in knowing and experiencing God and discerning the difference between The Only True God, as Jesus calls the Father, and the false, perverted perception of an angry, punitive, distant, aloof, list-keeping, retributive *god* of religion?

We start with the primary essence of God—as revealed to us by Jesus' closest friend, John, who tells us, "We have come to know and believe the love that God has unveiled within us. God is love. Love is who God is; to live in this place of conscious, constant love, is to live immersed in God and to feel perfectly at home in his indwelling. Love never brings fear, for fear is always related to punishment. But love's perfection drives the fear of punishment far from our hearts. Whoever walks constantly afraid of punishment has not reached love's perfection."

Take a few minutes in your secret place with your primary Teammates, Jesus, Papa, and Grace, and say (out loud if you can) several times slowly, "I am Just Like Jesus Is. I Am Perfect Love!"

PAUL ANDERSON-WALSH
Adding Conditions Negates Love!

> *"They say that we are what we choose to believe we are. I say that you are more than you can believe or see right now. Believe in you, and you'll soon discover that it is not that seeing is believing, but rather believing is seeing."*
>
> *~Paul Anderson-Walsh*

Paul Anderson-Walsh lives in London, England, and is a co-founder of the Center for Inclusive leadership. He is a broadcaster, an inspirational speaker, and the founder and director of The Grace Project. He is a well-respected commentator who is often called upon by the BBC. He is a regular contributor at Premiere radio. He travels internationally as a highly regarded keynote speaker and teacher. He has collaborated with many in his travels in the U.S., including Steve McVey and Grace Walk Ministry/Quantum Life.

Paul is also a learning and development practitioner, and his unique gift is being able to communicate to people their self-worth and expand their horizons. He has been teaching identity in Christ for many years. He believes that in addition to teaching the believer's identity in Christ, we are also focusing on helping those who don't yet have a revelation of their 'in-Christness.'

Many of us have come to know and believe that God is Love. Love is not just what God does; it is the very essence of who He IS. Paul helps us understand that although we say those words, we may not know what they actually mean. Agape means unconditional love, but Paul has found in his own life, and with his teaching others about their Christ identity, that making a slight twist in that wording has helped people to get that understanding.

Walsh teaches that when we use the term 'unconditional love,' people who have dealt with a lot of rejection can automatically make a presupposition that there is conditionality to it. The term 'unconditional love' can imply that something can be added to it or subtracted from it. However, by simply saying "Love is unconditional," it can seem more inclusive to all. Paul simply says, "Love is unconditional … it includes all and has no conditions."

Paul loves to experience synchronicity with like-minded, like-spirited friends. He often talks about his special friendship with Steve McVey, who lives in Florida. Although they are separated by an Ocean, they regularly visit via social media and always learn from each other. He describes humility as not about us thinking less of ourselves, but instead thinking about ourselves less. Being humble and open to learning brings unity in the body and a sense of community in Christ that transcends the borders of nations.

Paul Anderson-Walsh is quick to mention how the grace and inclusion of Christ easily resonates in his work in the corporate world. He has had the privilege of teaching leaders in large corporate banking environments, including Bank of America and Bloomberg. In these situations, he seeks to help clients create an environment in which people can be their best selves. He teaches corporate leadership how to create a culture of love in which people can live in a psychologically safe work environment where they can trust their leaders and be trusted.

The gospel of inclusion gives us all a sense of emotional belonging in the corporate world as in all of life. Paul knows and teaches that Christ included everyone in His redemption, and He loves all mankind. In corporate settings, he prioritizes helping people understand love that is unconditional. He knows that religion tends to be motivated by exclusion and separation, so his teaching is focused on life ... not religion.

Christ in Paul will always appeal to the Christ in others, even if they are not conscious of it yet. He seeks to remove the lines of separation and exclusion and to teach people that they are completely loved. As a result, he often sees Christ in them begin to emerge and flow naturally. He sees people gain greater confidence in who they are, which results in improved employee morale and soaring production. Once people learn they are loved, respected, and appreciated by God, they tend to flourish in all areas of their lives.

Last Christmas, Paul referenced Luke 2:14 and wrote: "Now is the time for peace on Earth and goodwill to all men–It surely is! What a beautiful, unspoiled word goodwill is. It struck me that this little verse from the scriptures is the very essence of the inclusive workplace. To be an includer, we need to have and maintain a disposition of goodwill.

"Imagine what our workplaces would look and feel like if they were characterized by expressions of friendlessness and service to one another.

"Imagine if nobody regarded their status as being anything, but instead served one another.

"This is precisely the vision that is presented to us in the Christmas story: goodwill by us all to us all—not just by some to some—and perennial goodwill not seasonal.

"In the inclusive organization, goodwill is something that you experience always and in all-ways not just at Christmas; it is about the sharing of eternal presence more than the giving of annual presents."

Grace I AM #3

In knowing and experiencing God and discerning the difference between the only true God, as Jesus calls the Father, and the false, perverted perception of an angry, punitive, distant, aloof, list-keeping, retributive *god* of religion, it's imperative that we know that God IS Grace! Grace is not a doctrine, not a concept, not a dogma. God IS Grace! Jesus personally taught a man named Paul, who then wrote to us, "The grace of God has appeared, bringing salvation to all people!" Grace is a person—Christ. The Spirit of Christ —Grace—lives in you! Grace is the antidote and answer to all our negative situations, the most powerful 'medicine' there is!

For a brief introduction to seeing how this works, let's look at Jesus. Not the historical, textbook, religious Jesus that's sort of a mascot for religious people; rather, the REAL Jesus—Grace personified—who is an example of (not for) you!

In Jesus' greatest time of trouble, facing the most brutal physical beating ever, the greatest rejection ever, the most hurtful accusations, lies and slander ever, the greatest embarrassment ever, and ultimate physical death, Jesus chose (in His mind) JOY! 'Joy' and 'Grace' are very closely related. They both come from the same Greek root word!

Before you say "Even if Jesus did choose joy, He's God … I could never do that," remember, we're starting to experience a totally new paradigm, one of actually believing the truth that (as written by Jesus' best friend, John), "As Jesus was here on earth, so are you!"

We'll continue fleshing that out, but for now, look at how Jesus faced the worst of the worst of the worst: "We look away from the natural realm and we focus our attention and expectation onto Jesus who birthed faith within us and who leads us forward into faith's perfection. His example is this: Because his heart was focused on the joy of knowing that you would be his, he endured the agony of the cross and conquered its humiliation, and now sits exalted at the right hand of the throne of God!"

No matter what we have experienced in the past or will ever experience, when we know The Truth, we can change our mindset and move from negative to positive and focus our attention and expectation on the best positive outcome we can even imagine!

As you come to know and believe the love that God/Grace has unveiled within you, you awaken to the full inclusion of your love union, where everything is perfect, and you start to see that what happens to you, what goes on around you, your circumstances and situation may not seem perfect, but within you, in your Secret Place, you are perfect, just like Jesus, the Son of God, God Himself!

Take a few minutes in your secret place with your primary Teammates, Jesus, Papa, and Grace, and say (out loud if you can) several times slowly, "I Am Just Like Jesus Is. I Am choosing Joy!"

RICHARD MURRAY
No Hatefulness Here

"God is not dread!" ~Richard Murray (You may need to read that again carefully!)

Richard Murray is an attorney—a career not normally known for a lot of 'God hugs,' but even there, Richard admits he witnesses God's goodness in action. He has seen Him soften a judge's heart to mercy. And he has seen perfect strangers help someone out of a jam in the courtroom because 'something moved them.' He says, "God is in it all, extending His kindness toward us. He cannot help it. It is who God is."

Richard says, "Goodness is the very nature and true essence of our God. It is the goodness of God that leads us to repentance and to come alive to the Christ dwelling within us." Richard Murray's journey into the all-inclusive grace of God leaves him captivated by this goodness. And he will never believe anything about God that is not consistent with Him being only good.

Awakening for this Southern defense attorney started at a local Baptist church when he was twenty-nine years old during a very difficult season in his life. It was there that Richard encountered God's irresistible grace, and he 'received Jesus.' "I got saved in the parking lot of a Cracker Barrel restaurant," he says, and although that sounds like the title to a country song, for Richard, it was where his life would change. He started his journey like a tiny, flickering flame, but God began a work that continued to burn ever brighter within him, fueled by the love of Abba Father.

Joy is exactly what Richard remembers experiencing in his own salvation story. "My pearl of great value was to remain locked and loaded on His character." But this joy would soon be vexed when he began hearing messages of wrath and hellfire while attending that same Baptist church. They no longer rang true. The pastor he had known did not even sound like himself through Richard's opened ears.

To Richard, these messages also felt contrary to the nature of the god he was experiencing personally. It certainly was not the father he was experiencing who could torment anyone in a place called hell.

Soon after this, he describes a pivotal moment that helped him move beyond this image when he attended the Toronto revival meetings. People prayed for him at the revival. He remembers coming under the weight of the Spirit of God and, in surrendering to it, simply falling to the floor. While on the floor, the Lord began to take him back to his childhood.

When in High School, Richard wrestled. He had an amazing coach who took him under his wing and 'fathered' him in many ways. He coached Richard to be a warrior and showed him what he was made of. Unfortunately, Richard's family moved, and although he continued wrestling, it was without the leadership of his first coach. It was there he would face the biggest wrestling match of his life, feeling nervous about facing a 'gorilla' of an opponent. He looked up and suddenly noticed his former coach was there, and he was cheering him on from the 3rd corner of the ring like a dad would.

God brought Richard back to this memory while being on the floor in Toronto under the weight of the Spirit. The weightiness was like God playfully put him in his own 'half-nelson.' And then the Lord quickened within Richard the revelation he wanted Him to see. That coach was allegorically Him. God was his Father and was always in the corner of Richard's life, including every pain and every failure. Richard couldn't see that before, but now, he could!

Being overcome by this kind of love changes your perspective. When God speaks to the very depths of your heart, you cannot unsee His goodness. The truth is, God is only love, light, and life. There is no darkness in Him. His wrath even flows from love, as it is a passionate NO to that which hurts us! When we catch this truth, when we see it, it causes us to live out of greater love and greater joy.

Richard writes: "In the Old Testament in Nehemiah, it says, 'The Joy of the Lord is our strength.' If our theology is not bringing us a lightness of being, a deepness of enjoying, a wildness of smiling and frequent belly laughs of ecstasy, what good is it? It is time to trade up for a better, brighter, and lighter view of a joyful God. It is time for us to embrace His embracing us and to continually receive and return His ongoing hugs. In other words, life is to be hugged out."

"God is our hugger! He enjoys us."

Richard Murray frequently posts his amazing insights into the real meaning of Scripture (as opposed to religion's doctrinal system of darkness). He is a tremendous researcher and connects with the reader in a way few can. He's truly a 21st-Century Mystic who will encourage, inspire, and give you sound reasons for challenging the cognitive dissonance you have experienced in religious settings!

From Notes From Papa, a 366-day devotional by Paul Gray:

A Note From Papa to you!

To My precious, beautiful child, whom I love unconditionally and totally,

Faith is absolutely necessary for you in Our relationship. Faith is seeing what really is in the unseen and eternal realm.

Now, I want you to know the truth about faith! So many people believe the lie of religion that it's up to them to work up faith. That's a lie straight from the pit of religious hell.

I always supply and provide what I require! Sear that in your memory!

I require faith for Our relationship, and it's impossible to please Me without faith … So, I have already provided all the faith you will ever need—the faith of Jesus!

You have, and you can live by, the faith of Jesus, who loves you and gave Himself up for you. There is only one faith—Jesus' faith!

There's no possible way you could ever come up with faith to believe the right things about Me or anything or anyone else! At best, your human faith is subject to situations, circumstances, well-meaning but misled teachers, and whispers from the deceiver/accuser.

That's why I have given you the one faith–Jesus' faith! Whatever faith you could conjure up about Me would always be deficient … I knew that before creation. That's why I have given you the only One Faith of Jesus—who lives in you!

Only Jesus' faith—what He believes about Me and about you and everyone—only Jesus' faith matters! You are to live from His Faith to your faith! Believe what He believes about Me, you, and everyone. That's it! I made it very simple. Get to know Jesus better and better every day and believe His divine promises that I have already given you everything necessary for life and godliness. Take sides with Jesus.

Believe Him. Live by His Faith!

~Love, Papa

ROBIN SMIT
It Is Finished!

"ALL humanity rose up out of the grave together with Him two thousand years ago as one new man IN Christ. Alive with His resurrection life. This is our newness of life. We are not inviting Jesus into a place; we are awakening to Him already within." ~Robin Smit

Robin Smit and her husband Steve have been married for 24 years, and they have 4 children, ages 17-22, and a new son-in-law. They divide their time between their organic farm in Northern California and their beach house in Southern California. Robin has a BS in Grace Theology and a master's degree in Biblical Studies from Global Grace Seminary.

Robin did not grow up in church and didn't have the religious baggage that many have. She did not even start to attend church until age 25, and the very first message she and her husband heard was about "Christ in you, the hope of glory."

She says, "That was great until things got a little more religious." Robin and her husband got involved in "The word of faith movement," and while religion started to take its toll on their joy, she remembers that her foundation was still 'Christ in you.'

Her understanding of a God of radical grace came after she was given a book by Steve McVey titled *Beyond an Angry God*. This helped her see the Father through a clearer lens of pure grace. Learning that God is not an angry punishing God, but that He is loving, gracious, and inclusive of all has made her relationships with people much easier. She is more relaxed now and can love freely, knowing there is no need to pressure people for Christ.

Knowing that He has already included all people, with no pressure involved, she can tell people the truth that they are already in Christ, and they are meant to live life abundantly. She knows now that our job is to tell people the Truth and let the Holy Spirit do the awakening.

Next, Robin became interested in pursuing an education and began attending Global Grace Seminary, where her studies would teach her of an even more glorious gospel. There, she learned new concepts.

Previously, she had been told that we have a fallen identity, but she learned the truth that we do not have a sin nature, and that our nature has always originated in Christ; we simply lost our sight and could not see the truth of our origin.

During this process, she learned to put her 'sacred cows' on the shelf and wait for the Holy Spirit to reveal truth to her. About 3 months into Global, she really began to understand it all and could see the gospel from an eternal perspective. She studied how the early church fathers always viewed the work of the cross as finished. They knew that it has always been a finished work. This was her inspiration for her first book appropriately titled *It is Finished*.

Robin's second book is titled *Awakened*. Her inspiration for it is a chronicling of her journey through Global Grace and awakening to the message of inclusion. *Awakened* includes her essays, tweaked here and there as her beliefs change. This book focuses on awakening to the Christ already in us. She writes, "The truth is, we are not inviting Jesus into a place. We are awakening to Him already within!"

Robin shares how some people will have trouble hearing God because of their own tainted image of the Father. She personally felt God was silent because her own dad would give her the silent treatment. Now she knows how good and loving our Dad is and how He knows each of our needs uniquely and will meet us there. He will speak to us the way He knows we will hear.

Robin is a lover of the study of Scripture and the languages they were originally written in Hebrew, Greek, and Aramaic. Francois Du Toit's Mirror Translation has special meaning to her, and she highly recommends it, saying, "It opens your eyes to deeper revelation."

Currently, Robin is preparing to write her third book, which will be about obedience. In her Hebrew study, she learned that there is no Hebrew word for obedience. And that instead of obedience, it is about hearing God and dwelling in seamless union with the Trinity.

She enjoys weekly zoom gatherings with like-minded and like-spirited friends from around the world.

Grace I AM #4

Did you know that Jesus called God 'Papa'? That's the word He used—translated into English. Jesus encourages you to use the same word!

Remember, as Jesus is, so are you in this world! Wait until you hear this! You and God are BEST FRIENDS! Papa may be the best friend you've never met (yet)!

Jesus hung out with his friends 24/7 for over three years. One time, He told them, "Papa and I are best friends! We have no secrets; Papa gladly lets Me in on everything He does and will continue to show Me works of most significant proportions, which will astound you!"

Another time, Jesus told the group (men and women), "You didn't choose me, I chose you and I call you My Friends. I treat you like Friends, I relate to you like Friends. We are Friends!"

Take a few minutes in your secret place with your primary Teammates, Jesus, Papa, and Grace, and say (out loud if you can) several times slowly, "I am Best Friends with Jesus, Papa, and Grace!

They call me Friend!"

CATHERINE TOON
Marked by Love!

> *"Allow love not only to frame but to saturate your world! Whatever is hindering you, throw it off! Whatever is causing you to stumble, throw it off. Lock your eyes on the eyes of Jesus. He authored the faith you started with; He will finish it. There's too much joy on the other side to give up now! Disappointment is the seedbed for re-appointment and for an upgrade. Let love joyfully do His work!" ~ Catherine Toon*

Catherine Toon, MD, is highly accomplished in a variety of careers. As an MD in residency, Catherine's life was radically transformed when she encountered the real Jesus, who walked her out of years of heavy bondage. In that process, He birthed deep compassion in her to reach out to others with the love and power of a wildly passionate God who heals, transforms, restores the broken, oppressed, and infirm and releases them into powerful destinies.

After practicing medicine for four years, she retired to raise her children and wholeheartedly pursue God's call on her life. She has ministered in numerous spiritual capacities, including prayer, healing, prophetic coaching, wholeness coaching, training, teaching, preaching, and equipping. She has served in a variety of organizations, including being Director of the Emerge Campus School of Transformation, Imprint LLC, and Catherine Toon Ministries are dedicated to restoring wholeness, revealing identity, and releasing destiny through the unveiling of God's imprint of Love uniquely expressed in every person. Her books include *Marked by Love*, *Rare and Beautiful Treasures*, and *How to Hear From God.*

Catherine teaches that there is a beautiful, sweet intimacy we can all encounter with Jesus. He enters our brokenness; He draws and woos with kindness until our heart awakens, and we see Him rightly. All the pre-conceived notions you once held about Him, including the image of a dark, angry God simply fall away. We are left glaring in the beautiful face of our Creator, who is Love and created each of us uniquely to be consumed by His Perfect Love.

Catherine Toon remembers having encounters with Jesus early on in life, but she never heard anything of the gospel. She grew up in a family that was everything but religious, and like so many families, there was no shortage of disfunction and trauma. In that disfunction, she listened to lots of voices telling her who she was.

She now knows that most of the things she heard were not from God. She says that she didn't feel any type of real love or affirmation, and she was very insecure. This created a desire for over-achievement, which let her to pursue an intense education and career as a Medical Doctor. It was while she was working as an MD, she says, that she began to encounter Jesus for real; He captured her heart. She says, "With Jesus, once you see, you really cannot unsee and certainly cannot resist His love. When the eyes of your heart open, it feels like you are finally home. The power of God begins to move in you!"

Catherine is a gifted author, writer, and teacher. She says, "Salvation is about our wholeness. God wants to have relationship with us and restore us to His original intent, completely whole."

Dr. Toon had great emotional pain from her past, which also included sexual abuse. "God is not afraid of our messes; in fact, He stepped into it and transformed my life. The love of God begins to unveil who you really are. When you can see Him, you will begin to see yourself through His lens." She found herself moved with great compassion for hurting people that fueled a desire to move into ministry.

In addition to being a wife and mom, her passion is to help many know about this same encounter of love that she discovered. She is a prophetic coach and has done much in the area of prayer and healing. Her life has been radically changed by God's unconditional love, grace, and healing. He has unveiled in Catherine His imprint. Scripture says that we were predestined before the foundation of this world. Catherine was marked by His love since then, and no matter what life's circumstances threw at her, she was always marked.

"Only God, only Love gets to define us. Anything else is a mere shadow at best, and an outright lie at worst" (from her book *Marked By Love*).

In *Marked By Love*, Catherine takes the reader on a personal journey. We get to dive into the deep end of the all-consuming fiery love of God that will stop at nothing in the pursuit of us knowing Him rightly. Inspired by her own personal journey, Catherine realizes our hearts are made for encounter.

Marked By Love encourages your own reflection, contemplation, and writing at the end of each chapter. You chronicle your personal journey in discovering the God who is Love, the God who knows us, and we get to know Him. We find we are each special to God, and in the unveiling of God is the substance of our true identity!

Catherine Toon is a delightful, engaging, brilliant, and winsome communicator of God's Unconditional Love and *Grace to ALL*. You'll be blessed as you connect with her!

Grace I AM #5

Ever been told you need more faith? Stronger Faith? Better Faith? Ever tried to have more faith? How'd that work out for you? Not so well for me either until I learned the Truth about Faith!

Jesus revealed to his friend Paul, who then wrote to us, "There is only One Faith! Christ's faith … the Faith of Christ! Christ is the author and perfector of all Faith. It's from Christ's faith to our faith! It's by the faith OF (not in) Christ that we live!"

Friends, that's really, really good news! That means all the pressure is off! We don't have to work up more faith or beat ourselves up or succumb to religious leaders who condemn us for not having enough or the right kind of faith! There is only one faith!

Take sides with Christ. Believe what God says is true about you. You have access to the One Faith of the entire universe. Any other 'faith' is nothing compared to the One Faith.

Do you have to have faith? Absolutely! And you're learning that whatever you need, whatever God requires, God provides! He has already provided you with the only real faith there is: The Faith of Christ!

Take a few minutes in your secret place with your primary Teammates, Jesus, Papa, and Grace, and say (out loud if you can) several times slowly, "I AM filled with the Faith of Christ!"

FRED YOUNG
Recovering Legalistic Pastor!

Fred Young has had circumstances and situations in his life that would seem to drain the joy from anyone; however, he's been empowered by Christ in Him to weather those storms and even write encouraging posts like this one: *Joy.*

Elusive Joy.

Lasting joy.

We all desire it.

Joy based on circumstances won't last long. We will be up and down like a roller coaster.

The secret to joy is understanding that it is the FRUIT of KNOWING what is true about you.

Loved.

Forgiven.

Accepted.

Holy.

United with Christ.

Child of God.

Fred Young has been the Senior Pastor of East Side Church, Independence, Mo. For the past twenty-two years, he previously Pastored in Aurora & Marshall, Mo., and is a graduate of Baptist Bible College, Springfield, Mo. Don't let his fundamentalist legalistic background scare you off! Fred is as 'gracey' as you can get!

Many of the 'Grace Restoration Team' folks profiled in this book have paid a heavy price to be true to their God-given calling to boldly proclaim the really good news about God's Perfect, Unconditional, never-failing Love; Pure Light with no trace of darkness; Complete Goodness; and total inclusion of ALL. Fred Young is no exception!

Fred was the 'poster boy' of his denomination, board member, keynote speaker, and widely viewed as a mega-church superstar until he started to question the world's doctrinal system of darkness. Since his denomination didn't tolerate questions, Fred secretly turned to the internet, where he found Steve McVey, Baxter Kruger, Peter Hiett, Paul

Gray, and others.

"Fred eventually invited me to lunch, where he told me I was the first pastor or spiritual leader he had talked to publicly about Grace in his (then) two-year journey out of toxic religion," said Paul Gray.

When he started publicly proclaiming the Truth about the Only True God to his congregation, like many others, Fred met with so much resistance that his church membership and giving plummeted, leaving him and the church with a huge debt. However, his steadfast ministering of *Grace to ALL* has steadily rebuilt their congregation, especially with young families eager to hear the REALLY GOOD NEWS!

Fred says, "I take great comfort this morning in knowing that my choices are not strong enough to alter the purposes or the character of our Father. He is powerful enough and loving enough to use every choice we make for good. Lovingly redeeming all of our sorrows and pain. Thank you, Father. I take great comfort in knowing you are good; all the time, you are good, and whether I see it in this lifetime or in the ages to come, I will see that you are a redeeming genius working all things together for good."

If you or a friend live in the greater Kansas City area, you'll be encouraged at East Side Church, Independence, Missouri!

Grace I AM #6

Does it seem like you're lacking in some areas, maybe even several areas? Grace doesn't ask us to stick our heads in the sand and pretend that things are better than they actually are. Instead, grace enthusiastically shows us where all good things reside and teaches us how to see how to manifest all good things. Really!

Peter, one of Jesus' three closest friends on earth, was a slow learner. I can surely relate! After Peter saw the truth, he wrote this to you: "Grace and peace (that special sense of spiritual well-being) be multiplied to you in the true, intimate knowledge of God and of Jesus our Lord. His divine power has bestowed on you absolutely everything necessary for a dynamic spiritual life and good living through a true and personal knowledge of Him who called us by His own grace, goodness, and power!"

Look at that again! God's divine power has already given you absolutely everything you need for a dynamic spiritual life and good living!

You already have everything you need! Where is it? It's in your imagination, which is the mind of Christ!

A mystic who was very intimate with God wrote, "Whatever you think or conceive of in your mind and imagination, that's what you really are!"

Another wrote this, "Faith is the assurance (title deed, confirmation) of things hoped for (divinely guaranteed), and the evidence of things not seen [the conviction of their reality—faith comprehends as fact what cannot be experienced by the physical senses]."

The scripture word 'hope' actually means 'expect!'

A mystic is simply someone who hears from the Only True God. That's you!

Take a few minutes in your secret place with your primary Teammates, Jesus, Papa, and Grace, and say (out loud if you can) several times slowly, "I have everything I need for a dynamic life! I'm expecting good things to happen!"

CINDY LAZOR
Jesus Bumps!

"God has placed us all in a Mission Field. It doesn't matter what you do in life; that's your Mission Field." ~Cindy Lazor

Cindy Lazor is passionate about coaching others to be the best version of themselves. She's a top producer in the health and wellness field and a wonderful encourager and inspiration conveyer on social media and in person. Besides posting daily fun, encouraging videos online, she is a 6-figure earner in her business and has earned top awards. She's been married to her husband Shawn for twenty-six years, and they have three 'Gifts from God,' as they refer to their three children, a daughter and two sons.

Cindy says that God has placed her on a path with purpose, and she's grateful to have the chance to impact lives daily. She was raised in a Christian home, but she feels that the big turning point was the day that her own personal relationship with Christ began. "There's a huge difference between religion and relationship," she says.

A Bible study on March 1, 2007, changed her life, and she began to develop that relationship with God. She recalls beginning to see God's grace daily in her life and truly falling in love with her Savior. Scripture became more relevant to her. One verse that spoke to her said, "In all your ways acknowledge Him, and He will direct your path."

"I started to realize that I couldn't compartmentalize my faith anymore or limit it to Sundays and Small Group," she said. "God has placed us all in a mission field. It doesn't matter what you do in life; it's your mission field." She saw that her business, her community, and her family were all her mission field. She started to look at her livelihood as an opportunity to be the light. She determined to bring as much light as she could to the world and tried to live that daily.

According to Cindy, "You develop a relationship by communicating. It's the same with God." When she started praying, reading Scripture, and listening, she began to hear Him. And once she became more sensitive to that and obedient to what she felt the Spirit was saying to her, more 'God moments' just started coming. "There's nothing better," she says. "I love a good God story!"

When asked about her business success, she had another 'good God story' to tell. She had been in Direct Sales for nineteen years. But she didn't feel like it was properly utilizing her gifts. She had been praying for a long time for a new path. After a lot of things happened in her life, she found herself in an unhealthy place. She was unhealthy physically and emotionally and started to feel herself withdraw from life.

Some of her best 'God talks' came on walks in nature. So, one day, she found herself out walking, going down a literal path, when she felt in her spirit that God was telling her, "It's time for you to go down a new path." She wondered, *Is that really Him saying that?*

She got home and pulled up Facebook, only to see a post on her feed from someone who hadn't shown up there in a long time. The title of the post was, "Sometimes you have to take down the old to make room for the new." It was a pastor sharing a message about not being sure what God's will for your life is and stepping out in faith anyway. He compared it to Peter, squinting through the mist across the water, trying to figure out if that was really Jesus walking toward them. He said, "Sometimes you just have to step out of the boat."

The next morning, she prayed, telling God that she thought He was telling her to quit her livelihood and step into something new, but she was really afraid. Then she picked up a devotional book, which opened on a devotion about fear! That was enough confirmation for her—she turned in her letter of resignation the next day, got on a plane, and traveled to what would become her new home. She is now, as she describes, a Health and Wellness Advocate. "I am privileged and honored to help people care for their temples. I know in my heart of hearts that this is my mission field. I made this switch about three and half years ago because God knew I needed to go to this new place, and it would broaden my reach for Him."

A couple of timely messages from her pastor helped confirm all of this for her, including one about Jesus coming upon the fishermen and telling them to drop their nets (their livelihood) and follow Him, and they did. "I'm getting 'Jesus Bumps' telling you this. Going down that path that day, He was asking me to drop my livelihood and trust and follow Him." It was the scariest thing she'd ever done, but she was obedient. And God has honored that and blessed her.

She concludes with this: "He has little gifts for us, ways that He wants to bless us in our lives along our paths. When we are obedient, these blessings come, but when we try to do it our way, we're going to miss some of those gifts He has planned for us along the way."

With God's help, Cindy's mission is to do whatever she can to make sure that the people she encounters are enjoying the gifts and blessings God has for them!

From Notes From Papa, a 366-day devotional by Paul Gray:

A Note From Papa to you!

To My child, whom I'm so proud of … always,

At times when you're thinking about an upcoming, potentially confrontational meeting with someone, you tend to fear the worst. You question if you will remember the right things to support your position. You have doubts that you won't be able to think quickly. You worry that you won't be able to express yourself clearly. You are concerned that you won't be strong and that you'll give in to what you believe is wrong because you won't be able to stand up to someone else's skills, knowledge, and power. You fear they won't like you if you disagree with them.

I'm not condemning or criticizing you for that. I'm aware of how you feel and know that the enemy uses those feelings to condemn you. Any condemnation you ever feel comes from him … not me! I am infinitely stronger than your feelings and infinitely stronger than he who is in the world!

When you focus on those feelings of doubt, fear, lack, and worry, you leave Me out of the picture and dwell totally on yourself and your perceived lack and insufficiency.

Here's what I want you to do—bring everything to Me first! Ask Me what I'm thinking about the situation and then listen to Me. I will tell you if your position on the situation is My position … and if it is, I will tell you what to do. If I show you that I feel differently about the situation, I'll show you My way, and we'll go from there. If you are believing correctly, then I will show you how to prepare for the meeting. I will remind you of the important points. I will be with you, and if you let Me, I will empower you and speak through you and show you what's going on with the other person. Then with and in love for each of you, because I am for you both, I will present the truth clearly. Then I am responsible for the results. The other person may resist and not see the truth, but you can rest in Me and trust Me and be confident that I am working all things for the good!

~Love, Papa

KEITH GILES
Reconstruction!

"Instead of asking 'What do you believe?' I wish we'd shift to saying, 'How much love do you have for others?' There are great verses about how we should outdo one another in acts of kindness and love for one another." ~Keith Giles

Keith Giles is a husband, father, author, blogger, and now former pastor. As a result of disillusionment with organized religion and his subsequent deconstruction, he has been on a journey of passionately pursuing the rediscovery of the true gospel message.

"I have written a brief synopsis about most of my podcast guests in this book, but Keith does a much better job of it than I. So, following is a recent post of his! My friend Keith is the real deal!" ~Paul Gray

Here is an account from Keith Giles, in his own words: "About five years ago, I published my first book with Quoir Publishing. It was about my journey from being raised as a Conservative Republican Christian in Texas who joined the NRA, owned a bunch of guns, and listened to Rush Limbaugh religiously. I ended up with a faith that couldn't be distinguished from my political party. The Holy Spirit eventually untangled me from all of that, and once I got free, I realized I was not the only person struggling with the distinctions between following Jesus and voting Republican.

"The book, *Jesus Untangled: Crucifying Our Politics To Pledge Allegiance To The Lamb*, was released on Inauguration Day when Donald Trump took his oath of office. The foreword was provided by Greg Boyd, author of *The Myth Of A Christian Nation*, which really blessed my socks off. That book was about how Christians cannot serve two masters and need to admit that they cannot convert a culture if that culture has already converted them.

"Little did I know how prophetic my warnings in that book would become over the next four years. I also didn't realize at the time that this book would become the first in a seven-part series of books dealing with different facets of Christian theology that many believers today wrestle with the most as they go through something called

'Deconstruction.'

"The second book, *Jesus Unbound: Liberating The Word of God from the Bible*, featured a Foreword by Brian Zahnd and dealt with the troubling tendency of Christians to confuse the Word of God [Jesus] with the Bible [a book we wrote about Jesus]. In that book, my goal was to demonstrate how confusing the menu with the meal or the map with the treasure leads to missing the meal and the treasure completely.

"This is also the book I typically recommend everyone start with in the series—even though these are not sequential books—simply because this book unpacks a foundational concept of approaching the Scriptures through the lens of Christ [rather than taking the usual Flat Bible approach]. So, if you understand this concept first, it will make all the other books in the series much easier for you to process.

"My third book in the series was *Jesus Unveiled: Forsaking Church As We Know It For Ekklesia As God Intended*. This one took one of my previously self-published books *This Is My Body* and updated the content with an additional forty-eight pages of new material on the subject of starting and facilitating an organic house-based ekklesia in your own home or community. This was based on our eleven years of experience doing exactly that, and it is probably one of the most personal books I've written, since it chronicles this entire experience from beginning to end.

"My fourth book was one my publisher strongly encouraged me to write. *Jesus Undefeated: Condemning the False Doctrine of Eternal Torment* takes a look at all three Christian views of Hell from the historical and scriptural perspectives. Honestly, it has been one of my most popular titles in the series, and I've had so many people thank me for writing it, so I guess I owe my publisher a huge 'thank you' for making me write it.

"After that, I wrote *Jesus Unexpected: Ending the End Times to Become the Second Coming*, which is one of my favorites in the series because it once-and-for-all exposes the false teachings of John Nelson Darby about the End Times Rapture and unpacks my view that we [the Body of Christ] ARE the second coming of Christ and that there is more of Christ in the world today than there was 2,000 years ago.

"Next, I wrote *Jesus Unforsaken: Substituting Divine Wrath With*

Unrelenting Love, which takes on the myth of Penal Substitutionary Atonement Theory as the Gospel and presents a better idea of the atonement, which underscores the fact that everyone has been reconciled to God through Christ, and all sins are forever forgiven and forgotten for all eternity.

"Finally, the book *Jesus Unarmed: How the Prince of Peace Disarms Our Violence*, with a foreword by comedian and radio host John Fugelsang [Sirius XM Radio's TELL ME EVERYTHING]. As you might suspect, this book takes on the question of whether or not Jesus was serious about loving our enemies and overcoming darkness with light. It also answers every single possible objection raised by doubting Christians [and it's always and only the Christians, for some reason, who doubt that Jesus taught and practiced non-violence] like, 'Why did Jesus say "Go and buy a sword"?' and 'What about when Jesus fashioned a whip and chased moneychangers out of the temple?' and 'What about when Jesus said, "I came not to bring peace but a sword?"' Etc.

"As I ponder the impact of these books, my hope is that they offer people real answers to difficult questions of faith. Based on the feedback I've received from so many of my readers, I'd say they've accomplished pretty much everything I could have hoped for.

"I always say that my ministry is defined as 'Introducing Christians to Jesus,' and these books are a huge part of how I've tried to do exactly that. There are so many man-made ideas, doctrines, and theologies that we've created and built up over the centuries that obscure, distort, and blur the message and the character of Jesus. My hope is that by tearing down these toxic and anti-Christian teachings, people can finally and fully see the beautiful face of Jesus without all the garbage we've constructed along the way."

From Grace Is ... by Paul Gray:

God Is Love

The most important foundational truth of all is to know that God is love. It is impossible for us to exaggerate or embellish God's love and His love for us. You won't see Jesus face to face and say, "Wow, I overestimated your love and grace, Jesus ... You're not nearly as good as I thought!"

1 John 4:8, 4:16– God is love.

God's very essence is love. Everything flows from His pure, agape love that always does what is best for the other person. Pastor Lee O'Hare's online post captures the essence of agape very well. He said, "The Greek word used here to describe and define God is the word 'AGAPE,' which is a very precise and unique word used to describe a kind of love that is totally foreign to human experience. It could easily be translated as 'the God kind of love.' It is not so much something that God HAS; it is rather who or what God IS. It is a love that is completely unconditional and that emanates from the very person and character of God, which is always seeking the highest and the best and is not motivated in any degree by the loveliness or worthiness of its recipient."

Malcolm Smith said, "I may tell you that I have a glass of water or a reservoir of water, but it is an entirely different category to say that 'I am water!' To have water means my possession of it is subject to change, whether by increase or decrease, but to BE water means I am never subject to change because that is what I am! God is the definition of love ... that is what He is!"

Frederick Buechner said, "God does not need the Creation in order to have something to love ... because within Himself love happens."

Love is also the ultimate prophetic purpose of God for us! For everyone's mutual benefit, God wants us to love each other as Jesus loves us—unconditionally and by giving up our rights, doing whatever is necessary to love!

John 13:34 (MIRROR), "I give you a new commandment, keep on loving one another just as I have loved you—my love for you is the source of your love for one another."

LISA WENTWORTH COUTURE
The Honey Love of God!

Lisa Couture is a delightful lady who has an amazing capacity to relate to and encourage an ever-growing group of worldwide friends! She is someone who manifests the prophecy of Jesus "You will do even greater things than I do!" Not that Lisa does more spectacular or powerful miracles than Jesus, but she uses social media to connect with and inspire exponentially more people than Jesus did when He chose to limit Himself to a human body 2,000 years before the world wide web!

For many years, Lisa was the National Sales Manager for a toy company based in Southern New Hampshire. She's a single mom of an adult son, Trevor. Lisa says, "It was through a devastating divorce about ten years ago, and when I was most broken, that I encountered the One true living God. Abba and my Father. His kindness toward me and beautiful grace was revealed to me, and I can only describe it as a relentless drawing of me into His loving arms. From there, my life began to be transformed, healed, and made whole."

While searching for unconditional love, grace, and acceptance, she experienced divine introductions to many of the people written about in this book.

Lisa did what I hope you ALL will do—she connected with these folks, got to know them, became part of their groups, travels to spend real-time community with them, and has organized live Zoom groups that meet immediately following the weekly teaching of Don Keathley and others. The groups are for those navigating the dismantling of religious doctrines. They study Scripture from a new covenant perspective. It includes a private inner circle group that has become a special community.

Lisa says, "I am in love with Jesus. I am passionate about people knowing who they are, walking in the freedom that Christ came to reveal and restore. We are FREE right now. But so many of us don't know who we are, which is 'Loved by God and in union with Him.' I want to spend my life telling people who they are, who God says they are, and that they are loved and affirmed by Him from the beginning.

"It is the Love of God that I often refer to as 'Honey Love of God' that consumed all the alienation I felt and lived out. I was blind, and now I see. Jesus did this. He is LOVE. In my very small way, I want to tell the world what I now know."

She also has a private woman's group called 'Honey Love of God' just for women who are also walking through religious detox. Her groups are small and intimate (about twelve to sixteen a week) and have been life-changing for people who didn't have any community. They are growing and sharpening each other. She also counsels women online.

FULL DISCLOSURE: Lisa has been an integral part of this book! She listened to every podcast episode and wrote the genesis of most of the following guest stories! I deeply appreciate her friendship, encouragement, and partnership in bringing to fruition *Grace to ALL*!

Grace I AM #7

What do you want? How do you want your life to be? What do you want your life to look like? Your relationships, your career, your finances, your health, your situation?

One of the wisest people ever, a person who knew God intimately, Solomon, wrote, "Delight yourself in God and He will give you the desires of your heart."

What are the desires of your heart? Rather than focus on what your current situation appears to be (and we're not denying the reality of your situation), Grace invites us to dream, to focus on what we want. Grace actually puts those dreams in our heart, to begin with, then delights in giving them to us!

Remember, "Whatever you think or conceive of in your mind and imagination, that's what you really are!" Remember, "You have been given absolutely everything you need for a dynamic spiritual life and good living! Remember, "You are just like Jesus was in the world!"

Take a few minutes in your secret place every day with your primary Teammates, Jesus, Papa, and Grace, and dream! Imagine! Get a picture of what you want your life to be like! Then picture it as already being that way! It actually is that way in the unseen realm where Grace has given you everything! Say (out loud if you can) several times slowly, "My life is good. I have 'x' (fill in the blank for what you dream it will be)!"

BILL THRASHER
U.S. Marines, Billy Graham Crusades & Grace

"God in His infinite goodness reveals His all-inclusive love to us each according to our personality." ~Bill Thrasher

Bill Thrasher, the author of the book *The Jesus Purpose* and host of the Facebook group by that same name, believes this scandalous grace was deep within him and always present. He loves life and walks in joy often and looks at people as inherently good. He believes that love never fails.

He didn't always have this understanding of grace, but he says that when he came into this revelation, everything aligned. What he was living then agreed with his theology. However, as do many who are featured in this book, those who he knew inside the traditional church began to look at him differently. "I was now the weirdo," he says, "who no longer believed in a place of eternal suffering by God. Even more weird (to them), I came to believe that instead of Jesus dying for us, He also died AS us."

Contrary to the religious teaching "you have to drum up faith," he knows now it is the faith OF Christ that allowed him to even begin to believe in Him. He says, "So, although my theology now aligned with my being, all these new beliefs caused many to pull away and look at me as if I had grown a third eye in the middle of my head.

"I owe a lot of how I love and my attitude to my upbringing and my parents. I am a little bit of a paradox, in that I have an insider's view with an outsider's perspective. I remember early on working with my dad when he was on staff with the Billy Graham Crusades. It was an amazing opportunity."

Bill remembers being in stadiums filled with as many as 100,000 people. He would be backstage and watch as the spirit of God would move people by the thousands into the aisles to make a 'decision' for Christ. Seeing Billy Graham on stage and knowing he was known globally gave Bill a sense of awe. Watching all those people was so encouraging.

"But to be honest, in the middle of witnessing it all, I realized even back then some of those religious traditions, like saying a sinner's prayer, for example, were from a paradigm that kind of did not make sense to me.

"I am the guy who sees more church in the everyday broken places. I remember attending a huge alcoholics anonymous convention in Toronto, Canada, where there were 80,000 'drunks' who knew they were broken and messed up. And you hear a person introduce themselves as an alcoholic, and then 80,000 people simultaneously yell back to them, 'Hi, Bill!' I mean, you cannot get any more inclusive than that! It was beautiful to me.

"I believe any time you see authentic joy, goodness, patience, faithfulness on display in a person, that is the Holy Spirit, whether we can wrap it around the Christian context or not. They are manifesting the fruit of the spirit coming from Christ in that person.

"This understanding allows us to relate to others in that cruciform image that we all are made in. One of my dearest friends is a project manager for me who tragically lost 2 teenage boys within just a couple of years. Like us all, He struggles with his faith, but nobody displays the nature of Christ more than he does. Despite his understandable questioning of God in all the pain that he has endured, he is one of the most grace-filled people you will ever meet. I continue to speak this truth to him. He knows I am the weird one and often asks me why I believe so differently than anyone else. It's this inclusive type of love that always causes people to question you but, in a strange way, will draw them too."

Bill will tell you he is the guy who experiences church more at places like a bar and grill with a bunch of roadies after a Billy Graham crusade. He says, "It's as if Christ is in that family around the table, eating hot wings and drinking a beer.

"I see Christ in the bond of brothers I experienced cleaning weapons with fellow Marines. I see Christ in the local tailgate party at a football game with friends. I know I am experiencing God's perichoretic love in all these places.

"I even have church every day at work. I have been blessed with an amazing team. There are people from every walk of life. There is joy, union, commonality, and we share life together. That is how Jesus did it. That is what true church is to me … seeing Christ in all."

Bill writes: "The Bible is one of humanity's greatest gifts and paradoxically one of its greatest inhibitors. We can get so lost in its pages that we fail to realize it is a very small part of God's full story … The most religious of Jesus' day had this same problem with the good book, their accredited word and way of God.

"These blessed people had the creator of the cosmos wrapped in skin, with a beard, standing them eye to eye, denying his infinite power to be as human as they were ... desperate to show them a new Word and Way about God. And yet, even today, we believe this book has some answer, some divine power to save us ... It doesn't.

"The book points to an answer outside of it, who resides totally independent of the leather-bound, gold-embossed cover it has to make it seem more necessary to your life. The Bible is an amazing resource for reminding ourselves of who Christ is. But, reading it religiously will not fully tell you Who He is ... Holy Spirit, within you, is tasked with that wondrous privilege ... and Jesus alive today may look much more like a next-door neighbor or some random stranger than you would have ever guessed.

"So, let's get our noses out of old, dusty, dead-letter scriptures, wasting life ... the scriptures are pointing us to a new life active and exploding inside of Humanity ... All in Christ, and Christ in all."

Grace I AM #8

How are you doing with dreaming? Remember Christ's friend Paul? Here's another Grace Nugget that He wrote to you (by the way, Paul knew from experience what he was talking about):

"The Father of our Lord Jesus, the Messiah, the perfect Father of every father and child in heaven and on the earth will unveil within you the unlimited riches of his glory and favor until supernatural strength floods your innermost being with his divine might and explosive power!

"Then, by constantly using the Faith of Christ, the life of Christ will be released deep inside you, and the resting place of his love will become the very source and root of your life. Then you will be empowered to discover the great magnitude of the astonishing love of Christ in all its dimensions. How deeply intimate and far-reaching is his love! How enduring and inclusive it is! Endless love beyond measurement that transcends our understanding—this extravagant love pours into you until you are filled to overflowing with the fullness of God!

"Never doubt God's mighty power to work in you and accomplish all this. He will achieve infinitely more than your greatest request, your most unbelievable dream, and exceed your wildest imagination! He will outdo them all, for his miraculous power constantly energizes you."

Thinking about, meditating on, and remembering those words of truth will bless you immensely! Take a few minutes in your secret place with your primary Teammates, Jesus, Papa, and Grace, and say (out loud if you can) several times slowly, "God's mighty power in me will achieve infinitely more than my greatest request, my most unbelievable dream, and exceed my wildest imagination! He will outdo them all!"

As you come to internalize this truth and Delightfully Expect Effortless Manifestation of God giving you the desires of your heart, get ready for Amazing Grace to change your circumstances and situations into the Life of the Ages … better than you ever thought possible!

MICHELE FRANCESCA COHEN
Inspiration for Life and Performing Arts

Michele Francesca Cohen helps us "Imagine a world where people feel secure, aware of their God-connection, worth, and significance!"

A gifted writer, poet, teacher, and encourager, online and in one-on-one conversations, Michele has a winsome way of making people feel as if they are the most important person in her life. Michele was born and raised in the beautiful county of Surrey, England. After retiring from the British National Gymnastics Team in her mid-teens, she embarked on a career in theater arts, coaching students, professionals, and lay folk of all ages.

As a director, writer, choreographer, and performer, and as a teacher at one of Britain's most reputable performing arts colleges in London, she's had the privilege of bringing Inspiration for Life to many, including casts of hundreds in high budget productions, students (young and old) in top-level training facilities, and millions via television broadcasting.

In the 1990s, she entered the world of ordained ministry and continued her mission of identity empowerment by sharing the good news of God's unconditional love in more than twenty nations. She was formerly an associate pastor at The Church at Trophy Lakes, in Trophy Club, Texas, where she led women's events, pastor's classes, prayer meetings, and online outreach. She is the author of *Eden Song*, *Arise*, and *LOVESONG—Poems of Connection.*

In 2020, Michele encountered a severe and long-lasting experience of toxic mold poisoning. Via her online platform, she received love, compassion, mercy, encouragement, and inspiration from friends around the world. She's used that platform to inform people of toxic mold poisoning and provided much-needed insight on how to detect it in its early stages.

Michele wrote: "Is there a place in your soul that emits a 'for sale' ad? Do you prioritize people's judgments toward you over your own inner integrity and spiritual alignment? Do you compromise yourself to external control and give away your emotional and mental autonomy?

"Now, these are hefty questions. But think about it for a second and make amendments where needed. Stop giving your voice and the best of yourself away like a bargain basement item in a clearance sale. Instead, become established in the clarity of your own personhood and start living your life to your highest potential on every level.

"Tears contain revelation within their mysterious waters. They hold keys of awareness to help us shed old patterns and graduate to unchartered levels of beingness. Not all tears are for sadness. In fact,

few are. What are your tears specifically saying? Have you ever asked?"

JOURNEY OF TEARS

Not all tears are for sadness—

Some are for sowing into hardened ground to nurture faith and irrigate hope.

Some speak of feelings, desires, and emotions buried in caverns of underground truth. Some release trauma, betrayal, and pain, bloodletting poisons from trial and abuse. Some fall in silence as tender honesty, cleansing guilt or comforting loss. Some are destined as rains of refreshing, wellsprings of joy in the dew point of time. Some are for words that can't find expression, the muted voice of a complex life. Some are for rivers of transportation by which to swim to new shores of trust. And some are for gladness and celebration, showers of thanks on a journey of love.

–Excerpt from *LOVESONG—Poems of Connection* by Michele Francesca Cohen

Michele is currently visualizing and establishing the *Inspiration for Life and Performing Arts Institute* in the greater Dallas, Texas, area. Stay tuned for really exciting things!

From Notes From Papa, a 366-day devotional by Paul Gray:

A Note From Papa to you!

To My wonderful child, who continually brings joy to My heart,

From your perspective, it's hard for you to comprehend that you bring joy to My heart continuously because you still entertain the lie that your behavior affects how I feel about you and how I view you. But it doesn't! Never has, and never will!

Think of it like this: you have a favorite sports team, and you're really for them. You want them to win and be successful, and you delight with and in them when they do well. They are still your team, even when they don't do as well. Then comes the big game, but you can't watch it because you have to work ... so you record it. Before you can watch it, someone tells you that your team won. So, you already know how it's going to turn out. As you then watch the recording, you don't get upset or worry when a favorite player messes up, the referee makes a bad call, or the other team goes ahead. You have confident joy in the midst of apparent defeat because you know that your team comes back and ultimately prevails and wins.

That's how I relate to you! I know the end of the story. I know that because of what Jesus, the Holy Spirit, and I did for you in our finished work at the cross, you have already won! Because Jesus prevailed and defeated and conquered sin, death, the law, and the enemy, so have you!

In My view, I can see that you have won—you are 100% pure, innocent, right with us, without fault and totally included forever in Our Triune circle dance of love, joy, peace, and everything good! We are together.

You overcame and are more than a conqueror in Christ! Sure, we're sad for a moment when We see you mess up, but the final score is the only thing that counts with Us, and it's settled! It's finished!

We continually take joy in you, and We want you to continually take joy in and with Us. Be joyful always; that's Our will for you in Christ Jesus! Always take joy, My child, because We are for you!

~Love, Papa

BOB INGLE
Be Blessed!

Bob Ingle is a musician/salesman who likes to say, in the words of Mercy Me's great song Wishful Thinking, "What I bought before, I just can't sell."

When he was seventeen, Bob became discouraged by the judgmentalism of his church as they preached "Don't vote for this man for president because he's a Catholic." He left the church and didn't go back until he was thirty-two years old.

That's when he bought evangelical religion 'hook, line, & sinker.' He was there every time the doors were open, and not just 'there,' he was all-in. He served as Sunday school teacher and superintendent, small group leader, board member, musician, worship leader, teacher, lending-library developer and provider, evangelist, and whatever else he was asked to do.

After a few decades, as happened to many of us, he started asking questions about things that didn't make sense. When he didn't get satisfactory answers, he started searching and researching and learning about a completely different version of God than he 'bought' before. Even though he's a very successful salesman in the business world, he could no longer sell the version of God that he was taught by religion.

In addition to being part of the Grace Restoration Team in Lawrence, Ks., Bob is very active on Facebook, has written and recorded a number of great songs, and regularly posts insightful and encouraging blogs about the Only True God.

"Lord, you are my Shepherd; I don't lack anything. You encourage me to rest in Your beautiful Creation and drink from its abundance: You remind my soul of who I really am. You honor me to walk the way that honors you. When I walk through the lowest places I'm not afraid because You're with me; Your Word and Works comfort me: You provide for me in front of all opposition. You pour Your Blessing on me and it spills out on all around: You've got my back, every day everywhere. Lord, You, and I will be together forever." —Psalm 23, *BIV* (Bob Ingle Version)

Note from Paul Gray: "My experience in coming to know Bob Ingle is one of the primary motivating factors for writing this book. I naively thought my little group were the only ones in our city who knew about and were experiencing and sharing the only true God and Their Pure Light, Unconditional Love, Abundant Grace, and Inclusion of all people. Then Mo Thomas sent me a copy of his great new book *Into The Abyss*, which included an endorsement by Bob Ingle, Lawrence, Ks. What!? I'd never heard of him. Mo introduced us, and I found a kindred spirit just a few blocks away! My goal for *Grace to ALL* is to connect other like-hearted people who are in their area!"

Grace I AM #9

You've now been introduced to the Mystical and very practical concept of Delightfully Expecting Effortless Manifestation of the dreams and desires Papa has already created in your heart. We call that 'DEEM,' which means to suppose, expect, believe.

Jesus saw something in His mind, then spoke it into existence! Jesus, of course, was the Master of this, and remember, Jesus was an example OF (not for) you!

Paul wrote to you that you actually have the very Mind of Christ! Just like Jesus did! Did you know that? You have The Mind of Christ! Christ, the Second person of the Trinity, along with Papa and Grace. Christ the Creator who spoke everything there is into existence. Christ, the One whom you are just like, shares His very mind with you!

Among other things, that means you can create—co-create with God. Really! What you dream and conceive can, and will, come into being!

The very simple process includes:

Delight yourself in Jesus/Papa/Grace. Delighting in Their Presence.

Expect, count on, see, visualize, dream about what you want your life to be like and then expect it to happen, feel the emotions, see it in your mind.

Effortless—don't try to figure out how to do it or make it happen yourself or by your own efforts.

Manifestation (coming from the invisible realm into visibility) –

Take a few minutes in your secret place with your primary Teammates, Jesus, Papa, and Grace, and say (out loud if you can) several times slowly, "I have The Mind of Christ! I Delightfully Expect Effortless Manifestation Of (you fill in the blank)!"

Don't just do this once! Continue to DEEM and wait for God to co-create with you and give you the desires of your heart!

Mike Popovich, Don Keathley, Michele Francesca Cohen, and Steve McVey all have excellent teaching on DEEM.

WM. PAUL YOUNG
Being Yourself is Easy!

> *"If we believe in penal substitution, then we have defined true love (for is not love the deepest and truest nature of God?) as violence, and thereby potentially justifying all acts of violence as acts of love and declaring the greatest model of love being that of punitive and retributive violence ... When the way of our being matches the truth of our being; that's wholeness ... Trust is always present tense. Love is the long game!"*
>
> *~Paul Young*

William Paul Young, worldwide best-selling author of *The Shack* has arguably been the greatest communicator of God's Unconditional Love, Grace, and Inclusion in our generation or in most any generation! Over 30,000,000 copies are in print in scores of languages across the world. The Shack movie has also impacted millions of people worldwide.

Interestingly, when you Google "world's best-selling Christian books," most sites don't even include *The Shack,* even though it's outsold all others by millions of copies. They may put up a thinly veiled smokescreen about the 'blasphemy' of God being portrayed (partially) by a black woman, but as one reads closely, that's not their real beef. It seems apparent to me (Paul Gray) that the real issue is that those who compile the lists don't want to accept God's unconditional love, grace, inclusion, and forgiveness of all people. Like the Pharisees of Jesus' day, they tend to hold tightly to the self-serving, self-righteous belief that we get the credit for pulling the handle of the divine slot machine to get blessed.

Paul Young was born in Alberta, Canada, but spent much of his early childhood in New Guinea (West Papua) with his missionary parents and three younger siblings (each of whom had passports from different countries). The family moved back to Canada while Paul was just starting elementary school. He attended thirteen different schools before graduating. In recent years, he has been open about the struggles he has dealt with as a TCK (Third Culture Kid) and survivor of childhood sexual abuse. Paul and Kim (Warren) Young have six children. Paul wrote *The Shack,* his first novel, as a gift for his children.

Young eloquently describes the truth about what salvation looks like experientially in our lives. It is wholeness and authenticity. Paul learned first-hand that religion falsely teaches us that our 'inherited sin'—the concept that we are totally depraved when we're born—has separated us from God. He's found that message to have been drilled into the very essence of humanity. As a result, Paul walked the road of self-hate for many years (as many of us have), believing the lie that we are all pretty much worthless excrement.

He says, "We grow up in this world, not knowing the truth of our being … that we are made in the image of God. We are kind because God is kind. We are patient because He is patient. We are love because He is love. While that IS true, it is not what we have been told. Instead of basking in the joy of who we really are, we learn to internalize a view of ourselves as a piece of dung. We form harmful behavior patterns of comparing our lives to others. Our lives become riddled with inauthentic behavior as we continue to exacerbate more damage to our identity. Then life becomes about performance, not identity. Our anxieties turn us into control freaks with lots of religious hoops to jump through to 'get back to God.' All of it produces shallow relationships with no real authenticity."

He often says, "Finding Grace for the day, one day at a time, is key to exiting the lie-life of self-degradation. There is something very freeing about authenticity!"

Paul remembers that authenticity was something that struck him when he first met his wife Kim's family. He describes himself at that time as being a very intellectual and religious young man, but he noticed Kim and her family seemed to have a real substance to the ordinariness of their lives, something he did not have. He also noticed they possessed integrity in their ability to tell the truth. Again, something he did not have, but that was extremely attractive to him. He states, "We all long to just be who we are, and being around people who are real gives us the very freedom to be real ourselves."

Paul teaches, "Wholeness comes in the unveiling of our authenticity in Christ … The truth of our being. As it was allegorized in *The Shack*, we all meet up and experience the Father, Son, and Holy Spirit inside our own 'inner shack,' which is the inner dwelling place where we meet our Papa face to face. There, The Holy Spirit unveils and begins to dismantle all the facades we walk in, and the substance of who we truly are unfolds and emerges from within. It is then, and only then, that we are home."

When asked "How does this change how we treat people today?" Paul says, "Knowing that people are not separated from God changes everything. You can be sure when you meet any person in your day-to-day life, that the Father, Son, and Holy Spirit dwell within them, and there is a story of their own unfolding inside of their own shack. Then you drop your agenda and no longer see people as projects whom you try to coerce to 'come to God' as religion has taught us. Instead, your only agenda is to live in the unforced rhythms of grace, to flow day-to-day out of the purposes of God, realizing that every encounter with people is a magnificent thing, a moment to show love freely and be a voice of healing."

Paul says, "God dwells inside of you. The river of living water flows from inside of you! As a result, you don't need to tell someone … you will no longer need words of convincing because you are displaying the fruit of God out of the truth of your being. Then when people ask, always be prepared to give this reason for the hope that is in you; yet do it with gentleness and respect."

Paul is a frequent guest on podcasts, interviews, and speaking engagements around the world. He has arguably had a positive impact on more people than anyone in the tsunami of Papa's Perfect Unconditional Love, *Grace to ALL*, Inclusion, and total goodness that's currently sweeping the world. If you haven't read or listened to or been with Paul Young yet, you're in for a divine treat!

From Notes From Papa, a 366-day devotional by Paul Gray:

A Note From Papa to you!

To My highly successful child, whom I'm so proud of,

I have a totally different view and concept of success than you, and most of My children, have!

You tend to view success as what you have accomplished in the areas of education, finance, relationships, sports, the arts, and business. I want you to do well in every area of your life, and I have given you My grace, in advance, to enable you to become all that I have planned for you to be. My grace brings about success in every area of your life.

Enjoyable as it is, that type of success pales in contrast to Jesus' success! Jesus was totally and completely successful in His finished work at the cross!

It's imperative that you know Jesus was completely successful! He came to seek and save the lost, and He did! We're not willing that anyone should perish; it's Our will that everyone should have eternal life with us; Jesus accomplished that! We hate sin, death, and evil. Jesus defeated them all and took away the sin of the world! We forgave it all! Jesus was totally successful!

I so loved the entire world that I sent Jesus to save you all—save you from sin, death, and the destruction that you were bringing on yourselves. Jesus did that! He is the savior of the world, of everyone! Jesus was and is successful.

Jesus came to reveal Me to everyone, and He did, and He continues to!

Jesus was completely and totally successful in Our big-picture plan of the restoration of all things! I know each of you wants to do your part, but you have no part! It's all Jesus! The only thing you did was to judge, condemn, crucify, and kill Jesus. You (collectively) did that. And We used that to bring about the successful completion of Jesus' finished work at the cross!

Think about, revel in, bask in, experience, and enjoy the fruits of Jesus' labor. He did it all for you because We love you, and We would rather die than live without you (so He did!).

~Love, Papa

DR. PAUL FITZGERALD
Invincible Preciousness!

> *"I shared this wisdom with someone today who is making a courageous decision to name hard truth. Since we all face that choice on many levels, I'm sharing with you this quote by Eugene Gendlin: 'What is true is already so. Owning up to it doesn't make it worse. Not being open about it doesn't make it go away. And because it's true, it is what is there to be interacted with. Anything untrue isn't there to be lived. People can stand what is true, for they are already enduring it.'"*
>
> *~Dr. Paul Fitzgerald*

Dr. Paul Fitzgerald has his doctorate in ministry, with dissertation research about Internalized Shame. He founded the Heart Connexion Seminars in 1998—which continue to this day. They feature Breakthrough Seminars—an experiential learning process to transform internalized shame into internalized grace. Over 5,000 have attended, and the number grows each month. Dr. Paul offers Heart Connexion Focused Coaching—an experiential process to expand your personal journey to find your inner wisdom that empowers courageous and confident choices to creatively express your Truest-Self.

His coaching includes a specific, well-researched process designed to equip you with tools and practices to deepen your access to your inner wisdom so that you can creatively respond to any personal life situation and be more effective in your leadership roles.

Dr. Paul says, "Each person we ever meet is what we can call Imago Dei. Made in the image of God. How does this change things for us? Having learned the difference from our eastern orthodox brothers and sisters, it has helped change our perspective about judgment. We all have fallen short from God's likeness, but we can look at every person we meet and know that deep within them is a place where the very intrinsic image of God resides. It's a precious pure place, reflective of the perfection God made us in as He created us all and called us good.

"Our core place has not suffered any victimization or trauma and is free from shame or condemnation. Knowing this about ourselves and others helps us look at people with the heart of unconditional love and grace. It is also why healing shame is so important, because as people heal, they can connect to that inner godlike image again."

When Paul is going about his everyday life, he sees the preciousness in others and says it takes him off his own seat of judgment. He often refers to a powerful scene in the book and movie *The Shack* and the impact of what judgment looks like. He says that we can go either way when we judge. We can think grace is too much, or we can believe legalism is too much. Either way, judgment is not the heart of the Father. Unconditional love and acceptance are. However, since judgment is what has been drilled into most of us through religious theology, and we have been taught the lie that God is an angry judge, we need healing.

Paul has devoted his life to a ministry that heals this shame. He talks about the very basics of shame-based communication and the language that we use. For example, the word 'should' carries a judgment. It is a contractual word essentially telling another that they are violating a contract with you. You have placed your values onto another and attached a judgment of expectation to it. We can even do this to ourselves. Anytime we are speaking in a shame-based language, we will hear the word 'should,' and Dr. Paul wants to draw this to light and change our narrative.

He helps us see that judgment is at the root of the perceived disconnection we experience with God. Judgment blinds us. Jesus himself made some very powerful statements about judgment. He talked about how we worry about the speck in the eye of our brother and yet walk with a log in our own eyes. Jesus reminded us not to think that God's grace is only for "we who are 'in.'" He said that Grace rains on the just and unjust.

Dr. Paul cautions us about the effects of judgment within a 'grace group' because we expect grace people to not judge. Many of us start our 'religious' journey full of excitement, hope, and joy, only to sadly fall victim to shame and judgment from the very religious institution where we go to "be healed from shame and judgment."

Dr. Paul, his wife, and his team are trained in counseling people to help remove the frequently unknown emotional blockages that keep them blind. They spend time with people, coaching and helping them to connect to the root causes of deep shame. Much of it points to internalized trauma, often reaching back to childhood. A classic example is people in a joyful environment being stunned when something happens that triggers a person to begin having a temper tantrum like a child. Dr. Paul's counseling helps expose this 'trapped trauma,' get beyond the emotional blockage to the root and be healed.

Dr. Paul offers many resources in his ministry, from one-on-one in-person coaching to group seminars and zoom groups. All his ministry is designed to help us uncover that which blocks people from seeing the True self redeemed by God!

"Paul Fitzgerald is a tremendously insightful and gifted counselor/ encourager who has helped me immensely. I'm very grateful for his help and friendship!" ~Paul Gray

Grace I AM #10

A major part of taking sides with Jesus, believing what He says about us, includes understanding God's perspective of 'sin.'

The bottom line is that 'sin,' as we've been taught, is not an issue with God!

First, 'sin' is not a word that scripture writers used. Their Greek and Hebrew words simply meant 'missing the mark,' and they specifically used it to refer to our "missing the mark of knowing and living out of the knowledge that God is Perfect Unconditional Love for All, God is Pure Light with no trace of darkness, God's Grace covers everything, God has already made us all right with God forever."

Unfortunately, religion has missed that mark totally and perverted and fixated on an absolutely wrong concept of God, us, and 'sin.' Scripture tells us that God Himself says, "I choose not to remember your 'sin,' I will not bring up your 'sin' to you, I keep no record of your 'sin,' I forgave all your 'sin' before creation, Jesus took away the 'sin' of the world, I put your 'sin' as far as the East is from the West."

God specifically says, "Yes, ALL humans 'missed the mark,' but I have made (the same) ALL humans right with me."

Any hurtful actions that we take that are the result of our 'missing the mark' of who we, God, and ALL people are are symptoms, not the root 'sin.'

Of course, God is saddened when we hurt ourselves and others, but that never affects our relationship with God! He's already taken care of that!

Take a few minutes in your secret place with your primary Teammates, Jesus, Papa, and Grace, and say (out loud if you can) several times slowly, "I Am right with God forever! 'Sin' is not an issue with God and me!"

ROB DECKER
From Tragedy to Triumph

Rob Decker's primary objective is to share his story of a failed suicide attempt that led him to a deeper relationship with God. He suffered many years of sadness, anger, and confusion fueled by drugs, alcohol, and bad relationships. With the help of God, he was able to turn his story from ashes to beauty. His desire is to inspire, encourage, and give hope to those who have had similar battles.

For many of us, the cycle of brokenness, chaos, and destruction of our childhood continues in our adult life. For Rob, this is a beautiful story of redemption and God's unconditional love and grace that not only saved a man from suicide but also led him to forgiveness. Rob always begins his story with his mom, who was the oldest of five kids and was beaten and abused as a child.

His mother grew up in a very dysfunctional home, and this pattern carried over into Rob's life when he was growing up. He was born when his mom was only a teenager. She was told to abort him, but thankfully, she did not take that advice. After he was born, she met a man that Rob would call his dad, and together, they had another baby, Rob's sister.

At the very tender age of five, he was told by a grandmother that he didn't belong. He was also told that the man he thought was his dad was not his biological father. These words had a detrimental impact on Rob's life that would affect his identity and set him on a path to destruction.

Rob shares how his identity was shaken when he felt for the first time he really did not belong. To compound the hurt, Rob saw the favoritism his sister would receive and realized this to be due to her being the biological child of both parents. Out of the pain of hurt and rejection, Rob began to live a life of destruction. From drug addiction to broken relationship after broken relationship with women, Rob did not care what he did or how he treated people. He just lived from a place of deeply rooted pain and did everything he could to try to numb it.

All this chaos, addiction, and brokenness would take a drastic turn when Rob met Jesus. As he began to change, he was still walking in and out of his past destructive patterns. A former girlfriend turned on him. She sent him pictures of herself, saying she was being beat up by another man she lived with. However, she then lied and told authorities that it was Rob who beat her and falsely accuse him of brutally raping her.

When police showed up at his home to arrest him, feeling completely cornered by her false accusation and feeling hopeless, Rob jumped out of the third-story window, trying to end his life. By the grace of God, he failed. An awning broke his fall, and instead of dying, he ended up in the hospital, alive, but his prognosis was not good. He was told he would never walk again.

Rob remembers waking up to a police officer holding a folder about his case in his room, and the officer telling him he was an awful man. Rob told the officer that while he had certainly done a lot of things in his life, brutally raping this girl was not one of them. After this conversation, something strange happened. The girl who falsely accused him of rape came into the room, completely disguised. The police officer immediately knew something was wrong and began to question her story. Why would a woman who was brutally raped disguise herself to go visit her 'rapist'? The police officer knew to ask questions and ended up escorting her out of the hospital.

Rob knew he was innocent. And God did too. Rob began to dialogue with God about the situation as he was facing prison, knowing he may never walk again and having no money to pay for recommended surgeries. In this desperation, he cried out to God.

Miraculously, he felt a peace move throughout his body, and the calming voice of the Father say three things: "Rob, these charges will be dropped; your bills will be paid, and you will walk again." That is exactly what transpired.

Rob heard from the police that the charges were dropped. Within days, he began to walk again, and his bills were paid.

Rob describes the greatest miracle; he forgave his mom for his childhood pain. He left the hospital completely in awe of a God of unconditional love and grace. This God turned his life from victimhood to victory.

Grace I AM #11

God is good, really! Have you (like me) ever been in religious groups that say in unison "God is good all the time"? Well, that's true. But religion actually teaches us a multitude of lies about its concept of God that are anything BUT good!

You can easily make up your own list, but here are just a few:

God is NOT good to 'sinners'—He causes calamity to come on them

God's 'goodness' has limits and an 'endpoint,' unless a person sincerely does whatever their specific religious group says

God's goodness doesn't include 'those people'

That kind of teaching obviously brings about cognitive dissonance: both concepts can't be true at the same time. Religion then comes up with a variety of nonsensical replies to questions. You may have heard:

It's actually GOOD for God to punish 'those' people

His punishment is for their own 'good'

God's goodness is only for certain groups

God's ways are higher than ours (please know that this phrase, in context, refers to God being way better than we expect!)

While we need to be aware of religion's false concept of God, it serves no good purpose to dwell on it or bash it or complain about it. Rather, Jesus and those who knew Him personally simply said, "Change your mind completely." Do a 180 in what you have believed that religion taught you. Instead, take sides with Jesus and go by what His mind in you reveals to you!

As you do, Grace reveals to you that God is indeed Good, 'gooder' than you can ever imagine! And His goodness is focused on you. He is continually working out all things, even (especially) things that aren't good, for the good!

Take a few minutes in your secret place with your primary Teammates, Jesus, Papa, and Grace, and say (out loud if you can) several times slowly, "God IS good! God is good to me! God is continually working all things for the good for me!"

DR. STEVE MCVEY
Inclusion Changes Everything!

> *"Science tells us that every person projects light from their bodies. It's not visible to the human eye but can be detected with the right equipment. Some people 'shine' brighter than others. Science also tells us that we unconsciously 'mirror' each other when we encounter one another. Make it your aim today to 'let your light so shine before men.' Choose to bring light into somebody's dark circumstances. 'Turn on your heart light.' Brighten the day of somebody who needs it. That is the grace walk experience." ~Dr. Steve McVey*

> *"You'll notice a prevailing theme throughout many of the stories in this book—acknowledgment and thanks to Steve McVey for his teaching being one of the first and most impactful transformational effects on the lives of the Grace Restoration Team! That's certainly true of me!" ~Paul Gray*

Steve McVey was a very successful fundamental legalistic Pastor, Teacher, and Leader of Calvinistic churches and denominations for over twenty years. In his first book, an international best-seller, *Grace Walk*, he tells about his 'crisis of faith' and God's comfort, counsel, compassion, and grace as He transformed Steve into one of the preeminent Grace teachers in the world. That journey has come at a great financial and loss of friendship price, as he was branded a heretic and false teacher by misinformed and misguided religious leaders.

Steve and his wife, Melanie, are gracious, loving, inclusive, welcoming, compassionate, and a lot of fun to be with!

Steve McVey is the author of twenty-seven books (translated into many languages); founder of Grace Walk Ministries; Vice President of Global Grace Seminar; and television, radio, and internet personality. He frequently does conferences with Don Keathley, Paul Young, Baxter Kruger, Paul Anderson-Walsh, and others featured in this book.

Steve says that our perception of God is foundational to how we will treat others. He's been teaching people's identity in Christ for over three decades and continues to do so with his newfound understanding of

Quantum Physics, which he says is also Quantum Spirituality. Quite unlike the angry, punitive, distant, wrathful, list keeping Zeus-type *god* of his religious days, Steve now passionately and informatively teaches about The Only True God, who is Pure Love, Light, Grace, and Inclusion for ALL people!

While he still loves and values scripture, he has come to agree with the Apostle John that Jesus is the Living Word of God, and we are to understand Scripture through the revelation of the Christ in us as opposed to understanding Jesus through scripture.

When asked the very legitimate question "How can we tell if we're hearing from Jesus or from some other voice?" Steve answers, "Love. Divine Love. The only Source of Authentic Love. If you're moving deeper into Love, you're moving in the right direction. Don't torment yourself with questions, doubts, and fears about whether you're getting it right or wrong. If you're growing in Love, you cannot be wrong because 'God is love,' and 'Love never fails.' Love. That is the grace walk experience."

Steve believes everyone and everything lives inside the inescapable atmosphere permeated by God's divine love. Everybody and everything are within this atmosphere. We are One with God and each other. He relates, "Knowing this oneness is everything in your relationships. It stops you from seeing people from an insider and outsider point of view." He references the Apostle Paul's words "There is neither Jew nor Greek, there is neither bond nor free, there is neither male nor female: for you are all one in Christ Jesus."

He is quick to point out that, of course, not everyone knows they are in Christ. "We treat everyone with the same kindness God does. We can also be assured God's got them! This allows us to be so much more accepting of people. We seek to love and understand, not convert; that's the Holy Spirit's job." He often quotes Julian of Norwich, "All will be well," and says, "We can relax and just love people as they are because God's Love never fails!"

Inclusion extends God's grace to all, whereas religion tends to judge and separate, leaving people feeling unloved. Steve says in the religious community, that is nowhere more evident than in regard to the LGBTQ community. He remembers a time when he was introduced to his friend's gay sister. She asked if he would speak at her church, which was primarily populated by people who were gay. He enthusiastically replied, "Of course!" She then asked him what he would say to them. Steve replied that he would share what he shares everywhere: "How much God loves each person there unconditionally."

Steve finds it interesting that the gay community has received a great deal of judgment from Christians, but often it's from a very overweight preacher who never mentions what his Bible has to say about gluttony! Steve says, "Exclusion has never been in God's heart." He laments that even in much of the grace community, there is still the attitude that "you are not in yet, and if you don't believe the same way as our group, you are judged an apostate, heretic, deceived, or even the anti-Christ." Steve knows there is tremendous freedom when we humbly realize that while none of us have it all figured out, we can walk in the all-encompassing love of Christ.

Dr. McVey teaches Quantum Spirituality every weekday in a private subscription-based Facebook group. He challenges listeners to think for themselves and not just take what he teaches as the truth. Although he once crisscrossed the planet, sharing his message of God's unconditional love to multitudes, he now reaches even more via the internet. He especially enjoys intimate settings where the group can interact, ask questions, and grow in grace and love in community.

"Steve McVey was my first (and continual) mentor in the 'Grace Movement' and has graciously accepted, included, and loved me through twelve years of moving with him into an ever-deeper understanding and experience of Papa's all-inclusive grace and love. Not a week (and hardly a day) has gone by in twelve years that I haven't listened to one of his videos or Facebook live-streamed teaching or read something he's written. In addition to all these, his personal calls, texts, and emails have continually encouraged, stimulated, and inspired me. He introduced me to many of the others whom I've interviewed and written about in this book, and I love him, even if he does smoke cigars!" ~Paul Gray

Grace I AM #12

"Forgiveness always precedes repentance."—T.F. Torrance

"Union is prior to faith and repentance."— C. Baxter Kruger

"The gospel isn't that you can receive Jesus into your life. The good news is, Jesus has already accepted you into His life." — C. Baxter Kruger

"Truth doesn't become the truth when we believe it. It is already truth; that's why we believe it."— Francois Du Toit

The following is by David Adams: "God's unconditional love and goodness toward us precedes our knowledge or experience of it.

"We get the cart before the horse so many times in our theology and doctrines. I believe this is why there is no power in what is preached in many places today. If we have a toy that needs batteries, and we put them in upside down, the toy will not work because it does not receive the power from the batteries.

"The scriptures say that the gospel is the power of God unto salvation, yet most people do not seem to be experiencing the joy of that salvation. I believe this is because most of the time, the gospel is presented as something that we must do instead of something that Jesus did.

"When we really hear the gospel, the real gospel, it will ignite faith within us. Faith that is already within us because God has already put it within our hearts.

"It may take a while for that initial spark to turn into a full-blown flame, but at some point, even if it is after we die, it will turn into a lake of fire, burning away anything that is ungodly out of us.

"God has already given you your inheritance. It is already yours! You don't have to wait until you die to enjoy it! Eternal life is for us to enjoy now and forever. Eternal life isn't about getting to heaven. It is about experiencing heaven within you."

Take a few minutes in your secret place with your primary Teammates, Jesus, Papa, and Grace, and say (out loud if you can) several times slowly, "I AM my Papa's child! I already have my Divine Inheritance! I enjoy it today!"

WES TARPLEY
Poetic Justice Outreach

Wes Tarpley is a rapper, poet, composer, gourmet chef, entrepreneur, special ed teacher, car salesman, biker, photographer, encourager, visionary ... a real renaissance man! He was formerly a poor student who loathed reading and writing, but after Christ opened his eyes to His Life and Love, he is now a voracious reader, writer, poet, psalmist, and photographer.

Wes and his wife, Karen, love traveling in their RV and motorcycle out into the wild Texas wilderness and small communities, being living epistles read by all and being an open door to the gospel of Grace Himself, where art and music become a manifestation of the presence of Father, Son, and Holy Spirit.

Having unique giftedness for taking the words of pop songs, scripture, and other writings and transforming them into poetry and song has spurred Wes to construct a unique multi-media platform for both in-person and online experience called Poetic Justice Outreach. If you'd like to have him and Karen come to your community, just ask!

Every winter, Wes and Karen spend a few months in West Texas, and he frequently posts pictures with his poetic journaling of their life experienced as union with Papa, Jesus, and Grace! Here's an example:

A Day in the Desert ~by Wes Tarpley

The mountains erupt out of the dry and thirsty ground. And the ground itself is as a parchment of what could be. The grasses are parched from the sun and lack of rain. As the rocks deflect the heat upon a ground that is ravaged and spent. And yet the beauty is iridescent in the splendor of Hope. For rain itself, seemingly ever on the horizon, yet seldom up close and personal, is more than a wish. Rain is the precipitation of Grace in the middle of nowhere, the conduit of Love Himself.

So many people are overwhelmingly tired. As if their lives were arid and rock-strewn. Exhausted and plum-crushed in the dire circumstances of an unfruitful life. Too many are worn out, stressed out, inebriated in solitude, and empty of fortitude. Memories are replete with failure and the dust on the road too frequently traveled is the noise of "it is what it is, same as it's always been, karma's a bitch, and what goes around comes around." Nothing seems to ever change.

But God, in the midst of desert mindsets, shows us that in Him, we live and move and have our being.

We drink of Grace Himself Immersed in His Love.

"But whoever drinks of the water that I shall give him will never thirst.

"Indeed, the water that I shall give him Will become in him a well of water

Springing up into eternal life."

We drink of Christ Himself Immersed in His Light.

"Come to Me, All who are weary and heavy-laden, And I will give you rest.

"Take My yoke upon you And learn from Me, For I am gentle and humble in heart,

And you will find rest for your souls. For My yoke is easy and My burden is light."

We drink of Christ Himself Immersed in His Life.⊠ "On that day You will know that I am in My Father, And you are in Me, and I am in you. He who has My desires And keeps them Is the one who loves Me.

"And he who loves Me will be loved by My Father. And I will love him and will reveal Myself to him."

We drink of Christ Himself Immersed in His Desires.

We know That we are now in Christ.

His Desires are ours. His Mind is ours. His Love is ours. His Hope is ours. His Peace is ours.

His Joy is ours. His Faith is ours. His Way is ours. His Truth is ours.

His Life is ours. His Righteousness is ours.

We have been baptized With the Holy Spirit and with Fire. The All-consuming Fire Is the River of Living Water That flows through every aspect of our being.

So drink deep of Christ Himself. And know that you are His Garden.

The Cross was the desert

And His Resurrection and Ascension Are His Ever-Present Reign.

And Rain.

From Notes From Papa, a 366-day devotional by Paul Gray:

A Note From Papa to you!

To My precious, beautiful child, whom I love unconditionally and totally,

Faith is absolutely necessary for you in Our relationship. Faith is seeing what really is in the unseen and eternal realm.

Now, I want you to know the truth about faith! So many people believe the lie of religion that it's up to them to work up faith. That's a lie straight from the pit of religious hell.

I always supply and provide what I require! Sear that in your memory!

I require faith for Our relationship, and it's impossible to please Me without faith. So, I have already provided all the faith you will ever need—the faith of Jesus!

You have, and you can live by, the faith of Jesus, who loves you and gave Himself up for you. There is only one faith—Jesus' faith!

There's no possible way you could ever come up with faith to believe the right things about Me or anything or anyone else! At best, your human faith is subject to situations, circumstances, well-meaning but misled teachers, and whispers from the deceiver/accuser.

That's why I have given you the one faith—Jesus' faith! Whatever faith you could conjure up about Me would always be deficient. I knew that before creation. That's why I have given you the only One Faith of Jesus—who lives in you!

Only Jesus' faith—what He believes about Me and about you and everyone—matters! You are to live from His Faith to your faith! Believe what He believes about Me, you, and everyone. That's it! I made it very simple. Get to know Jesus better and better every day and believe His divine promises that I have already given you everything necessary for life and godliness. Take sides with Jesus.

Believe Him. Live by His Faith!

~Love, Papa

BRAD JERSAK
A Different Agenda

"Letting go of making sure is a step toward mental health."
~Brad Jersak

Like most of the people featured in *Grace to ALL*, Brad Jersak's spiritual journey has included a hodge-podge of experiences. From fundamental Baptist to Evangelical, to Mennonite, to Eastern Orthodox, with periodic blessed relationships and learning from First Nation People and others, Brad has a unique and wonderful background from which he graciously and generously shares wisdom and knowledge with people around the world.

Brad Jersak, author and teacher, is based in Abbotsford, BC. He currently serves as the Dean of Theology & Culture at St. Stephen's University (SSU.ca/graduate) in New Brunswick and teaches peace studies courses with IRPJ.org and is a regular speaker with the Open Table Conference crew. He writes regularly for the Clarion Journal and CWR magazine. If you have a college degree in any subject, you can get a master's degree in 'Religion, Peace, and Justice' and/or 'Theology and Culture Programs' online at SSU with Dr. Jersak as your primary professor!

Through his books and seminars, Brad shares the good news that God is Love, perfectly revealed in Jesus Christ, and that God's love heals wounded hearts and empowers us to heal this broken world.

Brad is a frequent guest on podcast and video interviews and often appears with his close friend, Paul Young. Together, they have written the compelling novel *The Pastor: A Crisis* that draws from their personal religious experiences and those of people with whom they have experienced life together. It's not for the faint of heart!

Brad's research, studies, willingness to ask questions and be open to grappling with the cognitive dissonance that man-made religious doctrines and teaching espouse has led him to write a number of books that have been a tremendous help to people worldwide!

Here's a description of Brad Jersak's seminal book *A More Christlike God: A More Beautiful Gospel:*

"What is God like? A punishing judge? A doting grandfather? A deadbeat dad? A vengeful warrior? 'Believers' and atheists alike typically carry and finally reject the toxic images of God in their own hearts and minds. Even the Christian gospel has repeatedly lapsed into a vision of God where the wrathful King must be appeased by his victim Son. How do such 'good cop/bad cop' distortions of the divine arise and come to dominate churches and cultures? Whether our notions of God are personal projections or inherited traditions, author and theologian Brad Jersak proposes a radical reassessment, arguing for A More Christlike God: A More Beautiful Gospel. If Christ is 'the image of the invisible God, the radiance of God's glory and exact representation of God's likeness,' what if we conceived of God as completely Christlike—the perfect incarnation of self-giving, radically forgiving, co-suffering love? What if God has always been and forever will be 'cruciform' (cross-shaped) in His character and actions? A more Christlike God suggests that such a God would be very good news indeed—a God who Jesus 'unwrathed' from dead religion, a Love that is always toward us, and a Grace that pours into this suffering world through willing, human partners."

Following is a description of Brad Jersak's book *Her Gates Will Never Be Shut*, which was recommended to me by my friend Steve McVey back in 2010. It was the first book I read that gave me hope that the horrifying version of God and 'hell' might be based on lies! I highly recommend it as well as all of Brad's books!

"Everlasting hell and divine judgment, a lake of fire and brimstone-these mainstays of evangelical tradition have come under fire once again in recent decades. Would the God of love revealed by Jesus really consign the vast majority of humankind to a destiny of eternal, conscious torment? Is divine mercy bound by the demands of justice? How can anyone presume to know who is saved from the flames and who is not? Reacting to presumptions in like manner, others write off the fiery images of final judgment altogether. If there is a God who loves us, then surely all are welcome into the heavenly kingdom, regardless of their beliefs or behaviors in this life. Yet, given the sheer volume of threat rhetoric in the scriptures and the wickedness manifested in human history, the pop-universalism of our day sounds more like denial than hope. Mercy triumphs over judgment; it does not skirt it. *Her Gates Will Never Be Shut* endeavors to reconsider what the Bible and the Church have actually said about hell and hope, noting a breadth of real possibilities that undermines every presumption. The polyphony of perspectives on hell and hope offered by the prophets, apostles, and Jesus humble our obsessive need to harmonize every text into a neat theological system. But they open the door to the eternal hope found in Revelation 21–22: the city whose gates will never be shut; where the Spirit and Bride perpetually invite the thirsty who are outside the city to 'Come, drink of the waters of life.'"

Grace I AM #13

Here's what the Team spoke to me one day, and it's for you as well:

"You are and always have been on, with, and in Our team! Be constantly aware and cultivate the TEAM concept! We are all for each other! We all have your back! We all love you unconditionally! We all accept you unconditionally! We all made allowances for and forgave you of any and all things in advance and continually!

"We all teach you! We all energize you! We all appreciate and value you! We all do Our part to ensure TEAM success! We have unlimited resources! We have everything you need! We are continually working out all things for the good! We constantly and continually restore and make all things right for everyone! We are all working toward and for the same goal: the restoration of all!

"We all delight in you and each other! We are all good! We are all Grace! We have given you Our wisdom, understanding, and counsel! Now delightfully expect the effortless manifestation of all this and more for your life from your loving TEAMMATES!"

Take a few minutes in your secret place every day with your primary Teammates, Jesus, Papa, and Grace. Say out loud, if you can, "I AM so grateful and thankful to you ALL for everything!"

GEORGE W. SARRIS
Heaven's Doors ...Wider Than You Ever Believed!

"God will win in the end—His Love will have its final say."
~George W. Sarris

If you've ever listened to the audio version of the NIV via Bible Gateway, you've heard George W. Sarris's wonderful voice! He's an author, speaker, performer, and graduate of Gordon Conwell Theological Seminary. He served on the staffs of three missionary organizations. He's the creator of an award-winning series of CDs that bring the Bible to life. His book, *How Wide Are Heavens Doors? -The Biblical case for Ultimate Reconciliation*, was awarded the silver medal in theology in the 2018 Illumination Awards for exemplary Christian books.

George is a versatile communicator who works in New York City as a principal spokesman on local, regional, and national radio. In TV, he has done commercials for national companies, including AT&T, IBM, Pizza Hut, and Honda, and played a main part in the last episode of a TV program, Super Boy. Other roles include guest spots in Spencer for Hire and Spin City. He's a humble, engaging, and accessible man who lives with his wife, Suzanne, and their family in Trumbull, Connecticut.

George Sarris believes in the early church doctrine of Apokatastasis, also known as ultimate reconciliation, based on Acts 3:21, which says that God has promised that there will be a restoration of all things. "When you learn that God's love is unconditional, and it is extended to everyone, you begin to walk in this freedom to just love one another. You know God's intentions are to restore that person, and you can trust Him to guide and draw, as you have freedom to just connect."

George teaches how the message in the western church has been about getting people to say the *sinner's prayer.* Somewhere along the way, he says that the Great Commission went from making disciples to making converts. Unconditional love allows us to focus on building relationships. And, ironically, because the pressure to convert someone is gone, conversations about faith flow more naturally and organically. The very same people who would normally resist you see love instead of agenda and are much more receptive.

George shares what this looks like as he tells us about a friend whom he worked with in NYC, who was not a Christian. This man believed more in an eastern mysticism spirituality and was resistant to the gospel. But because George was not treating him like a project to save, the relationship grew close and was built on mutual trust. The two friends had numerous discussions; most of the time, they would banter about political issues and current topics. And then, one day, "at the right time," George remembers feeling led by the Spirit to nudge this man to "ask God to reveal Himself to him."

As the next few months passed, George visited his friend in the hospital when he was terminally ill with a brain tumor. Then his friend revealed to George that he did in fact have 'that conversation' with God, and George had the privilege of praying with him before he passed away.

George tells of another co-worker from New York, who was a casting person. George knew this man was gay but felt no need to mention it. He wanted to see this man through the eyes of love with zero agenda. And again, because he just loved the man, grace opened a space where George would eventually have an opportunity to pray for him. This man shared how he was moving to San Francisco, in part due to the pain he had because his family all hated him because he was gay. George remembers praying for him, just a simple prayer, that God would work in his life, and that He would guide him in the right direction.

George knows that we can all trust God's irresistible love to win in everyone's life. Our part is to share the message of the good news by building relationships with people and planting seeds of grace along the way.

The doctrinal belief in the restoration of all things is what most of the early church believed. However, through the years, especially through the protestant reformation, it was mostly removed from all western religious teaching. Since it's virtually unknown in the western church, those who teach it and even write about it meet much resistance.

George remembers feeling the pressure to leave his church after twenty years because he no longer aligned with their doctrinal beliefs. Although it can be painful, George also believes it establishes your integrity and is worth it for what he believes is the true message of the gospel.

Grace I AM #14

Jesus is Grace personified, and He lives in you right now!

Jesus' best friend, John, writes to you: "Jesus is full of grace and truth and the Word (Jesus) became flesh and dwelt among us, and we beheld His glory, the glory as of the only begotten of the Father, full of grace and truth. And of His fullness we have all received, and grace for grace. For the law was given through Moses, but grace and truth came through Jesus Christ."

Paul wrote, "Grace appeared! The grace of God has appeared, bringing salvation for all people!"

Jesus came so that we could experience LIFE right now, and He defines it as abundant life, life to the full, the state of one who is possessed of vitality or is animate; of the absolute fullness of life, which belongs to God; life real and genuine, a life active and vigorous!

That's what you have right now!

Jesus said, "I am the way, the truth, and the LIFE!"

Paul says, "The grace of the Lord Jesus Christ, and the love of God the Father, and the fellowship of the Holy Spirit, is with you all."

The three members of the Trinity are One, in essence, and they have different functions that they specialize in: Jesus—Grace; The Father—Unconditional Love; The Holy Spirit—fellowship!

Take a few minutes in your secret place with your primary Teammates, Jesus, Papa, and Grace, and say (out loud if you can) several times slowly, "I Am abundant Life! I Am full of Grace, Love, and intimate fellowship with God!"

MALCOLM SMITH
God IS (not 'has') Unconditional Love

> *"I may tell you that I have a glass of water or a reservoir of water, but it is an entirely different category to say that 'I am water!' To have water means my possession of it is subject to change, whether by increase or decrease, but to BE water means I am never subject to change because that is what I am! God is the definition of love ... that is what He is!"*
>
> *~Malcolm Smith*

Malcolm Smith, founder and leader of Unconditional Love Ministry, began to preach at age fourteen and has continued preaching around the world for more than 68 years! He's not an evangelist but, as he often describes himself, is an evangelist to the evangelized, teaching Christians who they really are in Christ, who God really is, and who ALL people really are!

You'll find his English accent as welcoming as his genuine love for all people. Malcolm has had several 'turning points' in his long and productive life. In the 1960s, he was a pastor in New York City in a neighborhood filled with broken lives. Frustrated at not seeing people really connect to the Father God whom he knew and loved, he stopped all the programs in his growing church and told The Holy Spirit that he was going to wait to do anything until He told him what to do.

In a rather humorous series of conversations and events, the approach that God revealed to Malcolm was so successful that he found himself traveling throughout the world as a leader of the emerging renewal of the Spirit in much of Christianity. He decided to travel less and have a home where he could teach locally and where people could come to him.

Several years ago, he settled in Bandera, Texas, where he conducts retreats and a non-residential Bible School. Malcolm has a huge presence online, with thousands of people watching his Webinars each week. He also travels throughout the U.S., conducting retreats and meetings in churches and organizations of all denominations.

A favorite verse of Malcolm's is John 17:3, where Jesus explained that to experience eternal life is to know God intimately. Malcolm says, "Jesus came to reveal incredibly good news that all of mankind belongs to God. He came to reveal that God is not mad at us. The gospel means good news. The word gospel originated in the 1800s and actually means 'good, glad, merry news that makes a man fairly leap for joy!'"

He challenges us to "picture that visual when someone wakes up to this! God is LOVE! He does not have love. It is not an appendage of Him. He IS Love. It is the outgoing energy of the very essence and being of who He is. That is The REAL Good News which often exposes the 'not-so-good news' generally portrayed by religion."

These days, Malcolm pulls no punches in what he has observed firsthand in organized religion during his eighty-plus years of having a ring-side seat. He says, "Sadly, I have met with thousands of people who have been taught a different kind of gospel, the one where we teach people that they must do something to get reconnected with God. Many people wonder if they have repented enough, prayed the right prayer, or could drum up enough faith to be accepted by God."

He explains, "Our word 'repent,' which comes from the Greek word 'metanoia' does not mean groveling at an altar; rather, it means 'to change your mind,' to see God in truth. And as we change our minds, we will see ourselves in truth the way God does. 'Repent' has nothing to do with our actions; it is the movement of the Holy Spirit to reveal what God did in Christ for all of us. So, faith becomes our response to this revelation. We respond and enter into the faith of Christ and receive God's peace. Joy begins to overflow from the revelation of this union."

"What religion has done is come up with formulas and rules," he continues. "The very word religion comes from a Latin word, which means 'to return to bondage.' Religion gets you to do something to reconnect you to its *god* and puts you on this hamster wheel of performance where you are never sure if you are accepted."

Malcolm talks about what he refers to as the faces of religious anxiety. In the many years of his ministry, he says that you can see it on peoples' faces. "You look into their eyes and can see the fear as if to ask, 'Have I done enough?' By contrast, faces radiate when they know they are accepted just as they are and always have been in the bosom of the

Father. The kingdom of God is, after all, overflowing in righteousness, peace, and joy."

Malcolm Smith exudes the love of God! You will experience Jesus when you hear his teachings. He explains Scripture's original languages (Hebrew, Aramaic, and Greek), the culture of the time, and reveals what the Holy Spirit is teaching us today, which he says all points to God's redeeming love for all of mankind as revealed through Jesus. He calls it a 'glorious wasteful love' that never runs out.

"The Hebrew word that we translate 'rejoice' means 'to leap in the air and spin around in delight.' That's what God does when He's thinking about us!" ~Malcolm Smith

Grace I AM #15

Grace, God's Unconditional Love and pure goodness, is perpetually in action, working all things for your good (divine influence) to help you know and enjoy and experience abundant life by relating to you personally and intimately!

God is not "up there, out there, over there somewhere."

God— Papa, Jesus, and Grace— are IN you and always have been! You, like us all, just haven't been aware of that. But now, you are!

Religion's foundational lie about its counterfeit *god* is separation. Religion wants you to believe you were born separated from its *god*, and you have to do whatever they say to get its *god* to come to you and stay with you.

That's the greatest lie in the history of mankind. The really good news is, it's just a lie! Like with a dark, bad dream, it seems real, then you awaken and see the Light of the Truth: God is with you, in you, and will never leave you or forsake you!

And Jesus, Papa, and Grace relate to you personally, 24-7. That's why They made you in their image and likeness so you can enjoy each other!

Take a few minutes in your secret place with your primary Teammates, Jesus, Papa, and Grace, and say (out loud if you can) several times slowly, "I AM relating to Jesus, Papa, and Grace intimately and personally right now and always!"

DR. SHARON BAKER PUTT
Razing Hell!

"'Study to show yourself approved unto God, a worker that needs not be ashamed, handling rightly the word of truth' (2 Timothy 2:15). These words from the Bible perfectly describe what I want for my students. By teaching them theology and religion on an academic level, I hope to motivate them to know not only what they believe but also why they believe it so that they grow in their faith and in their love for God and others."

~ Dr. Sharon Baker Putt

Dr. Putt says, "When I'm not teaching (or grading papers), I research and write in the areas of non-violent atonement theory, justice, reconciliation, forgiveness, and peace. I also work in the area of interreligious dialogue, comparative theologies of religion, and Continental Philosophy. As a professor in an academic institution, I teach diverse doctrines and views of Christians in various cultures throughout Christian history in as unbiased a manner as possible."

Sharon Baker Putt describes herself as coming from a fundamental Calvinist Christian background, where she was very rigid about who she thought God was. She was taught that God is only good to the 'elect,' and the rest of the world would have no chance for salvation and be confined to hell. She believed those man-made doctrines until her children were school age, and she decided to go back to school herself.

Then, she says, the eyes of her heart began to open, and she could see God in a new light. She experienced an awakening and began to see that He is a God of unconditional love, who is extravagantly gracious and rich in compassion. And He desires for all people to be saved. She makes the analogy that the journey for many who are deconstructing from fundamental religion often feels like Lazarus coming out of the tomb. She states, "Wrappings of all that you were ever taught come off one by one as you are standing face to face with God. Your whole life changes!"

Dr. Putt says that she went from being judgmental and meanspirited to someone who is loving and open-minded, even with those who disagree with her. The dismantling of the violent teachings of eternal conscious torment and penal substitution came easy for her. By digging into the context of Scripture, researching the Greek and Hebrew languages, learning that 'hell' is an English word retranslated from four different Greek words that mean something else entirely, her concept of 'hell' fell like a house of cards. Her new understanding of Truth empowered a great desire to help others learn the truth and be free from the bondage of fear of eternal conscious torment for themselves and others.

That desire led Sharon to write her book *Razing Hell.* She had already started to lose religious friends simply by leaving the traditional role of homemaker and going to school, but after writing her book, she recalls it got worse. She was being condemned by many people and getting death threats! As Sharon says frustratingly, it has been harder to tell people that there is not a place called eternal conscious torment than it would be to say that Jesus is not the only way to salvation. You just can't take hell away from some people!

Today, Sharon is a professor of theology and religion at Messiah University in Pennsylvania. Her approach is to be fair and open-minded. Not wanting to appear biased, she does not include her own book when she teaches about hell. She teaches the three main beliefs from the early church, showing that the majority believed in Apokatastasis, that God would reconcile all. She presents the belief in Eternal Conscious Torment, the belief that unbelievers simply no longer exist after human death, and then allows the students to make up their minds.

Her students write a final paper in which they state their own beliefs and must support it with Scripture. Despite what she has written about, she does not want to dictate to them what to believe or push her own view. Sadly, her view is not often found in religious settings. Most organized religious organizations tend to present 'their way or the highway.' Sharon believes her approach will help build confidence in her students, and they will grow in their own faith and can defend their own convictions.

Her teaching and research have provided her much joy, especially when researching female Christian mystics, including Hildegard of

Bingen, Teresa of Avila, and Julian of Norwich. She loves this research because it reveals those who connect to God in direct contemplative ways that are intangible. She says, "We do not have to fear mysticism. Mystics simply experience God through the openness of their heart through many different practices, including prayer, fasting, times of solitude, and other spiritual disciplines." She hopes this will be the subject of her next book.

"*Razing Hell* was a pivotal and extremely helpful message in my journey from a religious fear-based dark religion to the bright unconditional love-filled experiential relationship with Papa, Jesus, and Grace. I'm very grateful for Dr. Sharon Baker Putt!" ~Paul Gray

Grace I AM #16

Grace is God's Unconditional Love and pure goodness perpetually in action, working all things for your good (divine influence), to help you know and enjoy and experience abundant life by energizing and empowering you to be all God created you to be!

God is ALL-POWERFUL, and God always and only uses their power for good!

Every religion's counterfeit concept of God believes it is all-powerful, and they believe it uses that 'power' for both good and evil. Jesus, God Himself, reveals to us that God never uses power for evil. You can read every scripture about Jesus and never, ever find even a hint that He uses power against you.

The only True God always uses Their Power for good—for you! They continually energize you with Their Power and empower you to be everything they created you to be, which is ALL good!

Right now, this very day (and every day), you have the same power that created and sustains the universe IN you and working FOR you. That's a really good thing to know, isn't it?

Grace in you is continually revealing to you how to live by and use that power for your good! Take a few minutes in your secret place with your primary Teammates, Jesus, Papa, and Grace, and say (out loud if you can) several times slowly, "I AM being energized and empowered by God to do all God created me to do!"

PETER HIETT
Where the hell is Hell?

Peter Hiett likes to ask questions. He's found that it gets him in a LOT of trouble with religious organizations and their leaders! When he was his denomination's poster boy for being a successful pastor, building a mega-church, and recognized as an extremely gifted communicator, leader, and rising star, he started asking, "What does the Bible really say about hell?"

That got him kicked the hell out of the denomination, de-frocked, marginalized, labeled a heretic and other things too nasty to mention. Despite that heartbreaking and painful experience, Peter Hiett has continued to be a successful author, pastor of The Sanctuary in Denver, Colorado, an online teacher and long-distance mentor to many! He says, "God had given us a message to proclaim that, sadly, is rather rare. I think that message is the Gospel." In a nutshell (or a human shell), the Gospel means "God is Salvation." In the language of Scripture, "God is Salvation" forms a name 'Yeshua,' that in English is pronounced 'Jesus.' That's the Good News, the Gospel.

"Is it rare? Well, no, and yes! Most of us put our faith in 'me is salvation' rather than 'God is Salvation,' or, as I like to say, 'Me-sus' instead of Jesus. And so, of course, then, we don't really believe that God desires to save all or has the power to save all because we've come to believe that God is basically 'me.' But the Gospel isn't 'Me-sus' (my choice). The Gospel is Jesus (God's choice) for me.

"At The Sanctuary, we're beginning to believe that God in Christ Jesus saves all by creating faith in all through amazing Grace for all, and the Bible tells us that this is so. We preach the Gospel with two convictions that, together, seem to be fairly rare: That Scripture is trustworthy. AND that, through Christ, God reconciles all things to Himself, making peace by the blood of His cross. That's Scripture: Colossians 1:19. And that's what we mean by 'Relentless Love.' Quite simply, God is Love, and God is Almighty, and through Jesus, God conquers all. That's the Good News, the Gospel."

Peter Hiett is the son of a Presbyterian pastor, whom he greatly adored. After receiving a degree in Geology from the University of Colorado, Peter earned an M.Div. Degree from Fuller Seminary in Pasadena, CA. Peter has authored four books that you should read! He has been married to Susan, his high school sweetheart, since 1983. They have four wonderful children that Peter says he likes most of the time!

In describing his book *All Things New: What Does the Bible Really Say About Hell?* Peter says: "In several places, Scripture testifies to the idea that there is a reality in which everything is very good (Gen. 1:31); a reality in which all things are made new (Rev. 21:5); where 'every creature in heaven and on earth and under the earth and in the sea, and all that is in them,' praises God and the Lamb that was slain (Rev. 5:13); a place where Jesus, the Light, fills all things (Eph. 4:10) and every knee bows and every tongue gives praise (Rom.14:11, Phil. 2:1011, Isa. 45:23). Well, if that's the case—and Jesus said, 'Scripture cannot be broken' (John 10:35)—then where the hell is Hell?

"I mean, how do we reconcile Scripture with 'popular' notions of 'Hell,' an endless Hell? That question comes as a surprise for many; for we've been told that the popular view of Hell—a place where God tortures people or allows people to be tortured forever without end—is a biblical idea. The more I've studied it, the more I've become convinced that this 'doctrine' is a very unbiblical idea ... perhaps it's even a satanic idea. In this book, I'd like to offer some assistance in constructing this new mental paradigm—a biblical paradigm that allows for an eternal day in which everything is good. In the first section, 'Exegetical Paradigms,' I'll examine the three leading views of Hell in light of Scripture and offer a set of ideas that has led me to embrace the idea of redemption for all. In the next section, 'Theology,' I'll suggest a few ways in which the idea of redemption for all may relate to one's current theological system. In the last section, 'Pastoral Care,' I'll suggest some reasons as to why I think all of this matters."

You can watch Peter's teaching videos at www.thesanctuarydenver.org/sermons. You'll bc inspired, encouraged, entertained, challenged, and taken deeper into God's inclusive Unconditional Love for ALL people! Unless, of course, you haven't yet become awakened to the truth. In that case, you'll be mad as hell until The Light comes on!

Grace I AM #17

Grace is God's Unconditional Love and pure goodness perpetually in action, working all things for your good (divine influence) to help you know and enjoy and experience abundant life by continually showing you that God is PURE Goodness!

God is GOOD – period!

God is perfect – PURE Goodness!

Religion's myriad of false understandings about God say, "Well, yes, of course, God is good, BUT He's also just." Then religion 'justifies' (pun intended) its absurd false understanding of God by repeatedly saying things like "It's actually good for God to give you a disease to teach you a lesson; wipe out a city with a hurricane because of the 'sin' in that city; infect people with deadly diseases because they 'deserve' it; delight in punishing and tormenting people forever because they didn't believe religion's lies about their version of God."

I hope you've never heard or believed those heinous lies, but most of us have. That false belief is based on fear and perpetuates fear. That's why it's so important to know that God is PURE GOODNESS! A simple Google search of honest sources will show you that the Hebrew, Aramaic, and Greek words for 'just' and 'justice' mean "making all things right for all people."

Take a few minutes in your secret place with your primary Teammates, Jesus, Papa, and Grace, and say (out loud if you can) several times slowly, "I AM so grateful that God, who lives in me, is PURE GOODNESS!"

DEBRA WESTBROOK
Leaving the Echo Chamber of the Mundane

> *"Each of us has a brilliant reason why we incarnated for such a time as this. This reason forms the underlying beat of our heart, the focus of our expression, and energizes the underlying conscious awareness stream of how we live, move, and have our being in life. If we just take the time to 'be still,' there will come a divine whisper from our heart in coherence with the mind of Christ/Christ consciousness within. We then find that everything we are, in all ways that we live and in how we move in this life, is found in our particular creative expression. It is the 'me' that flows forth in authenticity.*
>
> *"Personal example: I find my focus, my bent, is always intent on helping people find their unique creative expression in this life, in this time. This is simple, yet I find it aligns with my focus in everyone I see. 'Who are you? How do you navigate life? What is your passion?'*
>
> *"Not 'What do you DO?' but 'Who are you? What makes YOU YOU?'" ~Debra Westbrook*

Deborah says each season of her life brings new experiences that lead her into beautiful transitions, continual change, and flowing transformation in Christ. She has a passion to see people rise into their creative expression in Christ Jesus, living a life that is uniquely and gloriously perfect within their flow and function. God longs to journey with us and within us to co-create a life that is full and abundant in Christ.

She is a speaker, leader, administrator, writer, creative seer, visionary, and travel scribe. Each season in her life has opened new doors to travel throughout the world. She has lived in Finland and in the Middle East for over eight years. She traveled to Africa to teach. She's explored twenty-five countries in unique and creative ways, and her curiosity and sense of adventure can consistently challenge her to know God in a deeper way through the realm of faith and science. She has a degree in education, with a focus on science and math, and she has a Master of Theology degree at Global Grace Seminary.

Deborah speaks on quantum concepts that impact and challenge spirituality and faith. She has lived in Northern California since 1980. Originally from Chicago, she has two beautiful French bulldogs named Chloe and Flynn, two adult children, and two grandchildren, all of whom live in California.

Deborah is an inspiring woman with a zest for life. She has a passion for each one of us to move out of what she would call "the echo chamber of the mundane" and into living out our unique and divine creative expression.

She began her own faith journey of 'leaving the mundane' when she began to get a deeper revelation of God's unconditional, all-inclusive grace. Her path would lead her out of a traditional denomination into her studies at Global Grace Seminary. It was there she said that God used a particular verse of Scripture to awaken within her a deeper revelation of our connection and inclusion in Christ. 2 Corinthians 5:16 says, "From now on, therefore, we regard no one according to the flesh."

Her studies opened her eyes to the greater truth that while all died in the first Adam, all were made alive by the second Adam—Christ Jesus. Then she realized she could no longer look at people through the lens of separation, holding an attitude of 'in versus out,' or by judging what she saw in a person's actions. She could instead see all people as they are really in Christ! She says that as a result, her love grew deeper for other people, and she started seeing Christ as universal.

Seeing our interconnectedness fostered Deborah's exploration of Quantum physics (quantum spirituality). Her study of Quantum has unfolded a greater and more glorious view of this world in which we all live. She has found a natural synergy between Quantum science and our faith.

Quantum includes terms such as field, energy, frequency, and entanglement. In spiritual terms, we say spirit or kingdom or faith. Her study has shown that God has intricately woven all of mankind together. Science and faith are not a contradiction.

In Quantum, we learn how science and spirituality harmonize

beautifully! Both point to a God who loves us all and intended for us all to be connected by One Spirit. We can safely conclude that the science of Quantum does not conflict with God at all; rather it points to Him. Quantum entanglement confirms Scripture in Colossians 1:16–17 "For in Him all things were created and in Him all things hold together."

Her progressive understanding has dramatically impacted her day-to-day relationships. She lives in San Francisco, a diverse area totally unlike the 'Bible belt.' As she relates to people of all walks of life, Debra has the unique gift to pull out of people their own treasure. She does this by looking beyond natural barriers to see us all as one in one Spirit. So, whether she meets a Buddhist or Muslim, atheist or agnostic, gay or straight, black or white, she knows there is no separation and only love. We are one in Christ.

Debora says, "In this place where science and faith have collided, we may have just scratched the surface into how this world is beautifully woven together. Perhaps there is still so much more to discover. I am 'all in' in the discovery!"

From Notes From Papa, a 366-day devotional by Paul Gray:

A Note From Papa to you!

To My delightful child, whom I have made perfect in every way in My economy,

You tend to focus on your supposed flaws—physical, mental, emotional, spiritual, and behavior/character. I call that having a 'sin-consciousness.' I do not want you to ever have a sin-consciousness!

Religion focuses on sin and behavior management because it believes the lies that you are all sinful; you displease Me; sin has separated you from Me; and you must work at managing your behavior in ways that will then please Me in order to cause Me to bless you.

Every one of those is a lie! First of all, I took all the sin of the world away, forgave it all, don't hold any of it against you, choose not to remember it, and will never bring it up to you. How much clearer can I make that? You are not sinful; you are sanctified (made pure, holy, innocent, without fault and right with Me). I know that because I did all that!

Your sin does not displease Me! Of course, I am saddened when the actions of any of My children hurt themselves and others, but never mistake that for Me being displeased with you.

You have never been separated from Me. I put you in Christ before creation, and Jesus, the Holy Spirit, and I have always been in you. There is nowhere you can go that I'm not there in you and with you.

You don't have to work on or change anything to please Me or get Me to bless you. I am already pleased with you, and I bless you because I am love, and I am good, not because you do anything!

Once you know the truth about Me and you, and the better you get to know what I am really like, I will change your *want to*, and you will find yourself wanting to live differently than you did before. Then you will enjoy and experience the abundant life I have given you more and more every day!

Sin is not a terrible crime. It is a terminal disease that I cured in Jesus' finished work at the cross. I am the Great Physician, not the Terrible Judge!

~Love, Papa

DR. KAY FAIRCHILD
The Father's Love Changes Everything!

"Several places in Scripture (Matthew 3:2, Mark 1:14–15, and Revelation 1:3) state that 'the kingdom is at hand.' The word for 'hand' in Greek means: The throttle. Therefore, the phrase, 'the kingdom is at hand' means that we have the advantage to experience the kingdom (since it is within us) as quickly as we desire to subjectively experience it from within ourselves. The verse in Matthew 3:2 also states: 'REPENT ye: for the kingdom of heaven is at hand.' The word 'repent' does not infer repenting for sins in one's life, but it denotes changing the way one thinks or to draw our thoughts from the realm of spirit, our Christ Mind." Kay Fairchild continues, "Then the verse in Mark 1:15 also uses the word 'repent' in conjunction with the kingdom being at hand. Consequently, 'the throttle is in our hand,' which indicates that we can subjectively experience the kingdom within us as quickly or slowly as we want, depending on our becoming aware. That, my dear friends, is the Good News of the Gospel of the kingdom of heaven/our Father!"

Dr. Kay Fairchild is the president and founder of New Life Ministries. She has traveled abroad and across the U.S. for more than forty years, teaching the grace of God and the inclusion of all people. She is a pastor, television show host, author of twelve books, professor at Global Grace Seminary, and has hundreds of YouTube presentations. She is currently in the high triple digits of her series called Mind Brain Connections, where she helps us interpret the Bible through spiritual allegory as much of it was written and intended!

Kay says, "It's the love of the Father. That's really what is it all about, isn't it? He loves us all so much." The Scripture says, "We love, because He loved first loved us." In her personal journey, she vividly remembers awakening to unconditional love and grace when the Spirit revealed to her "The Creator of the universe loves all of mankind so much that He predestined us ALL before the world was ever formed to be One with Him!" She states, "Nobody can resist this type of love!"

One of Kay's favorite scriptures that led her to see that God includes everyone is Psalm 24:1, "The earth is the LORD'S, and the fullness of it, the world, and those who dwell in it." She says, "This declares all of mankind belongs to God, and I'm so thankful that across this planet, people are waking up to realize they are included, and the Father loves them!"

Knowing the Father's goodness motivates Kay to challenge many of the traditional western doctrines of religion that have kept people from seeing the truth and kept many in the bondage of torment and fear. She has found that these doctrines were not believed by most of the early church and were, instead, formed out of paganism, violence, and a false message of separation from God.

Kay's exhaustive studies have led her to dismantle the sacred cows of penal substitution and original sin (vs. original blessing), which both completely contradict the true nature of our Father, who is love. Kay teaches, "God did not change in the garden toward His creation. He changes not. It was, instead, we (mankind) who became blind and took on amnesia and forgot who we are. In Ecclesiastes, it says God brought us all here upright, but it was us who sought out schemes. And the schemes we searched out only came from our forgetting."

Kay has an incredible gift for interpreting Scripture parabolically and allegorically. She relates that Jesus spoke in parables, and those who sought truth would be given even more. When we start to read Scripture parabolically and allegorically, the Spirit reveals deeper truths to us. Kay says that then we can begin to live out of the right side of our brain, which is the Christ identity. Our Father has given us everything to live our lives right now whole, healed, and prosperous. We don't have to wait for some future end-time event or when we 'get to heaven.' She has learned and teaches, "Because we have been taught to read Scripture from only the historicity of it, or what Paul calls the letter, we miss out on so much of the richness of what was actually being said."

In her latest series called "Mind-Brain Connections," Kay has led many out of the prison of living out of the left side of our brain (ruled by the 5 natural senses) and, instead, moving into the right side, where we live not by sight but by the Spirit.

Kay shares how she is quick to correct and encourage her grandchildren when they begin to believe lies of lack/poverty/or sickness. She reminds them of the truth that they are whole, healed, and prosperous today. She reminds them that before the foundation of the world, they are found in Christ. She repeats often that God is not mad at them, and there is no distance or delay in Christ!

She says, "This is the real good news! God is not mad at humanity. He is only love!"

In addition to her numerous blogs and videos, Dr. Kay leads and teaches two fellowships in person and online each week. Check her out—you'll be blessed!

Grace I AM #18

Grace is God's Unconditional Love and pure goodness perpetually in action, working all things for your good (divine influence) to help you know and enjoy and experience abundant life by continually showing you that God is totally for you!

God is absolutely, totally, always unwaveringly FOR YOU! God created the best for you, has given you all things for life and living like God, and really wants you to know that they are for you!

We've all had things happen in our lives that make us think that not only is God not for us, but He's also actually against us. When that happens, They want us to know that we simply don't yet see Their big picture.

Religion's lies include insane teachings like "God can't hear your prayers if you have 'sin' in your life; God can't do anything for you after you die if you haven't done whatever that branch of religion says you have to do to get God to be for you; God is against you because of your lifestyle or your sexual preference or your political beliefs or your color or your ethnicity or your business practices."

Jesus, Papa, and Grace aren't 'for' you hurting yourself or others, but that never means they are against you. God is the same yesterday, today, and forever. God is not bipolar! God is ALWAYS FOR YOU!

Take a few minutes in your secret place with your primary Teammates, Jesus, Papa, and Grace, and say (out loud if you can) several times slowly, "I Am so grateful that Jesus, Papa, and Grace are always totally for me!"

DAVE CARRINGER
Human Treasure Hunter

"It was the courage I found to ask all the 'What ifs' that changed my life and set me free. Without them, I'd still be stuck, nodding my head to the ideas and opinions of others, who, I, later on, realized had never asked any 'What ifs' of their own. Since truth has nothing to hide, it loves all the 'hard questions' you throw its way, and if someone tries to discourage you from asking them, or always circles you back to one single source to prove their point, well, you might wanna rethink that whole scenario altogether," says Dave Carringer

In 1996, at the age of twenty-four, desperate from being involved in a life of drugs, violence, and danger, Dave Carringer had an encounter with God that dramatically changed the trajectory of his life. He soon started ministering to those in jail, teenagers on the street who were drinking and doing drugs, the abandoned elderly, and a host of others. Eventually, he came to realize that the world doesn't need more Bible teachers; rather, it needs more carriers of the Father's heart. He describes himself as an "ordinary guy on an extraordinary journey."

Dave Carringer is the author of *Born From Above (Waking up to our Genesis)*, where he writes, "MAN HAS ALWAYS been connected with his divine Source. It's in our authentic design, and it didn't come through our natural birth or any ability our earthly parents passed on to us. It was born of the will and passion of the heavenly Father who never lost sight of our true origin. For too long, we've missed the deeper foundation that Jesus told Simon Peter the entire ekklésia was built upon. Not only did the Son of Man reveal the Christ to us ... he unveiled the joyful truth of the incarnation in us—that all sons of men might recognize their paternal Source from within and become active participants with this divine nature … as One. Men and women all around the world are waking up to an inner realization that the heavenly Father has been with them all along … and the most passionate desire of God is to enjoy a life of intimacy and Oneness through us and as us—as divine treasure in earthen vessels. I invite you to join us on this journey, where we can't help but see the undeniable and unchangeable truth of our authentic origin as born from above, and we begin waking up to … our true genesis. Life will never be the same. You'll see."

Dave recently posted, "I remember when I thought this meant reaching a place of ultimate surety in my beliefs, as they rested on a solid foundation that could never be moved. Today I can't help but chuckle at ideas suggesting some pinnacle destination where my feet were firmly planted with dogmatic concrete poured around traditions and opinions. I now know I had been trained 'what' to think, and not 'how' to think and explore for myself.

"Most everything I'd been taught actually came from a foundation of fear, accompanied by warnings of impending doom if I happened to venture down the 'wrong road.' As I began seeing things which made much more sense than what I was trained to believe, my entire outlook on Life began to be 'remodeled.' As I dismantled rigid walls that obstructed a wide-open view which I was previously never 'allowed' to explore, sincere friends began warning me 'not to throw the baby out with the bathwater.' I now know these thoughts (sincere as they were) are merely covert tentacles of fear which only serve to keep us bound up in the same old tub of service to the same walled-up fear.

"As I pulled the plug on that tiny one-tub mentality I'd bathed in for 20+ years, I realized there was no baby in that water worth saving, and that 'water' never made me feel clean anyway. I've traded in that tiny tub peep-hole mentality for an endless river of beautiful adventures waiting for me to explore. My eyes have been opened to see that the 'approved' list of things I was taught were OK were, in fact, backward, upside down, and diametrically opposed to all the adventurous Real Life out there just waiting to be enjoyed.

"I Love this Life of waking up every day and surrendering to all the universe has to show me. I've learned to trust that more than anything I was taught—and I've found more life in what I was warned to stay away from than I ever did from those who issued the warnings. I now believe 'Growing in wisdom and maturity' means becoming like a child again and exploring adventures of which the true River of Life has no end!

"I am pretty open and vocal about my beliefs ... which are now (most of the time) opposite of all I was taught to believe for 1/3 of my life. I'm not ashamed of that, and I won't back up. I just want to say, whoever you are, whatever you believe, no matter how different our thinking may be on certain topics, I love you as a precious brother or sister. I'll never push you away. I'll stick my hand out, hoping you'll grab it, and we can learn about this journey of life together. We have much to see.

"I'm gonna be me ... and thanks for being you!"

Grace I AM #19

Grace is God's Unconditional Love and pure goodness perpetually in action, working all things for your good (divine influence) to help you know and enjoy and experience abundant life by continually showing you that God has forgiven, accepted, and included you in Their relationship and chose you before creation to be one with Them and in Their family!

You are IN! And you've never been out! And you can never be 'out!'

The Apostle Paul wrote to you what Jesus Himself personally taught him: before creation, before time and space, before the foundation of the world, They focused Their intention on you, dreamed you up, created you in Their image and likeness (in spirit form), chose you to be one with Them and in Their family forever!

The Apostle Paul also revealed to us that the whole process was because of their Unconditional Love for us and manifested as a result of their Grace! Not only that, but They also took great joy, pleasure, and delight in doing that.

Knowing that you (and all of us) would forget that upon coming to earth at the appointed time for us, they made it their stated plan before creation to ultimately reconcile and restore ALL people and ALL creation to our original genesis … who we have always been!

Take a few minutes in your secret place with your primary Teammates, Jesus, Papa, and Grace, and say (out loud if you can) several times slowly, "I AM IN! I AM accepted, included, and forgiven forever. That's not because of anything I ever did, but totally because of what They did before creation!"

JAMIE ENGLEHART
Encountering the Liquid Love of Abba!

Jamie Englehart is the author of the book *70 Myths & Mistranslations: Unpacking 70 Misconceptions about God and the Bible.* What started with simple Facebook posts that dismantled common myths many have been taught but never questioned grew into a wonderfully helpful book! Jamie is the president and founder of Connect International Ministries, a worldwide family of churches, ministries, businesses, and leaders. He is widely sought after for his unique, multi-dimensional understanding of the kingdom of God, the New Covenant, and the heart of the Father revealed through Jesus Christ.

Jamie's wife, Wendy, is a recording artist, and they have ministered across the globe, serving as elders, church planters, Bible school teachers, spiritual parents, and itinerant ministers for over thirty years. They have two adult married children, Brittany and Brandon, and have two beautiful granddaughters, Caydence and Ariyah. Jamie and his family desire to see future generations empowered, affirmed, fathered, and guided into their kingdom purpose by releasing inheritance and connecting generations.

Jamie's personal journey into the radical love and grace of God began about eleven years ago. Prior to that, he was active in a "classical Pentecostal denomination that was hyper-focused on holiness." According to him, they were taught that you don't drink, you don't smoke, and staying right with God was dependent on abstaining from forbidden things. God seemed dark and distant. And God help you if you didn't say the right sinner's prayer because that *god* of religion had a special place of eternal torment for you to go to in the name of his 'justice.' Jamie preached an angry fire and brimstone gospel for many years.

"We don't just read the Bible; the Bible reads us." *What does this mean?* he wondered. He concluded that it meant that the God we preach reflects more about us, and if we are angry and judgmental people, we will be drawn to every scripture passage that speaks of a *god* who is angry and filled with judgment.

The beginning of his transformation occurred while Jamie was ironically in the middle of preaching a series on the love of God. He began to read a book a friend suggested titled One Way Love by Tullian Tchivijian. While sitting at an airport, he downloaded the book and dove right in. As he began to read, he remembers experiencing and being overcome by what he now calls the Liquid Love of Abba Father. God's Love in this moment consumed him and brought him to tears. Next, in what would seem like a conspiracy from God himself, another friend suggested a book titled Loving our Kids on Purpose by Danny Silk. As Jamie read it, the printed words seemed to open his heart, and again, it was like God was pouring in that Liquid Love. As a result of his reading, he began to see how much his tainted image of God had negatively affected his own parenting, especially with his son.

"In Ephesians, Paul prayed that the eyes of our heart would be enlightened that we would know the hope and the glory of our inheritance. And by the power of the Holy Spirit speaking to me through these two books, an unveiling was taking place. My heart was seeing a deeper level of a God who is benevolent."

This powerful revelation prompted Jamie to gather his family when he got home from his trip. Being humbled by love, he apologized for how he had treated his own children. He says that he realized that religion caused him to want his own kids to believe just like him and ride the coattails of Jamie's own faith.

Now, however, Jamie saw the alienation he had caused. He says that the Perfect Love revealed this to him. He began to learn that divine Love is never a demand. God is not Zeus; He is Jesus, full of Grace, mercy, and a fiery all-consuming liquid love. It's the kind that brings a grown man to tears. According to Jamie, those relationships were repaired that day. He knows that reconciliation is the beautiful picture of the kingdom of God!

Today, Jamie is traveling the world, preaching and teaching the gospel. Only, now, he is passionate about advancing the kingdom on earth as it is in heaven. He is also very passionate about clearing up so many myths and misconceptions that keep us bound to a false, dark view of Abba. He teaches that God is Pure Love, Light, and Life.

Jamie has a large number of resources that help, encourage, and inspire us as we come to know The Only True God!

Grace I AM #20

Grace is God's Unconditional Love and pure goodness perpetually in action, working all things for your good (divine influence) to help you know and enjoy and experience abundant life by communicating with you how They see you and everyone!

Just as Jesus, Papa, and Grace focused Their attention and intention on creating you in Their image and likeness and forgave and accepted and included you in Their relationship and chose you before creation to be one with Them and in Their family, THEY DID THE SAME THING WITH ALL PEOPLE! God's Perfect, Unconditional Love, Grace, Goodness, Joy, Peace, and Inclusion is and has been since before creation.

Perhaps the tell-tale sign that you are coming to intimately know the Only True God is when you start to see how They not only see you but how They see everyone! You have never locked eyes with someone who was not included before creation just like you! You have never met or heard about someone who Jesus didn't die for and include as Savior of the world!

In God's economy, there is no one 'other,' 'less than,' 'outside,' 'not included,' 'not right with God.' In God's economy, there are only those who are 'in the dark' or 'blinded to the Truth' or 'not yet aware,'—and those who are becoming more and more aware of The Truth!

At the cross, Jesus prayed (talked to) His Father (and your Father) about those who rejected Him, humiliated Him, lied about Him, slandered Him, beat Him, tortured Him, and were killing Him and said, "Father, forgive them, they just don't know what they're doing!"

Take a few minutes in your secret place with your primary Teammates, Jesus, Papa, and Grace, and say (out loud if you can) several times slowly, "I AM becoming more and more aware that ALL people are loved, accepted, forgiven, and included just like I Am!"

JOEL HOLC
The Eggshell Effect

Joel Holc is an energy awareness coach and emerging author in the healing arts. His book, *The Eggshell Effect*, reveals the story of how he discovered his source of illness and powerfully transformed his health beyond the limitations of conventional medicine. In his book, he creates a space for others to become self-aware in a way that enables them to tap into their own energy source, a source that empowers them to choose freely throughout their life's journey.

Joel discovered his approach to self-healing while battling a severe auto-immune disease, one that had conventional medical practitioners hand him a debilitating prognosis. Transformation came by an altering of his lifestyle, which included a plant-based diet, spiritual awareness and connection, and emotional growth.

Born in Argentina in 1967, the son of a holocaust survivor, Joel Holc and his family immigrated to Israel when he was three years old. He grew up in a kibbutz, a communal farming settlement. In his twenties, he traveled the world through South America and Europe and eventually settled in Pittsburgh, Pennsylvania, in the USA. He has two grown children.

'The Eggshell Effect' is a phenomenon that all human beings can fall prey to. It is an all-encompassing state of being, leaving one protected from the world, yet severely limited in life. Through acute awareness of self, Joel has managed to break through the eggshell with our greatest weapon—love. Armored in God's love, he has overcome great adversity in life through the power of awareness, which he shares with you.

Joel says: "1 John 4:18, 'There is no fear in love; but perfect love casts out fear.' Fear can be very paralyzing. And what if this kind of fear can cause a person to walk in reactionary survival mode for most of their life? What if this survival mode you are unaware of and which goes into adulthood is rooted in a single event that happened at 7 years old? What if it went undetected and affected life in such a way that it was like being inside an egg, behind the protective walls of a shell?

What if sickness entered in through all that fear, followed by broken relationship after broken relationship? What if it kept you from living your life the way God wants you to live, in fullness?"

These 'what-ifs' happened to Joel, then ultimately became a part of a greater story that would lead him to write *The Eggshell Effect*, his journey to self-healing.

Starting in first grade, when Joel was only 7 and going to school in Israel, he was held back. He remembers how crushing it felt, like his teachers and classmates had abandoned him. This may seem small to adults, but to a seven-year-old boy, it was devastating. In Israel, Joel lived in an agricultural community where he loved playing with horses. The horses did not judge him. One day, while watching an egg inside an incubator begin to crack, he was struck with wanting to help the little abandoned chick inside break through the shell. As he began to reach, he was stopped by an adult who counseled him that the chick needed to go it alone, to exercise his growth muscles. A profound moment that day became the inspiration to write about the eggshell effect of self-protection in his own life.

As an adult, Joel became sick with muscular dystrophy. He was diagnosed by a medical doctor and told he would soon find himself confined to a wheelchair. Then one day, at a conference, a powerful statement was made to him by a speaker who spoke words to him about the root cause of his illness. She looked at Joel and asked him if he knew he was the root of his MS. As harsh as this was, it was what opened his eyes and began a series of changes in his life, starting with examining unhealthy patterns, broken relationships, and fear.

Joel realized that he was living in a world inside the eggshell of self-protection, consumed in fear-based survival mode. Later, grace led him back to that day and the trauma he endured when he was kept back in first grade. He remembers feeling so stupid and how deep the abandonment had impacted him. Thus began a pattern of self-protection.

This discovery led him on a journey of self-healing. He started with his physical body by modifying his eating and drinking. Then he moved on to examine his spiritual health and discovered the relationship of fear as an energy that ruled him. Fear drove him into unhealthy relationships and kept him from breaking through that shell.

When he was forty-five years old, he experienced supernatural healing from MS and many other physical maladies, discovering that the antidote to all fear is found in the perfect love of God that casts out all fear. Joel Holc is an engaging speaker who is comfortably relatable and who has a great personal story of healing and joy. You will be inspired and encouraged as you connect with Joel!

From Grace Is ... by Paul Gray:

High Love

Ephesians 3:16–19 says, "I pray that out of His glorious riches He may strengthen you with power through His Spirit in your inner being, so that Christ may dwell in your hearts through faith. And I pray that you, being rooted and established in love, may have power, together with all the Lord's holy people, to grasp how wide and long and high and deep is the love of Christ, and to know this love that surpasses knowledge—that you may be filled to the measure of all the fullness of God."

'High' means above all; God's plan that supersedes everything else; God's ways are higher than ours.

We, all humans, tend to think, *God loves us and those in our group. But He can't possibly love other people. Look how bad they are. Look at the wrong beliefs they have. They don't believe in God.*

We think that, but the truth is, God's love is at such a high level it's hard for us to comprehend it. It's unconditional and way better than any example of human love! It's the same for you and everyone!

LYDIA DU TOIT
Unconditionally at Home

Every now and then, you will meet a special person who just simply oozes pure, unhindered grace. They live and move with the sweet fragrance of the unconditional love of God. Lydia Du Toit has a smile that is inviting and most assuredly is that person.

Lydia did not grow up in a religious family or know Jesus in the traditional sense. Nor did she participate in a traditional church environment, where she notes people may only meet once a week, and the experience is often a quick 'in and out' meeting with little substance. However, she says she was blessed because she was raised in a family that spent a lot of time with a lot of different people, and they just loved freely. To say her early years were different from most families would be a tremendous understatement! Lydia's papa worked in the drilling field in South Africa, and the family would go with him from place to place. They traveled in caravans, like gypsies, sleeping in tents, which was their home for many years.

She remembers a childhood filled with sitting around campfires and talking among family and friends. It would not be out of the ordinary to wake up and find a whole new family staying with them that her parents had connected with and invited to join them along the way. "We just never thought of any people as silly or stupid, and every single person was valuable," she says.

Lydia describes having an incredible encounter with Jesus. She suddenly found herself face to face, like in a mirror, with Perfect Love. "We can experience Him intimately," she says. "There is nowhere we can run, even in our imagination or self-judgment, that we can we hide from God. We can simply look around, and He is right there. Even in our tough times."

She recalls that a friend recently asked, "Was God there in my own childhood and suffering?"

Lydia replied, "Yes, God is with us in our suffering. He is not the source of our suffering, but He feels the very pain with us in those places. And although we do feel separated in our darkness, He is the

Light within, always giving us strength even when we cannot see. God's love, when you encounter it for yourself, you realize you are now home. This is the incarnate Christ. He is not just in the tolerating business. He is in the 'at homeness' business." She continued, "It is nothing you can earn, but you are changed. You will begin to see Him in everyone. And even when you encounter people who are walking in a place of judgment, you realize your urge to judge back is not there because there is no judgment now, only love."

The Apostle Paul describes this by writing that we no longer see anyone from the human point of view; rather, through the eyes of Perfect Love—Jesus Himself. Lydia says that this breaks you away from all performance and eliminates competition. The cross is a level highway.

Lydia and Francois have enjoyed many years of spreading the gospel together. She describes mission work in the remotest parts of Africa where they started Bible schools and training centers, spreading the message of God's all-inclusive love for everyone. They did this for 14 years until their hearts drew them to start their own business. The Lord released them from the mission field to pursue that desire, thus providing income, while Francois began his translation of the Mirror Bible.

Lydia loves this cherished verse: 1 John 4:7 (The Mirror Translation), "Beloved, love always includes others, since love springs from God; its source is found in the fellowship of the Father, Spirit, and Son. Everyone who encounters love immediately knows that they too are born of the same source! It is not possible to fully participate in love without discovering God. To love is to know God; to know God is to love."

Today, Lydia lives in South Africa, where she and Francois spend time with their family. She enjoys tea, gardening, and marvels at the beauty of creation. She also enjoys writing children's books inspired by her own childhood adventures, where she says they often would do plays and invent their own stories. Titles include *KAA of the Great Kalahari*, *Little Bear* and *The Mirror*, and most recently, *Stella's Secret.*

Lydia is a delightful person who is blessed with the most amazing imagination! Through her books, adults, as well as children, learn to let go, be free from the performance-driven life and enter into exploration, where we meet the God of unfailing love in the everyday layers of our daily adventures.

"Three of the most amazing days of my life were spent with Lydia and Francois and a small group of friends in Kansas City a few years ago. Out of that grew a long-distance friendship of mutual encouragement and love. Through the help of our fellow Grace Restoration teammates Gene and Charlene Fritzel, we have provided hundreds of gratis copies of the Mirror Bible to friends around the country. Lydia, Francois, their books, and the Mirror Bible are grace gifts that Papa has lavished on us all! I'm so blessed to be part of His team with them!" ~Paul Gray

Grace I AM #21

Grace is God's Unconditional Love and pure goodness perpetually in action, working all things for your good (divine influence) to help you know and enjoy and experience abundant life by producing an effortless change in you as you dwell in seamless union with the Trinity!

A huge part of Grace is that it's ALL God! There's nothing you can do to get Them to love you anymore, and nothing you can do to cause Them to love you any less! They love you because they are love.

You never have to work or strive to become a better person, let alone a 'better Christian!'

Peter wrote to us that God has already given each of us everything we will ever need to live and experience the abundant life God has for us and to be the 'godly' person God made us to be. God wants us to 'rest' in our knowledge and awareness of who we already are, then as we rest and are aware of what we already have, we simply access all the 'treasures' that were already lavished on us before creation. It's like we effortlessly go to the storage room inside us and supply ourselves with whatever we need for the moment: love, joy, peace, patience, kindness, goodness, gentleness, the faith of Christ, the power of Grace, compassion, mercy—and much, much more!

Living in seamless union means partnering with Christ as He lives as us, using our mind, personality, voice, and actions. Paul calls that the Divine Mystery: Christ in you, the hope of Glory! That's when life gets really good!

Take a few minutes in your secret place with your primary Teammates, Jesus, Papa, and Grace, and say (out loud if you can) several times slowly, "I AM continually manifesting effortless change for the better as Christ in me lives as me!"

BRIAN LONGRIDGE
Seeing Christ in those in prison and in leprosy camps

For the last twenty-seven years, Brian Longridge and his Dutch wife, Mirte Anisha, have shared the Father's love in music and song in heavy crime prisons in the Philippines and in leprosy camps in different countries. Here's one of Brian's posts: *Engrace us ...*

Grace to see what you want us to see Grace to know what you want us to know Grace, grace, grace ...

Grace to process; grace to think straight grace to see the silver lining Grace to hope for a better world

Grace to be present in the small, be more intimate with loved ones

Grace to transcend to share our global pain

Grace to ponder, 'Could that which is of most IMPORTANCE for us now flow out from our IMPOTENCE?'

Can Light and transforming insight possibly be veiled within shroud of darkness?

Creativity and innovativeness bubble from a Love deeper than every hell

Grace to know that Christ bleeds in the furnace of our pain and weeps torrents .... grace, grace, grace

Not mere transaction but a Person

We cling to You as You embrace us in our night ...

Mirte treats lepers with physical therapy while Brian plays soothing, healing music on his portable keyboard. Together, they minister God's unconditional love, grace, light, goodness, and inclusion to those who are considered 'untouchables' by even their family.

Brian Longridge was born in Belfast, North Ireland. He is a trained classical/jazz pianist who studied at the Berklee College of music, Boston, and, after having a beautiful encounter with God in his early twenties, felt called to use his gift as an instrument of deep healing for broken people. Brian is also a writer and poetically articulates the love of Father, Son, and Spirit. He has released several instrumental CDs.

Brian's deepest heart is to help people to see the beautiful union they have been freely given in Christ and see them experience the intimacy they are made for.

Grace I AM #22

Grace Is God's Unconditional Love and pure goodness perpetually in action flowing:

From the Trinity to us

From us to ourselves

From us to others

From others to us

THIS PERPETUAL MOTION OF GRACE IS THE KINGDOM OF GOD/KINGDOM OF HEAVEN!

Paul reminds us, "The grace of the Lord Jesus Christ, and the love of God, and the fellowship of the Holy Spirit, be with you all." He also wrote, "For from Him and through Him and to Him are all people. For all originate with Him and come from Him; all live through Him, and all center in and tend to consummate and to end in Him."

We tend to forget these truths, so it's important that we continually remind ourselves and each other. Many of us don't have others in our homes, neighborhoods, or even community who are yet aware of the real Good News. Unfortunately, you won't find many (if any) of the wonderful truths you're seeing in this book in organized religious settings.

So, I want to encourage you to connect with one or more of the people highlighted in this book. They regularly remind each other, encourage each other, comfort each other, celebrate each other, and share things God is revealing to us. The TEAM reminds us that God is working continually in every situation in the world for His ultimate purpose: The restoration of ALL things.

Take a few minutes in your secret place with your primary Teammates, Jesus, Papa, and Grace, and say (out loud if you can) several times slowly, "I Am becoming more and more aware that the Grace of God is continually flowing from the Trinity to me, from my heart/spirit to my mind, and from me to others!"

JULIE FERWERDA
Raising Hell!

Julie Ferwerda's journey into knowing God's unconditional love and grace for all began with what she describes as a crisis of faith. After attending a church for years, being both active and loyal, and thinking she was doing all the right things, she realized that she did not know love.

One day, while out on a walk, she remembers becoming overwhelmed with emotions, and she cried out to God in her frustration, "God, I don't know how to love. After all these years serving You and being devoted to You, all I feel is this void of not being able to love others." She made a heartfelt, sincere plea and asked Him to teach her how to love people and love Him.

A few months later, Julie was studying the Hebrew perspectives on Scripture when she began questioning the doctrine of eternal conscious torment in 'hell.' She learned that the writers, teachers, and people in the 'Old Testament' did not believe in a place of eternal punishment and that they read Scripture quite different from the way we do today.

Next, she started researching the doctrine of 'hell.' She meticulously studied for over a year. The more she studied, the more the doctrine unraveled, and in the process, her life began to be tremendously transformed for the better!

Previously, she had a strong desire to know the experience of being 'born again.' She states that although she had been in church for years, she never experienced anything other than 'head knowledge,' most of which turned out to be false! Once she saw that Eternal Conscious Torment in 'hell' was a false, man-made doctrine, she says that it was like she felt she completely came alive and felt the elation of a 'born-again' experience.

By looking at her own past actions, she was shocked by the 'ugliness of her subconsciously judging people.' She would go to the grocery store and see a burly man with tattoos and think, *He is not worth sharing the gospel with.* Meanwhile, she judged, "That little old lady over there; she is deserving." Julie says that she realized she had always been judging people.

However, her new perspective and experience of the beautiful inclusive love of God revealed to her that every single person that has ever been born is a beloved child of God. Julie relates that this change of thinking set her free from judgment and made her able to love freely! Instead of seeing darkness in people, she began to see them filled with light. Suddenly, the world felt safe, and she had a different view of everything. She compares the whole experience to living in a world of only black and white to suddenly seeing everything in full color.

As she grew in excitement and joy, she wanted to share all of what she learned about deconstructing 'hell' to help others get free. As a result, she wrote *Raising Hell: Christianity's Most Controversial Doctrine Put Under Fire*. She knew she was taking on a very controversial subject, one that the church does not want to let go of, and she expected much push back.

To her surprise, there was very little rejection, and instead, she felt insulated from condemnation. She believed there was favor on this book as she began to get plugged into the right communities on Facebook, where people were receptive and hungry for truth. She realized God's grace was clearly manifesting and using her book to help set many people free!

Eventually, Julie and her husband moved to Puerto Rico, where, through a series of 'God moments,' they found a beautiful place in the mountains that they plan on making into a spiritual retreat where people can come and heal. For a time, Julie also took a traveling nurse's job on a Zuni Native American reservation in New Mexico. She has always had deep compassion for Native Americans and for people in general. Now, her revelation of the lie of 'hell' has impacted and unveiled a richer, more healing gospel that manifests in her nursing practice, helping people experience both spiritual and physical healing!

"In the last year, Spirit has been teaching me to tap into the many messengers in my surroundings (in Puerto Rico) that are offering me instruction, guidance, encouragement, and comfort. One day, orange dragonfly, orange butterfly, and honeybee showed up while I was in the yard, and they all flitted around me for several minutes, as if delivering a message.

"I already knew that dragonflies and butterflies represent death and transformation, leaving the mud or the cocoon for a higher state of consciousness and a liberated purpose. Orange promotes a sense of general wellness and emotional energy that should be shared, such as compassion, passion, and warmth. Orange aids in the recovery process from trauma or bad events. Lastly, honeybee symbolizes community and creating a conscious field of energy within that community. I was impressed with the importance of my state of mind and how it impacts my neighbors, my city, and even the island. I felt as if Spirit was telling me that one person standing in steady hope, fearlessness, and a positive energy field could potentially impact a whole region, resulting in a shift of consciousness for all. This is not really some 'woo-woo' teaching; this foundation stone is being proven with quantum science experiments!

"All of these 'wise guides' were there to tell me this morning, 'Stay strong; stay grounded; create a conscious field of positive emotional energy (orange, bee) so that you and those around you can be transformed by this experience (dragonfly, butterfly) rather than victimized by it."

Grace I AM #23

Richard Rohr wrote *Grace Fills in the Gaps* in his newsletter on August 6, 2021. He says: "The goodness of God fills all the gaps of the universe, without discrimination or preference. God is the gratuity of absolutely everything. God is the 'Goodness Glue,' the love that holds the dark and light of things together, the free energy that carries all death across the Great Divide and transmutes it into Life. Grace is what God does to keep all things God has made in love and alive—forever. Grace is not something God gives; grace is who God is. If we are to believe the primary witnesses, an unexplainable goodness is at work in the universe."

He wonderfully reminds us that Grace is to, for, and in ALL! He reminds us that Grace is Love, Free, Life, Energy, and always at work in everyone everywhere!

I (Paul Gray) haven't had the privilege of interviewing Richard Rohr, so I don't have a section about him in this book. But I do highly recommend his books and his daily newsletter. You can find his writings at www.cac.org.

Take a few minutes in your secret place with your primary Teammates, Jesus, Papa, and Grace, and say (out loud if you can) several times slowly, "I AM becoming more and more aware that Grace fills in all the gaps in everything!"

CHARLES SLAGLE
From Despair to Joy

"God talks to ME!" ~Charlie Slagle

Charles Slagle and his wife, Paula, both gifted musicians, have traveled the world, ministering God's unconditional love and grace to hundreds of thousands in numerous countries. God has given Charlie the supernatural ability to see with great precision physical, emotional, financial, and other challenges in people whom he's never even met! Coupled with this insight, God works through Charlie in healing and meeting people's needs in miraculous ways. As a result, a multitude of people's lives have changed, and they have come to know God's goodness and grace for ALL people! Charles also created and facilitates a group on Facebook called "Abba Calling," an online community inspired by his own relationship with Abba, where people can share their prayer requests and discuss the unconditional love and grace of Abba.

Charlie is motivated by the unveiling of the inclusive saving love of our Father. He wants to share this love with others and encourage everyone to know that they can have intimacy with God. His ministry page explains it like this:

"This group has been inspired by Charles Slagle's devotional book *ABBA CALLING*. The group has been created to help people become more secure in the infinite goodness of ABBA through experiencing that He yearns for them to enjoy a literal and real relationship with Him, resting assured that He has created them with the capacity to enjoy His fellowship. 'ABBA' is the Hebrew name for 'DAD' or 'PAPA,' and our FATHER wants to relate to us on these intimate terms—just like JESUS did when He walked this earth (Romans 8:14–16). He longs to commune with us (Isaiah 55:1–3, 10 & 11) and lavish His love upon us (1 John 3:1–2)."

Charles and his wife, Paula, share Abba's love with others from the local waffle house to faraway nations. They joyfully share the good news about how He has saved us all, how He included everyone as family in Christ and the message that anyone can enjoy intimate communion with Abba.

Like many, Charlie did not always believe the message of the good news for all men. He speaks of a season of life when he was facing depression, inner struggles, and addiction—all while being right in the middle of full-time ministry. He says his wife, Paula, introduced him to the true character of God and his infinite Grace. Although he says she believed in the doctrine of hell at that time too, it was as if it didn't exist in her consciousness. It was always about His unconditional love, grace, and healing.

Charlie soon learned of inner healing prayers, journaling, and the gift to really hear directly from the Holy Spirit. These divine inspirations, by way of words of knowledge, became a part of his life. All the while, he was getting to know God deeper and coming into a greater understanding of true Grace.

But Charles is also a thinker, and while he was experiencing and growing in the knowledge of the love and character of Abba, he found himself not being able to easily shake the belief in hell as eternal torment. Like many of us, he experienced the problem of the irreconcilable difference between the God of universal love and the heinous concept of hell.

He soon began to receive answers to his questions as he began reading the letters of George MacDonald, who believed in universal reconciliation, the primary doctrinal belief of the early church. This belief states that God will eventually reconcile all of mankind. And as he read more and more, God began to lead him into a place of peace and understanding. He started to see that 'hell' is not a place of eternal torment and suffering!

Today, Charles knows the intimacy of God, and it flows from within. He has a gift to encourage and is known by many for his encouraging 'God words,' including at the local waffle house where they look forward to seeing him visit. On one occasion, he was able to share an encouraging word with a teenage boy who was dealing with much disappointment. As he heard Charlie's prophetic words, the boy's entire countenance changed, and he could be seen running through the parking lot, excitedly declaring, "God talks to me!"

In addition to being a great prophetic encourager, Charlie is also a world-class pianist, and he and Paula radiate joy and perfect harmony as they sing duets. You will truly enjoy and be inspired as you connect with them!

We all long to know and be known by God. Charlie Slagle helps us on that journey by showing us that Abba is calling each of us. I can attest to that personally because, for two years, I was inspired, blessed, and encouraged every day by reading a page in *Abba Calling*!

From Notes From Papa, a 366-day devotional by Paul Gray:

A Note From Papa to you!

To My very special child, whom I totally adore,

I know that you, and most of My children, have been told religion's lie that there's going to be a day of reckoning with Me, a horrible day of judgment.

Know this straight from Me: There was only one judgment day, and it has already happened, all to your benefit!

I set the day of Jesus' resurrection to raise you and everyone to new life in Christ. As the Apostle Paul told the pagan idol worshippers in Athens, I judged you all righteous—right with Me forever! I judged you to be pure, holy, right with Us, innocent, and totally without fault. I reconciled the entire cosmos to Myself and don't hold anyone's sins against them. Christ took away all the sin of the world!

That means there is literally nothing for Me to judge! That is good news for you and everyone. Remember, good news is not good unless it's good for everyone, and my good news is for everyone!

Yes, there are Bible verses that can seem to say that there's going to be a judgment and that some people will fare well, and others won't. There are other ways to interpret those passages, as you know. So, you, and everyone, get to decide which scenario to believe—because they can't both be true.

I want you to take sides with Me and believe Me! Believe what Paul told the Greek philosophers in Athens. Believe what My original words in 2 Corinthians 5:14-21 say. Believe Me when I tell you that judgment day has come and gone, and your 'judgment' is total good news for you and everyone!

You have all been reconciled to Me already. I have made you My Ambassador of Reconciliation. Now you get to proclaim My good news to all others: "Be what you already are—reconciled to God!" ~Love, Papa

PHIL DRYSDALE
The Quest of Questioning

Phil Drysdale lives in Sale, England, with his wife, Tilly. His primary message is the grace of God, His goodness, and our perfection in Him. He says, "I'm never scared to ask questions of what I believe. If what I'm standing on is a solid foundation, then it will stand. If not, then I'm glad to be rid of it! This quest of questioning everything has taken me on an incredible journey. One in which I've been discovering God's goodness and who I am in Christ. My heart is to get you to think for yourself. To challenge everything you've ever been taught, driving you to a conversation with God and a study of the scriptures to find out if any of your beliefs need to change."

Phil produces regular blogs, podcasts, videos, and books for free. His primary focus is his free site "The Grace Course," which has dozens of videos on a variety of different topics. He is involved in his local community with both church leadership and running a ministry school. He also works throughout the week with pastors and leadership teams he has met during his travels.

He travels around the world, speaking in churches, conferences, universities and colleges, pubs, coffee shops, and homes. His heart now is to build a community online where people have a safe place to share their journey and help one another. That primarily happens on Facebook, but also on a variety of other networks.

Phil Drysdale was a pastor's kid and is now a pastor himself. He grew up in churches in the UK. Early on in his teens, Phil says he learned a love for the Bible and Scripture. Today, as he looks back, he admits he does not agree with most of the doctrines he was taught. It was actually his knowledge of Scripture that provoked him to question those doctrines. Phil makes the strong point that he doesn't know how anyone can read Scripture and not question the doctrines we have been taught. It was an integral part of the awakening process for him.

"You read about a *god* portrayed as a genocidal maniac killing innocent people, especially in the old covenant, and you think, *This looks nothing like Jesus.* Jesus, who is the full representation of God, and who said, 'If you have seen me, you have seen the Father.' And you end up with so many questions, and it does not take much digging to realize how off these teachings are. Things like penal substitution and eternal conscious torment do not line up with the God as we know demonstrated through Christ." And in all this digging, he soon began to dismantle many fundamental beliefs and eventually came to understand the true nature of God.

"Jesus leveled the field completely at the cross. All were included, raised to new life, and when you begin to see clearly, you cannot unsee His inclusive love is for all. Loving people gets to be a lot easier when you start to realize that God looks like Jesus, and so do we. We were all reconciled and designed to be carriers of the fullness of Christ. There is no place God does not dwell. And in Him, there is no haves and have nots."

Phil describes how the result of this paradigm shift begins to force relationships in places where maybe before you could not see a person's value. "You won't walk past the homeless person anymore, but instead, you see Jesus in them. Jesus frames this well in the parable of the good Samaritan. He dismantles the idea of religious privilege as He tells about a priest and a Levite who passed by the beaten person in need of help. Instead, we see a person considered to be out of the circle and the lowest of the low that day—a Samaritan—demonstrate love like Christ when he came to the rescue. God's unconditional grace and love for everyone forces us out of our bubble."

Today, Phil sees people all included in God's embrace and family. For him, life is no longer about being inside a self-imposed Christian circle. He says, "Knowing the true love of God today, we can even look at the child rapist or Muslim terrorist, for example, and think about that circle we have kept them out of and know that Jesus Himself will respond by saying, 'I am going to stand outside the circle right next to that person. I am going to hang with them like I did the adulterer, and the tax collector.' He made the circle bigger. Jesus dismantled religion and accepted all, especially the marginalized."

Phil Drysdale uses Facebook and other media outlets to help people come aware of the Truth of the Really Good God! He's always challenging us to step outside that old religious circle.

Grace I AM #24

You are the "Apple of God's Eye!"

Moses relates a poetic description of God's care for Israel: "In a desert land he found him, in a barren and howling waste. He shielded him and cared for him; he guarded him as the apple of his eye." Other versions say, "God kept circling around him, He scanned him [penetratingly], He kept him as the pupil of His eye."

The 'apple' in the apple of the eye is a translation of the Hebrew word for ishon, which is related to the word ish, meaning 'man.' Etymologically, the ishon of the eye is "the little man of the eye." Several times Scripture tells us that wonderful truth!

Have you ever looked someone in the eye and seen your own reflection in their pupil? That's the 'little man,' right in the center of the eye. The deep meaning of that is that Jesus, Papa, and Grace are so close to you (and in you) that They look you in the eye and see themselves reflected!

Picture your Loving Father, your Special Older Brother, and your Best Friend smiling with joy and pride as they look you in the eye and see themselves in your eyes, and you see yourself adoringly in their eyes!

A great definition of 'worship' is "love responding to Love!" This truth totally demolishes religion's false belief that God can't stand to look at you, or God can only stand to look at you because He sees you through the blood of Jesus.

Jesus, God Himself, came and lovingly looked everyone right in the eye, including the proud religious leaders who taught that God couldn't stand people. Jesus even loved them; He just revealed the Only True God isn't at all like they thought and taught.

Take a few minutes in your secret place with your primary Teammates, Jesus, Papa, and Grace, and say (out loud if you can) several times slowly. "I Am the Apple of God's Eye!"

JUDI MCCALL
G is for Grace

"God did not need you; He wanted you!" ~ Judi McCall

Judi McCall is the author of the Grace and Unconditional Love-based curriculum *G is for Grace.* She is bi-lingual (French) and studied in France. She is a mom and grandmother who taught in public schools for ten years and went on to homeschool her grandchildren for seven years. Judi lived most of her life in a religious environment, always feeling that God was far away. It was when she first encountered a message of pure love and grace that the awakening began in her.

Judi says, "When God told me to write a curriculum for children founded on His love and grace, I knew that I wanted all children to discover the unconditional love of the Father. My teacher's heart and my heart for God made for the right combination to allow *G is for Grace* to be born."

Judi McCall grew up in a church environment that taught a works-based gospel—where she heard, "You must work for your miracles, and you never seem to have enough faith to ever 'arrive.'" It was not until her adult years that her son Lane would introduce her to Houston Pastor Don Keathley, and she would hear about the finished work of the cross and God's all-inclusive love and grace for all. Overjoyed by what she was learning, all she could say is "How amazing it is!"

She remembers hearing these messages and thinking, *You mean God is right there inside of me, and He will never leave me? She went on to learn that the Truth is*, God is our very DNA, and He did not need us; He wanted us! He is who we are made of. This revelation completely changed the meaning of the gospel for Judi. It changed how she looks at friends, family, and all people! Love and tolerance grew in her because she started to see all people as included, which is exactly how God sees them.

Judi grew up believing in a distant far-off *god*. When she discovered God lives inside of her, it brought her tremendous peace. With this peace, she 'lives in the now' and knows that God has her. She enjoys knowing that Christ is within, and she can live in the present, in total freedom, instead of fearing her future. When she felt separated from God, she did not have that peace.

Her new knowledge and understanding of God's unconditional love, grace, and inclusion started to fuel a desire to teach young people the same message.

G is for Grace was written and created based solely on God's unconditional grace.

A summary from the back of the book reads, "For a generation. For all ages. God is Love, and in Him is only Love. We all have His unconditional love. We are His sons and daughters. We are His glory. As we awaken to who we really are and realize the finished work of the cross, we can then begin to live out of God's love and grace."

Judi knows and teaches that Grace focuses on God's love, His goodness, and our being found in Christ before the foundation of the world. She believes in also teaching young children about prophecy, that they can hear God because He lives within them, and that heaven is within each of them. She knows that when you teach children these truths at a young age, they will be rooted and grounded in their true God identity. They learn that their DNA is love. That love is God.

Although her curriculum is geared toward six- to twelve-year-olds, it can be easily modified for both younger and older children and adults. It has fifty-two lessons, one for every week of the year. Each week includes a teaching, a fast-paced game, a craft to do, and things to take home for discussion. The discussion subjects are also great for adults to use in interacting with their children. Although this was created for Sunday Schools, Judi is getting much interest from homeschoolers as well.

You will not hear sin, hell, or the devil in this book. She also did not include Scripture, although there is room to add it. She wanted to focus on the love of God so that a wide group of people could hear without preconceived ideas about Scripture.

G is For Grace is currently being used in God's House in Houston and by many homeschool families as well. Children are learning how much they are loved, who they are in Christ, how to hear God's voice, and are even prophesying over each other. It is very encouraging for Judi to see kids get prophetic words that edify and build each other up.

She loves seeing the fruit of her labor impacting future generations.

I have given *G is For Grace* to our adult children to use with their children and have found it to be a wonderful resource to impart truth to them all! Thanks, Judi McCall, for writing and publishing it!

Grace I AM #25

Want some MIND-BLOWING GOOD NEWS?

Listen to what Jesus prayed to Papa about YOU!

"I pray that they all may be one as You, Father, are in Me, and I in You; that they also may be one in Us. I pray that they realize the glory which You gave Me, I have given them, that they may be one just as We are one: I in them, and You in Me; that they may be made perfect in one."

Think about the ramifications of that!

Jesus—God in the flesh—who is One with the Father and Grace, prayed that you would be one with Them just like They are one with each other—Christ in you and you in Christ. ALL OF JESUS' PRAYERS WERE ALWAYS ANSWERED!

And that's not all! He asked Papa to make sure that you realize that you have the same glory that Jesus has! He asked Papa to make you perfect!

As you begin to wrap your brain around this good news, you will start to see who you really are, the real you, and see how wonderful you really are. Then things will start getting really good!

Take a few minutes in your secret place with your primary Teammates, Jesus, Papa, and Grace, and say (out loud if you can) several times slowly, "I Am One with Papa, Jesus, and Grace! I realize I have the same glory They do! They made me perfect!"

MO THOMAS
A Garden in the Abyss

> *"I would suggest that it's our broken experiences in life (body and soul) that allow the Unbroken, Uncreated, Essential, and Truest part of our being (spirit) to be freely and authentically released in and through us." ~Mo Thomas*

Mo Thomas has been a Crash Safety Engineer in Detroit for over thirty years. He played and coached basketball and tennis, taught piano lessons, tutored college math, is a lover of children's literature (Dr. Seuss is his favorite author; *Little Prince*, his favorite book), and recently published a wonderful book *Into the Abyss.*

From his book, *Into the Abyss*:

"At some point along our journey, some of us who grew up in a religious tradition start questioning our long-held beliefs. Sometimes, these questions lead us down pathways that are unfamiliar to our minds and hearts. This is perfectly normal, and God LOVES our authentic questions. I'm not sure that true growth can take place without them. At times, however, this process can be frustrating, frightening, and fiercely confrontational. Perhaps our questions are offensive to friends and family members who now see us as careless heretics because they perceive our doubts and questions to be dangerous. It might feel like we're losing our foundation and that all we've known has become uncertain. Our souls may experience the unbearable weight of loneliness as we go through the process of faith-deconstruction."

Mo Thomas' journey into the abyss began when he started to question God's goodness after a season of trials. He remembers feeling he did everything right and thought, *Shouldn't God be giving me favor? I mean, that is what we are taught, right?* Why is all this happening in my life? It made him start to question the God he was taught and opened him up to questions.

Into the Abyss is about a discovery of finding your identity in the infinite depths of Christ. It contains revelation Mo received over thirty years of his mystical journey. "It took me a long while, but They, the Trinity, invite us into this mystery," Mo recalls. "One fundamental shift before writing this book was challenging the idea of our separateness; this foundation that we are separated from a holy God because we are unrighteous creatures He cannot look upon. The false belief that there is this unbelievably large chasm we all need to cross is foreboding, fear-inducing, and always requires self-effort to do something to get us back into the favor of God."

Mo had many questions as he began to process things. He experienced resistance to the seemingly ever-shifting paradigms, and he experienced considerable spiritual and emotional pain. Previously, Mo was religious and self-righteous, believing that he was always right in his beliefs about God. He says that the pain he experienced was a very necessary part of getting his stubborn self to allow the Truth to be revealed.

Mo remembers a question a friend's daughter asked: "If God, at the end of the day, is going to send the majority of those who are created in his image to hell, this place of an eternal torture chamber, how are we ever going to enjoy heaven?" Mo says, "*I heard this and thought, YIKES! This puts things into a different perspective.* It makes it personal. It becomes about friends and family. We do not have to dismiss hell. But go after the truth, and you will find that early orthodoxy framed hell as the all-consuming fire of God's love, not a place of eternal torment."

Questions like this provoked Mo, but it was really his love for science that God used to leave a trail of scientific breadcrumbs pointing to the eternal truth that all of man was joined intricately to God before the creation. Colossians 1:16–17 says, "For in him all things were created: things in heaven and on earth, visible and invisible, whether thrones or powers or rulers or authorities; all things have been created through him and for him. He is before all things, and in him all things hold together."

Mo says, "Scripture says all things were created by Him and in Him. Christ is our origin. All of creation was created, held together, and sustained in Christ. He is our starting point. To connect this to a science term, we are inside of the Christ singularity. Paul called it our 'in Christ-ness.' We were born there, before the foundation of the world, in union with Them."

This beautiful journey has taken Mo to a deeper knowing of God.

He now knows that spirituality is not a series of religious boxes to check. It is about being willing to ask those painful questions and to surrender total trust to the Spirit within to guide you into truth. He states: "What you find is a God in which there truly is no shadow of turning. We are all encompassed in God's total love for all mankind!"

Grace I AM #26

Want some more Good News? Listen to what else Jesus prayed to Papa about YOU—specifically!

"Father, I pray that they know that You have sent Me and have loved them as You have loved Me."

Did you catch that? Jesus asked Papa to make sure that YOU know that Papa loves you just like He loves Jesus, just like He loves Jesus! God the Father, The Only True God who knows everything about you, who is everywhere present at once, who is all-powerful and all good, loves YOU just like He loves Jesus!

Papa, Jesus, and Grace want you to know that They love YOU as much as is possible, and nothing you can do can cause them to love you any less, ever!

We all come into this life hard-wired to crave unconditional love. Until we know The Truth, we'll look for it in all the wrong places. Now you know The Truth.

Take a few minutes in your secret place with your primary Teammates, Jesus, Papa, and Grace, and say (out loud if you can) several times slowly, "I AM loved by Papa! He loves me just as much as He loves Jesus!"

KERRY GOOCH
Free Indeed!

Kerry is a self-described 'Joyful Kiwi,' who is absolutely delightful to be around! She's from Waipawa in Central Hawkes Bay, New Zealand.

Kerry had a spiritual 'awakening' in 1997 that was so radical that her mind was transformed overnight! She says, "Regardless of the situation we start with, 'In Him we live, move, and have our BEING.'"

Kerry has an ever-growing understanding of Quantum Spirituality, especially in the areas of our Oneness with God and all people, God's unconditional love and grace for all, and healing. She has been healed of addiction, debt, sciatica nerve, twisted ankle (twice), headaches, pulled hamstring, teeth problems, and many other things. In addition, she has lovely personal stories about the healing of debt and addiction.

Her husband died of cancer fifteen years ago, five weeks after his initial diagnosis. Kerry says, "This was an amazing time where God did beautiful healing work, as I was left with three little children. Having an opportunity to share some of how my understanding in Him, the gloriousness of ONENESS in Christ that ALL share, is an honor."

Kerry is a single mom who radiates the Love of Christ to the teachers, staff, students, and their parents at the school where she works. If you're a fellow 'Kiwi' (or otherwise), you can connect with her on Facebook.

Grace I AM #27

Want even more Good News? Check out what else Jesus prayed to Papa about you. "Father, I desire that they also may be with Me where I am!"

Jesus told Papa that desire days before he ascended back to heaven, where He went to prepare a place for you! Jesus, All-Powerful God, the One who created the heavens and the earth, desires that YOU be with Him wherever He is, and He has prepared a place just for you to be together!

That's already happened!

The Holy Spirit of Christ—Grace in Person—lives IN you right now. Always has, always will. (I hope you can see the folly of religion's lie that you—or anyone—are separate from God, has to ask and do things exactly right to get God to 'come into your heart,' and you'd best be really good, or He'll get really ticked and leave you alone forever.)

Take a few minutes in your secret place with your primary Teammates, Jesus, Papa, and Grace, and say (out loud if you can) several times slowly, "I AM the dwelling place of God! Christ is one with me and lives in me right now! We are together forever!"

DAVID ADAMS
We are all God's beloved children!

> *"God is Love. Love is not what God does; it is who He is, His very nature and essence. His love is unfailing, long-suffering, kind, and patient. Many of us grow up hearing this message (God is Love), but few of us ever see it being worked out. And most of the time, it is presented in a way that is followed up with exceptions, leaving most people to believe in a double-minded God and never being fully assured of that love. Unfortunately, the religious system keeps people trying to earn or maintain the love He has freely given us all." ~David Adams*

David Adams could very well be named God's Love Prophet of Facebook. He grew up in Alabama and now lives in Lakeland, Florida, where he enjoys spending time with his son, daughter-in-law, and five grandchildren. When he is not doing that, you can find him on Facebook, encouraging people daily with the unconditional love of God. He loves to share the true gospel that proclaims that Jesus is the Savior of the whole world, and we are all His kids. David believes in the doctrine of Apokatastasis or ultimate reconciliation. This is what most of the early church believed—a promise from God that He will restore all mankind.

When David pastored a church, he had different beliefs than he now has. He taught a mixture of law and grace and believed in hell, a place of eternal conscious torment. But after leaving church in 2010, his son invited him to a Bible study at his home. David was eager to attend. It was at this Bible study that he first learned about God's grace. Messages from Andrew Womack and Joseph Prince about grace were new to him. He recalls leaving the home, reflecting and concluding that it was probably a false grace message. He even thought that people believing this grace message were probably headed to hell. God was certainly not as good as they were saying.

While he couldn't seem to shake the grace message, he also felt that he had to show those who believed in it that they were wrong. He decided to study the scripture afresh. He was postured with a heart to help set people back on the right path. Ironically, what would happen next would begin to change him instead and have him discover that God is that good and even better than he thought!

He discovered that God did include all in His salvation. Then one doctrine after another began to tumble down like dominoes with each study of the scripture. This former fundamental evangelical, who set out to prove others wrong, was now having his own eyes opened to the more beautiful, victorious gospel—that God was in Christ, reconciling the entire cosmos, and He was not holding our sin against us. He learned of the incarnation that all of humanity was in Christ when He went to the Cross. He saw that we have all been co-crucified, co-buried, and co-resurrected in Christ. All of humanity was raised with Jesus and reunited with the Father.

Knowing this changed David forever. First, it changed how he viewed other people. It opened his heart to love all people freely. He no longer saw people as insiders and outsiders or feared that people were going to a place called hell. It removed the pressure to get people 'saved.' It opened his spirit to freedom and to love all people, trusting the Holy Spirit to open their eyes because, as David often says, "We are all God's children."

David loves to help people see who they are in Christ. As he explains, 'sin' is simply missing the mark of our original identity. So, when he sees anyone acting outside of that, he knows that they are not bad but simply people who do not know who they are yet. He loves to show people the love of God by offering prayer, kind words of encouragement, and especially, he says, by being a good listener. Listening shows people their value as God sees them.

David is known by many through his daily Facebook posts. Ironically, when his daughter-in-law encouraged him to create an account, he did not really want to. But today, he loves to minister what he knows about God to thousands of people. He posts daily teachings and encouraging prayers that both provoke and encourage people and bring healing. David is bold in proclaiming this good news of inclusion. He admits it sometimes brings criticism, even name-calling, but he doesn't care because the perfect love of God compels him to tell the world, "We are all His beloved children."

From Grace Is ... by Paul Gray:

Wide Love

Ephesians 3:17–19 (MIRROR), "17This will ignite your faith to fully grasp the reality of the indwelling Christ. You are rooted and founded in love. Love is your invisible inner source, just like the root system of a tree and the foundation of a building. (The dimensions of your inner person exceed any other capacity that could possibly define you.)

"18 Love is your reservoir of superhuman strength which causes you to see everyone equally sanctified in the context of the limitless extent of love's breadth and length, and the extremities of its dimensions in depth and height.

"19 I desire for you to become intimately acquainted with the love of Christ on the deepest possible level, far beyond the reach of a mere academic, intellectual grasp. Within the scope of this equation God finds the ultimate expression of himself in you. (So that you may be filled with all the fullness of God, awaken to the consciousness of His closeness! Separation is an illusion! Oneness was God's idea all along! He desires to express Himself through your touch, your voice, your presence; He is so happy to dwell in you! There is no place in the universe where He would rather be!)"

God's love is so wide it encompasses everyone to the ends of the earth!

BOYD C. PURCELL
Christianity without insanity

You want to talk about 'hell' and the plethora of mistranslations, misunderstandings, and outright lies that religion has used to abuse people with? Boyd Purcell is your man!

Boyd C. Purcell, Ph.D., author of *Spiritual Terrorism: Spiritual Abuse from the Womb to the Tomb and Christianity Without Insanity: For Optimal Mental/Emotional/Physical Health*, is a well-studied academic researcher who knows firsthand what it's like to be abused by 'hell-believing' religious leaders who don't like to have their sacred cows tipped.

Dr. Purcell is a National Board-Certified Counselor, a Licensed Professional Counselor, an Ordained Honorably Retired Presbyterian Minister, and a Board-Certified Chaplain. Educationally, he has a

Bachelor of Science degree in Comprehensive Social Studies (World/ European/American History, Economics, Geography, Political Science, etc.).

He also has a Master of Arts Degree in Counseling, a Master of Divinity degree in Biblical Studies, and a Doctor of Philosophy degree in the integration of psychology and theology. In terms of experience, Dr. Purcell has over 40 years of ministry in counseling: agency, clinical, pastoral, psychiatric hospital, school, substance abuse, private practice, and chaplaincy—providing spiritual care at the end of life for hospice patients.

Those credentials and $6 couldn't even get him a mocha latte at the 'organized religious coffee shop' once he started questioning their cherished belief in 'Eternal Conscious Torment' and unwillingness to even acknowledge how the phrase 'salted with fire' could mean anything but non-stop eternal punishment from a *god* of religion, who is 'good all the time.'

Since he came awake to Truth, Boyd's books and pamphlets have helped deliver multitudes of people from spiritual abuse and are required reading for Grace Seminarians worldwide. Boyd writes: "Some people have a nonchalant couldn't-care-less attitude to the horror of human beings being tortured forever in literal hell fire. This is my response to such a callous elitist non-loving non-compassionate non-Christlike attitude. This is exactly the attitude of so many, who identify themselves as 'Bible-believing' Christians, with whom, in the last 30 years, I have shared the truth of Christian Universalism (CU).

"Compassionate persons have said that they hope I am right about CU, but most believers in eternal conscious torment in the literal fire of hell have been resistive, angry, and downright hostile. And, yes, some have been quick to call me a heretic to the Christian faith. As long as they think they are saved, and perhaps close family members, they don't give a damn about all fellow human beings whom Jesus admonished us to love as ourselves—neighbors and even our enemies.

"A question of utmost importance I asked in my second book, *Christianity Without Insanity*, is 'Does God love all people as He loves Himself?' If so, God cannot and will not torture anyone at all, much less forever! If not, then God is the biggest hypocrite in the universe!"

Dr. Boyd Purcell has blessed us all with his research, concise writing, commitment to The Truth, and willingness to endure persecution from organized religion to the point of financial loss and rejection from former 'friends.' He is generous and gracious with his time and resources and is a delight to know! I highly recommend you check him out!

Grace I AM #28

There's way more mind-blowing Good News than you can ever imagine or comprehend. In fact, Papa, Jesus, and Grace reveal more and more to you every day, and now you can hear and believe their revelation of Truth!

There's a place Scripture calls "The Throne of Grace." It's a place that you can confidently go to, where you receive mercy and find grace to help in your time of need.

Where is "The Throne of Grace"? It is IN you! You are the Temple—the dwelling place of God! Paul wrote that to his friends in Corinth and to you. He said, "Do you not know that you are the temple of God and that the Spirit of God dwells in you?" They were a jacked-up group of folks who were into some despicable things that even unscrupulous mobsters would never even think of doing! That certainly means there's hope for you and me!

The THRONE OF GOD IS IN YOU! Jesus, Papa, and the Holy Spirit are all IN YOU!

We go to Christ in us, the hope of glory, to obtain mercy and find GRACE to help us in time of need! There is no 'bad' judgment throne of God. There is only the THRONE OF GRACE, where we are reminded and assured daily that we have already been judged and made right, forgiven, justified, sanctified, purified, included, and accepted into the Divine Triune Circle Dance of God's Unconditional love and all that flows from it! All our sins have been taken away!

Be sure not to listen to religion's terrible lie that one day, God will get off The Throne of Grace, go to a Great white Judgment Throne, change His disposition totally and no longer be love and grace but, instead, be wrath and judgment! That's not Jesus at all!

Take a few minutes in your secret place with your primary Teammates, Jesus, Papa, and Grace, and say (out loud if you can) several times slowly, "I AM the home of the Temple of God where the Throne of Grace is, and I can confidently go there any time to receive mercy and find grace to help in my time of need!"

JERRY (J.L.) GRAY
Twin Brothers from a Different Mother!

When my friend J.L. Gray and I meet new people, they often ask if we're related. With a straight face, I tell them we're twin brothers. We probably are related through some Gray ancestor generations ago, but J.L. is six foot five and has trouble finding clothes that fit his XXXL+ body size. I'm a foot shorter and buy my clothes in the boy's section. Okay, I might be exaggerating a little with the clothes, but we're definitely not twins! We certainly are brothers in our ministry together to our group in Lawrence, Ks., and online.

J.L. grew up on a farm/ranch in the southern Flint Hills of Kansas, where he started a business hauling hay at an age young enough that his mom had to drive for him. He was an all-state football and basketball player and played football at Kansas State University until an injury ended that career.

He then became a professional bull rider on the rodeo circuit before joining the United States Air Force, where his first assigned duty station was at the Air Force Academy as leader of an elite special forces unit named RED HORSE. He spent most of his Air Force career on temporary assignments in covert places around the world.

After being discharged due to injuries, he raised a large family and owned and operated a building contracting business where, he states, "All of my children learned how to work!"

After marrying his second wife, Develle (her three sons expanded their family to seven children), they opened and operated a dinner theatre. During that time, God gave him a revelation about faith, specifically teaching others about living in faith and by faith. Teachings by Jerry Savelle and Jesse Duplantis were instrumental in prepping him for this new journey.

J.L. says, "We subsequently sold our place and moved to Lawrence, Kansas, where we 'stumbled upon' a church that really fit where we were. Many in that church were going through a transition from legalism to hyper-grace. This transition has brought about a different way of thinking and relating to others. We now see others through the lens of Christ in us." In addition to him and Develle being part of New Life in Christ, he posts a Facebook 'thought for the day' on his personal page and at Faith RX Ministries.

J.L. is a huge presence, not just in physical stature but also in knowing, receiving, giving, and teaching unconditional love, grace, and inclusion to everyone he's around. I used to say that he is "Larger than Life." Now I know he experiences new life in Christ, the largest life there is, and we all have it!

Grace I AM #29

Do you ever wonder why life seems so hard? Do you ever feel like there's an invisible force that's against you? I have good news and bad news for you.

Bad news first: There is an invisible force that's against you, and it is not what religion has told you it is!

Good news: You're about to be enlightened as to what it is that's against you and see the Light of the Really Good News.

Darkness is against you. Darkness is not true; it only claims to be true. Darkness is the absence of LIGHT. There is NO darkness in PURE LIGHT. The foundation of darkness is the great lie of separation. Darkness's entire force emanates from the lie that you are separate from GOOD—separate from GOD.

The doctrinal system of darkness is what is AGAINST YOU! It is The Enemy!

The Grace Restoration Team's purpose is to reveal the Truth of The Light to you. LIGHT'S message is: You are NOT separate from God. You have never been separated from God. You will NEVER be separate from God!

Since darkness is a lie, it only exists in your mind! It's not real! And it's incredibly simple to overcome the darkness. The Really Good News is, someone has already overcome the darkness for you! And that Someone is part of your VERY OWN TEA!

Take a few minutes in your secret place with your primary Teammates, Jesus, Papa, and Grace, and say (out loud if you can) several times slowly, "I Am Not Separate from God. I Am closer to God than the air I breathe!"

ANDRE CHAISSON
On a mission in a Street Mission

"Separation between God and humanity has only existed in our mind. God is ONE with His creation." ~Andre Chaisson

Andre Chaisson's journey to experiencing the revelation of God's unconditional love for ALL people, their pure light (with no trace of darkness), Their unlimited Grace for ALL, their perfect goodness, and inclusion of ALL people is unusual, to say the least!

Andre now lives in Kelowna, British Colombia, Canada. His journey started a thousand miles from there in Eastern, French-speaking Canada, when he experienced a dysfunctional, militaristic childhood as the youngest boy in a family of eight. There, his life was steeped in ritualistic Catholicism. He had no concept of God as a loving father.

He eventually moved further west, married, had children, and joined the workforce. Then, as a young adult, turned to a life of drugs. He lost his family, became homeless and, while going to a street mission for help, got 'saved,' which he now knows is simply believing the truth that Papa, Jesus, and Grace 'saved' him before creation.

Andre managed to get off drugs for a while, had gainful employment and functional life, including twenty years in organized religion, but then turned back to hard drugs, leading him to be homeless for five years.

During those years, he tried to change his life but wasn't successful. Later, he would write: "Trying to change the outside of our lives is working backward!"

Change has to begin from the 'inside.'

It's the 'inside' that transformed the outside.

Only God can transform our 'inside.'

Good News, the creator and Father is already in His creation! In the incarnation of the DIVINE SON, GOD has become 'ONE' with our humanity! As it has been written before: "Let GOD be GOD 'IN'

YOU!"

Finally, when he was at 'rock bottom,' to escape the elements of a hard Canadian winter, he went back to the mission and ended up finally meeting "The Only True God" who had been in him all along!

Andre had what some would call 'mystical' experiences—hearing from God personally about God's goodness. One of the volunteers at the mission eventually became his wife, and together, they have since been finding out every day that God is even better than they imagined the day before!

However, they were unable (and still are) to find a church in their area that taught about the Only True God (as Jesus refers to the Father). Eventually, they started searching online for people who taught Grace, the Fatherhood of God, and Unconditional Love and Inclusion for all.

Their searches led them to others in this book, including Steve McVey, fellow Canadians Paul Young and Ron Wright, and many more. Andre says, "Salvation is when you discover the Joy that GOD is already in you and always has been!"

In one of his insightful posts, he says, "The ego will often try the futile and impossible task of living 'for' God." It's IMPOSSIBLE to live for God. You can only live 'FROM' God!

God, in the incarnation of His Divine Son, is waiting for our surrender to the indwelling Christ so that the Divine Trinitarian Life can be lived and expressed through our humanity. Then, like Jesus, we will be able to say: "If you have seen me, you have seen the Father as well!"

Looking back on his life, Andre now writes, "We are born into a fallen materialistic world. From the time we're little babies, we are preconditioned by all the conditions surrounding us. Before we are old enough to see and assess the world for ourselves, we are told how to behave and what to believe. We grow up in the culture and religion where we were born. Then, there's all the things that happened to us, good and bad.

"All of these things mold our beliefs about ourselves, the world, and God. Being born in a dysfunctional world, it's a natural conclusion that our perception of ourselves, the world, and God is most likely screwed up!

"The Eternal Truth in the midst of all these distortions of reality is that we are 'spirit beings' created in the image and likeness of God. We are spirit beings having a human experience for a few years on planet earth. Our beginning is in the heart of God before time began. We always have been in God. Like the prodigal son, we are looking for our way back home to the father. Yet we never left, only in our mind. In the incarnation of the DIVINE SON, the Father has united Himself to us in our pigpen. We are already Home! The kingdom of GOD is WITHIN YOU!"

Grace I AM #30

You've heard the phrase "The Word of God." People use that phrase a lot. I don't think they know what it means! The doctrinal system of darkness, which is AGAINST YOU, perpetuates the lie that scripture, written words about God, is the word of god. It's not

Jesus Christ is the Living Word of God. Everything written in Scripture and other 'religious' books is words written about God.

To know the truth about darkness (which is against you) and PURE LIGHT (which is totally FOR you), the most fundamental revelation is that The Word of God—Jesus—is IN you and always has been!

You are not alone, you never have been, and you never will be! Jesus, the Living Word of God, was face-to-face with God the Father before They ever created anything!

Before They ever created anything, they thought about you; they conceived you in their Mind, the Mind of Christ; and They included you in their TEAM.

You, Papa, Jesus, and Grace have ALWAYS BEEN together. NEVER separate! Darkness doesn't want you to know that. Darkness lies to you. Darkness lies that you were born separated from its god, and it's up to you to get its god to come to you and stay with you.

THAT IS THE GREAT LIE OF DARKNESS: SEPARATION.

The very first and most primary revelation that Jesus wants you to know is, "God is Pure Light, with NO Trace of Darkness!" Jesus is the Light of the World, who is in the process of enlightening, shining the Light in ALL mankind, revealing the darkness.

Be aware that the lie and deceit of darkness is against you. Don't take its thoughts. Instead, live where you truly are: In The Pure Light!

Take a few minutes in your secret place with your primary Teammates, Jesus, Papa, and Grace, and say (out loud if you can) several times slowly, "I AM in PURE LIGHT! My Team IS Pure Light!"

BISHOP DR. BILL HANSHEW
Digging Deep into the well of God's Mind

I (Paul Gray) was a guest on a December 2021 episode of the *Kingdom Dynamics Show, with Dr. Bill Hanshew*. He began by quoting Hebrews 1:3 from The Passion Translation: "The Son is the dazzling radiance of God's splendor, the exact expression of God's true nature—his mirror image {or, exact expression}! He holds the universe together and expands it by the mighty power of his spoken word. He accomplished for us the complete cleansing of sins {mistaken identity}, and then took his seat on the highest throne at the right hand of the Majestic One."

He continued by explaining, "The word splendor is also interpreted as the out-shining [effulgence] of God's glory." The Aramaic can be translated as "He is the Sprout of God, the image of his glory." Also, we find that "the Son is God's mirror image and exact expression" or the reflection of God. And as He is, so are you. If As the Eternal Christ is, so are we, then we also are a divine portrait of the true likeness of the invisible God. I really hope you were enlightened and inspired to "dig deep into the well of Father's mind within this show with Paul Gray and me!"

Indeed, Dr. Bill digs deep into spiritual matters!

Bishop Dr. Bill Hanshew is an author, teacher, webinar speaker, and founder/president of World Bible School Online University, where he and his bride, Dr. Faye Henshew, provide wonderful leadership.

The Hanshews live in Joplin, Missouri, where the famed Route 66 once connected Chicago to Los Angeles. Today, Dr. Bill and Dr. Faye connect people spiritually all over the world!

Bill grew up during the days of great Pentecostal revivals. He started preaching at the age of seventeen, was a youth pastor at the age of eighteen, and was a senior pastor at the age of twenty. He has always pursued the knowledge of God by studying the Bible, other commentaries, and historical data,, and today, he is still experiencing continuous downloads from the Holy Spirit, bringing fresh biblical insights in a challenging, yet understandable, way to the body of Christ.

In addition to having a Bachelor of Biblical Studies degree and a Master of Theology degree, he has doctorates from two different prestigious schools. In affiliation with the Church of Grace International Ministers Inc., Liberia, West Africa., he was chosen as an Ordained Bishop.

Bill is the host of several live shows throughout the week on Facebook and YouTube. Tuesday evening is a panel discussion titled "Healed Because God Says So." Wednesday morning's show is called "Take Another Look," where Bill dives into the richer revelation of the scripture. Thursday nights is Kingdom Dynamics, and rounding out the week is a more casual show titled "Friday Morning Conversations." All of these shows flow from the Spirit and the heart of Bill to teach, inspire, and motivate us all to dig deeper, question our theology, and ultimately know who we are in Christ.

Dr. Bill started preaching as a teenager and then journeyed through many traditional church denominations, including charismatic and word of faith. After a decade, he found himself frustrated with the system and dissatisfied with what he was learning. He remembers asking God, "Isn't there more than just this?"

Bill remembers even at a young age receiving downloads of revelation from God. God was always revealing deeper things, especially about Scripture. As he was learning and growing, it all would eventually lead Bill down a path to an awakening to the finished work of the 'Eternal Christ.' In the process, all his learned doctrines of separation, including eternal damnation, rapture, and other futuristic eschatology, were now being challenged.

He would eventually learn what most of the early church believed—Apokatastasis, the restoration of all things.

In 1988, Bill and Faye began to have the vision to start their own Bible school. They wanted it to be accredited worldwide and offer a curriculum that would begin to change generations, teaching truth and the finished work of Jesus Christ. They have a passion to get this truth out to as many people as affordably as they can. What started as just a vision now has hundreds of students from all over the world attending. Students are being freed from doctrines of man and learning instead theology that lines up more with the early church.

Dr. Bill is not only the founder of WBSU, but he personally teaches several subjects there, including his favorite, the book of Revelation.

He says, "The traditional futuristic interpretation of this book brings many images of destruction, torment, and fear, including the mark of the beast, a lake of fire, and the anti-Christ. I was taught to stay away from it!" However, the Holy Spirit taught him the beautiful grace and joy of the symbolism revealing the eternal love of God for ALL people! You will enjoy, learn, and be challenged in a wonderful way by Dr. Bill!

From Notes From Papa, a 366-day devotional by Paul Gray:

A Note From Papa to you!

To My special child, whom I am continually growing in grace,

I want you to know up front that I am responsible for your spiritual growth, not you! Religion has propagated the lie that each individual is responsible for their own spiritual growth.

Depending on which denomination, para-church, or religious organization one belongs to, they are taught some combination of 'spiritual disciplines,' which are said to be what will bring about desired spiritual growth. These can include prayer, Bible study, attending religious services, and giving. Those aren't bad, but they won't produce spiritual growth. That kind of thinking says that by a person's own effort, they can grow and improve. That's actually the false self, ego, or flesh—which are all illusions and are not the real you.

Who is responsible for a child's growth? Its parents are responsible for shelter, protection, food, clothing, educational opportunities, and the like. Children can't provide those things. But even parents can't affect a child's height. Physical growth and spiritual growth are both provided by Me!

The 'Fruit of the Spirit,' which are character traits that all flow from My pure agape love that always does what is best for the other, includes joy, peace, patience, kindness, goodness, gentleness, faith, and Spirit power. No one can produce them, grow in them, or mature in them by their own self-improvement plan. The Fruit of the Spirit can only be produced and manifested in a person by the Holy Spirit! Your part is simply to be available and aware that you are living in seamless union, or oneness, with Me. Listen to Me, and let Me teach you. I will! Be aware, ask, and allow Christ in you to live as you in relation to the world and everything in it. Responsibility means having the ability to respond. Respond to Me.

Grace is My supernatural divine ability to enable you to be and do all that I have envisioned for you since before the foundation of the world. You were conceived by grace, given life by grace—and you live, move, and have your being by the power of My grace! Relax, rest, and enjoy the experience of Me providing your spiritual growth. It's a much easier and the only effective means of growing. Grow in grace!

~Love, Papa

DR. FAYE HANSHEW
I can. I can. I know I can!

"I have never in my lifetime felt that Father God has been mad at me." ~Dr. Faye Hanshew

Dr. Faye Henshaw has an Associate of Arts degree from Mineral Area College in Park Hills, Missouri; a BMS in Management; and an MBA in Business. She is the senior producer and editor of the five-year magazine *Faith Unlimited*. She's had her own talk show, "Live Talk with Faye." She is currently the founder and CEO of Inspired Creations Publishing Co. LLC, and Cofounder, Managing Director, and Graphics Designer for World Bible School University (WBSU), USA. Faye also has a heart for children and education and will do anything within her power to help keep children safe and to help adults learn the truth of God's word. Faye has served in many different ministries. She has served as Nursery Director, Children's Pastor, Youth Pastor, and Co-pastor with her husband Bishop Dr. Bill Hanshew. She was the Administrator and Graphics Designer for Grace International Bible University (GIBU) in Liberia. She and Dr. Bill have been married forty-eight years. They have two children, eight granddaughters, two great-granddaughters, and one great-grandson.

When you meet Faye, you right away find her bright, dynamic, and wholly devoted to all that she is involved in. She works hard and loves well because she knows the Father's unconditional love. Like many, she journeyed through a more traditional church environment for years. She and Dr. Bill even co-pastored a church. They once believed the lies about the false *god* of separation. She admits, though, that despite all those beliefs, she always knew the Father loved her.

As she began to learn of God's unconditional Grace for all, she said that she was filled with light. Knowing that we all belong to God enabled her to love easily. Faye is a woman who proudly wears many hats, but one of her favorite passions is children, both advocating for protecting them and helping with healthy child development. She does this by teaching them that Father loves them and shows them their God-given identity. She has written a children's book titled *I Can. I*

Can. I Know I Can.

This book gives parents a tool filled with God's truth to help their children, among other things, handle real, situational fear. This book takes children through scenarios, including bullying, nightmares, coming home to find your parents are not there and the resultant fear. Faye writes in language that is relatable and employs Scripture that teaches ways to experience God's help with fear. Children are reminded that God never leaves or forsakes them, and they are never alone. Faye believes that when children are taught these foundational truths, they will be equipped to conquer the giant of fear.

She and her husband have also founded and manage together World Bible School University. They have found that with so much awakening going on worldwide to the victorious finished work of the cross, there is a real need for a curriculum that correctly aligns with the truth. The western gospel has drifted far away from what most of the early church believed and, instead, wrongly taught a *god* of separation. The Hanshews know that God is not separated from any of His kids and that He is certainly not a God who is planning on destroying the planet or sending people to a place of eternal conscious torment. Their teaching reveals and exposes pagan doctrines rooted in the false idea of separation that have become pervasive in most churches. They remind all that Jesus tore the veil and fully restored our union with the Father for all.

Faye and Bill's mission at WBS is to 'right this ship' that has kept so many bound in wrong teaching for years. They offer a complete and comprehensive scripturally sound curriculum that not only corrects these doctrinal errors but enables people to walk in the freedom that Christ came to establish while also obtaining a degree. WBS is truly 'worldwide,' and they employ and work with leaders and teachers in many countries, especially in Africa.

Faye is the behind-the-scenes catalyst who keeps WBSU running smoothly. She continually works at recruiting paraprofessionals, hiring professors, and organizing the classes. Since they have many overseas students, it is normal to find her up at 2:00 A.M., fielding their questions. She does not complain and fully enjoys her work. The college is growing rapidly with enrollment, increasing exponentially in just a few years to hundreds of students.

In her spare time, Faye loves to be with family, cooking, and listening to music. She reminisces about once being in a traveling gospel group called The Gospel Crusaders. Dr. Bill is also a great singer, and they enjoy singing together.

Faye radiates the Father's love and blesses everyone she comes in contact with, including me!

Grace I AM #31

Jesus' best friend John says to you: "My conversation with you flows from the same source which illuminates this fellowship of union with the Father and the Son. This, then, is the essence of the message: God is radiant light, and in him, there exists not even a trace of obscurity or darkness at all.

"His life is the light that defines our lives. In his life, we discover the light of life. Jesus/Light came to earth and pierced the darkness! It could not comprehend or diminish this light. Darkness represents mankind's ignorance of their true identity as original TEAM members!"

The doctrinal system of darkness, which is AGAINST YOU, perpetuates the lie that you are far from God. Know the Truth that there is NO DISTANCE at all between you and the Only True God!

Jesus tells you that there will be a day when you know that Jesus is in The Father, The Father is in Him, and They both, along with Grace, ARE IN YOU!

If you didn't know that before, TODAY IS YOUR DAY! Now you see the Light of Truth!

Take a few minutes in your secret place with your primary Teammates, Jesus, Papa, and Grace, and say (out loud if you can) several times slowly, "I AM in The TEAM. Jesus, Papa, Grace, and I are in The Light together!"

FLORIAN BERNDT
Wading in the mystical flow

"It's the passion of my life to share the Unfailing Love of God, our Abba Father." ~Florian Berndt

Florian Berndt is a breath of fresh air blowing around the world from Germany! Prior to moving to their home on the Swiss/French Border of Germany, he and his Irish-born wife, Clare, lived in England for several years. They have two beautiful children.

Like many, Florian grew up in a dysfunctional family. He met Jesus for the first time while in his teens. In this encounter, he describes feeling like he was home, that he belonged somewhere and was loved and accepted. Florian also experienced the pain of his parent's divorcing. That situation brought division culminating with Florian's dad moving out to live with a new family, taking Florian with him. Until then, Florian had felt like he was the apple of his dad's eye, but with the divorce, he began to feel that he had to prove himself to his dad. He sensed a strain in their relationship that left him feeling guilt and shame. Florian found that he would project his own inner world onto his image of God.

He soon began getting involved in religious fundamentalism and quickly became a 'good evangelist,' who was able to motivate people to 'accept Christ.' He both experienced and employed fear, shame, and guilt, the staples of a fear-driven gospel. Eventually, the Spirit of God began to awaken Florian to the unconditional love of Abba. With this revelation of grace and inclusion, he was naturally provoked to question much of the theology and doctrines he had been taught and that he taught.

Florian began to look afresh at Scripture and started researching what the first church believed. He was pleasantly surprised to find that what his heart had been showing him about God and His goodness is also what was believed when the church started!

His fundamentalism background caused Florian much-suppressed trauma, but with the Holy Spirit's comfort, help, and guidance, he moved through the trauma and eventually found himself entering back into ministry.

Today, Florian and Clare are both journeying on the beautiful road of radical grace. They want others to know the love of Abba as well. Motivated by hearts for gathering people together, they bought a spacious old schoolhouse, which was built in 1875. They spent a couple of years cleaning, remodeling, and adding a guest room. They currently live there as well as provide a place for the community to gather. They invite others to come in for fellowship, friendship, and worship. Florian and Clare are both musicians and often lead worship.

They have had the pleasure of having the Trinitarian theologian Baxter Kruger come to encourage and teach their friends about our inclusion in the Trinity. Their environment is one of acceptance, love, and grace and provides a place for people to connect directly with Abba. Florian loves the prophetic gift but really enjoys teaching others that God is already speaking to them.

He emphasizes that anyone can hear from Him directly and that He is always speaking to us. Florian knows that those who come from a dogmatic fundamental Christian experience can have a separation mindset that becomes a stumbling block preventing them from making friends 'outside their group.' He knows from personal experience that those who believe that unless a person says the 'magic prayer' and believes the same as your group are labeled as 'outsiders.' He also knows that is not the true gospel and that it comes from religious adherents projecting their own image of God onto others. Florian often says, "God is not separated from anyone. In Him, all things are made that were made, and in Him, all things exist. His love is unfailing, and He is always speaking to each of us."

Florian writes, translates, and teaches about the Trinitarian Inclusion of Papa, Jesus, and Grace. He and author Charles Slagle started a Facebook online community named Abba Calling based on Charlie's book with the same title. It's a community for like-minded people to gather, share, and seek prayer amongst an online community.

I've had the wonderful experience of facilitating my PURE LIGHT WALKER course with Florian and a group of his German friends (who have now become my friends). He's now in the process of translating the course into German and plans to be teaching it in person and online starting in the spring of 2022.

Grace I AM #32

Paul, the Grace-Man, wants you to know when and how you joined the Light Team. It was a mystery until Jesus revealed it to Paul in person about 2,000 years ago. By the way, Jesus is still revealing things to us, to you specifically. The Living Word of God, Jesus, is continually speaking words of Light to You!

Paul wrote to a group two thousand years ago and, by extension, to you: "Your hearts can soar with joyful gratitude when you think of how God made you worthy to receive the glorious inheritance freely given to us by living in the light. He has rescued us completely from the tyrannical rule of darkness and has translated us into the kingdom realm of his beloved Son. For in the Son all our sins are canceled and we have the release of redemption through his very blood."

Another translation renders it as follows: "The Father, who has qualified us to share in the inheritance of the saints (God's people) in the Light. For He has rescued us and has drawn us to Himself from the dominion of darkness and has transferred us to the kingdom of His beloved Son, in whom we have redemption [because of His sacrifice, resulting in] the forgiveness of our sins [and the cancellation of sins' penalty]."

The doctrinal system of darkness, which is AGAINST YOU, perpetuates the lie that 'living in bad behavior' is living in darkness. It's not! It's actually the doctrinal system of darkness itself!

Take a few minutes in your secret place with your primary Teammates, Jesus, Papa, and Grace, and say (out loud if you can) several times slowly, "I AM in Christ's Kingdom of Light! I have already been transferred from the denominational system of darkness! And I'm never going back!"

WAYNE MCDANIEL
Everything will work out in the end

Wayne McDaniel is a successful businessman, teacher, leader, and giver. He teaches and mentors people in "Expanding Opportunities for Living Generously" through his organization Generous Vision, Inc.

In addition, much of Wayne's ministry involves serving on Tom Bassford's board at Significant Matters.

An avid bicyclist, Wayne rides several miles a day from his hilltop country home secluded in the woods outside of Lawrence, Kansas, to meet with and encourage a variety of people. In addition to cycling over much of the United States, he and his wife, Jude, are world travelers and supporters of several ministries.

Wayne has a decades-long history of religious involvement, including teaching, leading, serving on boards, giving, and mentoring. His transformation away from traditional evangelical thought into embracing what most of the early church fathers believed, taught, and wrote about apokatastasis (God's restoration and reconciliation of ALL people) has led him (and the others who are featured in this book) to question religion's portrayal of a seemingly bi-polar, dark, angry, punitive, list-keeping god, non-relational *god.*

He is continually exploring new ways to convey the character of the Only True God and our identity in Christ to adults and children alike!

He's a storyteller, and his stories are written within the Christian tradition and mystical experience but with respect toward all religious traditions that believe God is Love and the Source of Life. He's currently working on children's books where principles are presented without the dogma, which sometimes stunts instead of facilitates human flourishing. Current understandings of physics, biology, and psychology are incorporated into his writing so parents and guardians can feel confident about the messages conveyed.

In teaching healthy spirituality to kids (and adults), his objective is to instill core concepts about God, the world, and oneself, which promote spiritual and psychological well-being. Watch for an exciting group of children's books in the near future!

At the close of Wayne's emails, he emphasizes his belief in God's ultimate restoration of ALL people with this phrase he picked up on an exciting adventure to Iceland:

'Betta reddast,' an Icelandic phrase that encapsulates the idea that everything will work out in the end.

Wayne is indeed a generous giver in all aspects of life.

Grace I AM #33

What can you expect to experience in The Light Team?

Jesus' friend Paul wrote this to you: "The amazing grace of the Master, Jesus Christ, the extravagant love of God, the intimate friendship of the Holy Spirit, is with all of you!"

You can expect to continually and always enjoy and experience extravagant, unconditional Love that never fails, never ends, and continually works out all things for the good!

You can expect to continually and always enjoy and experience intimate friendship with Deity! You can expect to enjoy and experience the amazing grace of Christ to provide everything you ever need for a continual right relationship with God and provide everything else you need for life!

The doctrinal system of darkness, which is AGAINST YOU, perpetuates the lie that you have to work to gain and maintain the love and grace of God, and you'll never be 'friends' with God—at best, He will 'tolerate' you because of what Jesus did.

Take a few minutes in your secret place with your primary Teammates, Jesus, Papa, and Grace, and say (out loud if you can) several times slowly, "I AM now and forever best friends with God, loved unconditionally by God, and always have more than I need for God's abundant life!"

JOHN CROTTY
I died for 45 minutes!

"On December 7, 2014, I died for 45 minutes. My heart stopped beating; then God started opening my eyes to see Jesus in a clearer light! What a ride I've been on ever since. Currently, I'm studying Quantum Physics to see how it mirrors God as revealed in the Bible." ~John Crotty

Since that life-impacting event when Papa gave John spiritual eyes to see what really is, he says that his passion is to allow Jesus to live through him to touch others with His love. Galatians 2:20 is a pivotal verse for John. "My old identity has been co-crucified with Christ and no longer lives. And now the essence of this new life is no longer mine, for the Anointed One lives his life through me—we live in union as one! My new life is empowered by the faith of the Son of God who loves me so much that he gave himself for me, dispensing his life into mine!" He says that his reason for living is transformation—to be like Jesus.

John grew up in Dallas, Texas, then graduated from VMI with a degree in Electrical Engineering. He subsequently flew F-105 planes for the United States Air Force for the next thirteen years (both in active duty and guard), including in the Vietnam War, where he attained the rank of Major.

After his military service, John was a Captain for Delta Airlines for thirty-one years. For several decades in the Dallas suburb of Flint, Texas, he taught about the Unconditional Love and Grace of God. He now teaches a local group in Tyler. You will find John to be a very engaging, positive person whose unconditional love, grace, and inclusion mirrors that of Jesus!

"When Jesus died, there was a violent earthquake, and the veil in the temple was torn from top to bottom. The Bible says that tombs were opened, and many bodies of saints arose from the dead. It says that after Jesus' resurrection, they went into Jerusalem, where many people witnessed their return to life. And in three days, He followed them. Jesus is all about life—life-affirming, life-restoring, life-enriching, life-protecting."

From Grace Is … by Paul Gray:

Long Love

Ephesians 3:16–19, "I pray that out of His glorious riches He may strengthen you with power through His Spirit in your inner being, so that Christ may dwell in your hearts through faith. And I pray that you, being rooted and established in love, may have power, together with all the Lord's holy people, to grasp how wide and long and high and deep is the love of Christ, and to know this love that surpasses knowledge—that you may be filled to the measure of all the fullness of God."

Psalms 100:5, "For the Lord is good; His lovingkindness is everlasting, and His faithfulness is to all generations."

Psalms 118 says five times that His lovingkindness is forever!

God's love is long love. It lasts forever, for all eternity. We can never be separated from God's love!

Contrary to what religion has incorrectly taught, there's no cutoff date at the end of this life. Death can't separate us from God's love!

Romans 8:35–39, "Who shall separate us from the love of Christ? Shall tribulation, or distress, or persecution, or famine, or nakedness, or peril, or sword … Yet in all these things we are more than conquerors through Him who loved us. For I am persuaded that neither death nor life, nor angels nor principalities nor powers, nor things present nor things to come, nor height nor depth, nor any other created thing, shall be able to separate us from the love of God which is in Christ Jesus our Lord."

MIKE ZENKER

Did I have my keyboard off by one letter?

Mike Zenker is the National Director of Growing in Grace Ministries, Canada, and has a passion for sharing the Life, Love, and Grace of Jesus. He is a spiritual leader, speaker, writer, and encourager. He is also the Sr. Pastor of Hope Fellowship, in Waterloo, Ontario. Mike is the Chaplain for the City of Kitchener Fire Department and a Funeral home Chaplain. This has given him a tremendous opportunity to love and care for people who are experiencing some of the worst times of their lives. Previously, he was the National Director for Grace Walk, Canada, for thirteen years.

In all these many roles, Mike has had a tremendous opportunity to love and care for people often at the most difficult times of their lives (when they lose a loved one). Mike considers all of this to be an honor for him.

In his teaching and ministry, Mike shares with all a pastor's perspective on the journey into the revelation of God's unconditional love and grace. He believes one of his most profound shifts was in simply having the true nature of God unveiled in the unlearning and relearning process. The unlearning he admits brings with it much pain, but the upside of it is in the great rejoicing that you received in learning the truth about Jesus. "I'm still growing in Grace; after all, no one ever arrives.""

Mike hosts a wonderful weekly online show titled "Still Growing in Grace!"

Mike employs a great analogy to describe the process of dismantling old fundamental doctrines when he compares it to feeling like you are always typing with one letter off on a keyboard. It just feels disjointed throughout, and you wrestle, but then, miraculously, the letters shift, and you embrace the joy of seeing and knowing God as truly all good!

His earliest revelations of the inclusion of all in Christ began through teachings by Steve McVey and Rudy Zacharias. He found it most interesting to realize that these are not new teachings but, in fact, incredibly old teachings. He next connected with Australia's Dr.

Bruce Wauchope and his multi-part series on what is the true gospel. It was then that all the pieces seemed to fall into place for Mike, and he was able to understand how the doctrines he had been taught in the western church were contrary to what the first church believed.

Dr. Wauchope taught Mike the early orthodox beliefs and carefully exposed where the doctrine of separation, and dualism became central to the western gospel. His thorough knowledge of the early father's belief led him to see how most of the western church changed, as it was influenced by Augustine and embraced a distorted, punitive picture of God. Mike reminisces on how he felt as he watched Wauchope's teaching series, and tears flooded his eyes when he saw the dark doctrines of separation and punishment come tumbling down one at a time.

Mike subsequently found that when one begins to learn about a more victorious gospel, they often get push-back. The gospel is a proclamation that declares that Jesus Christ saved all and that in Christ, all were made alive again. Mike clarifies that not all experience this truth because many still walk in darkness. However, he knows that Christ's Light shines in everyone's darkness! In John 1, Scripture proclaims that Jesus is the life and the light that shines in every man.

Learning all of this has changed how Mike approaches much of his personal life as well as being a pastor and chaplain. As a pastor, the shift went from having to have all the answers to now giving every person in his 'flock' the freedom of knowing that the Holy Spirit speaks to each person, and he encourages people to listen for themselves what God is saying.

Mike says, "People are no longer just an agenda for me to get them to believe what I believe. Instead, each is loved, valued, and known by Jesus, and I can speak love and light into them." Today, when Mike speaks to people at a funeral where there are many grieving people who need hope, or day-to-day with his own family or with people on the street, his speech is always from love that is motivated to call out that Light that is within—the Christ in them that lights every man.

In January 2022, I had the wonderful honor and experience of being part of a panel of presenters for Mike Zenker's four-week "Understanding Forgiveness Conference." Similar to our goal of connecting unofficial members of the Grace Restoration Team in this book, Mike coalesced a super team consisting of Brad Jersak, Andrea Rabe, Catherine Toon, Libby Briscoe, Richard Murray, Rannie Childress, Francois Du Toit, Bill Thrasher, Reg Chute, Stuart Johnson, Safi Kaskas, Paul Anderson-Walsh, and Ken North. Mike and I—along with the others featured in this book—want to help YOU connect with these wonderful people from across the globe!

Grace I AM #34

How do I know my Light Teammates accept me?

Jesus revealed to His friend Paul (who subsequently wrote to you) "Papa, Jesus and Grace accepted you and included you on their team before They even created the cosmos!"

They knew all about you, everything you would ever think, say, and do … good, bad, and ugly. And They TOTALLY ACCEPTED YOU!

The doctrinal system of darkness, which is AGAINST YOU, perpetuates the lie that you must do the right things to gain and maintain God's acceptance. Not at all!

Take a few minutes in your secret place with your primary Teammates, Jesus, Papa, and Grace, and say (out loud if you can) several times slowly, "I AM completely and forever accepted by Papa, Jesus, and Grace!"

JENNIFER SMITH
It DOES get easier!

Jennifer Smith is a single mom who has a mission and ministry to provide Grace for Single Parents.

As is the case with most moms and dads, parents don't expect to one day have to 'go it alone.' But stuff happens.

Stuff happens, and it's not easy.

Transitioning from two incomes to one, while still having many of the expenses that were once shared, is hard enough.

Being solely responsible for children's well-being and upbringing, along with the pressure of worrying about keeping your job (and insurance) when you have to miss work to be with a sick child, only adds to the financial stress.

Jennifer Smith knows first-hand what those pressures, stress, and lack of rest and privacy can do to a person physically, mentally, spiritually, and emotionally.

She thanks God that with the help of relatives and friends, she's now able to say "It does get easier!"

Jennifer is doing her part to help other single parents through the organization she founded, *Grace For Single Parents.*

Her mission is to uplift single moms to live their best life with God's grace and love. She provides a variety of helpful resources (most of them at no cost), including affirmations, a Single Mom Survival Kit, weekly encouraging emails, and more.

Jen is a podcast host, and we've had the honor of interviewing each other. She's a delightful lady with a wonderful family, and I highly recommend her offerings at Grace For Single Parents!

Grace I AM #35

Now that you know you're on The Team, you may be wondering, *How do I learn? Do I get a manual? A set of rules? A guidebook?*

There are many good teachers around the world who are coming to know Papa (The Only True God), Jesus, and Grace better and better every day. Many of them are profiled in this book!

However, The Teacher lives in you! Grace, the Spirit of Christ, lives IN you! One of the primary things your teammate Grace does is to teach you!

One of Jesus' friends wrote, "Each person will not teach his fellow citizen, and teach his brother or sister, saying, 'Know the Lord,' because they will all know me, from the least to the greatest of them.'"

While we can and do each learn from each other's relationship with The Team, you can only intimately and personally know what someone is like by spending time with them and hearing them talk to you personally and individually.

Grace does that!

How do we know what to do and what to say? We listen to Grace in us and do what Grace tells us to say and do! The doctrinal system of darkness, which is AGAINST YOU, perpetuates the lie that their interpretation of their version of the Bible is your manual for how to live and what to say. It's not and was never intended to be! Grace can and will reveal to you what, if anything, Grace wants you to know about any particular scripture.

Take a few minutes in your secret place with your primary Teammates, Jesus, Papa, and Grace, and say (out loud if you can) several times slowly, "The Teacher, Grace, lives in me and teaches me. I AM listening to Grace!"

STEVE KOSCHELLA
Feeling the Presence of God

Steve Koschella and his wife, Carole, live in Adelaide, South Australia, where he has been a Tele Officer at the Australian Red Cross, working as an encourager to the community. The program allows Steve to connect with people who live alone and have no family support. Many have health issues and are vulnerable in the community. As part of his job, Steve works in collaboration with the government to reach out to people and connect with them to bring them love and encouragement.

Steve's journey into the inclusive love and grace of God began simply but powerfully with a pentecostal prayer and personal encounter in his own home. It was a difficult season of his life in his mid-twenties. He felt totally broken due to a failed marriage and didn't think he had much to look forward to. Wanting company, he remembers going with some friends to a service that ended up with them praying for him at the end.

Sensing Steve needed encouragement, his friends told him that Jesus would help him where he was at. As they began to pray for Steve in the Spirit, he remembers feeling something also immensely powerful; he could literally feel the presence of God.

A few days after that experience, on Easter Sunday, Steve was home, cleaning his kitchen, when he again felt a presence invade him, causing him to cry. Feeling overpowered, he cried out, "I don't know who you are, but I need you." God was invading Steve's very life and making Himself known. The God that he never really knew was wooing his heart. It was so powerful that Steve fell to the floor under the weightiness of God.

He shared with his friends, who had prayed for him at the service, what happened. Like has happened to many of us who encounter God and the rich presence of His love, Steve was told that he needed to get into a church. He then joined a local Pentecostal denomination and began to get involved. He says that while some of his church experience was positive, he saw that much of it did not reflect the God of Love whom he had experienced.

He was told at church that he had to give his heart to Jesus, read his Bible, tithe, and do a plethora of other things. They said he needed to repent and confess all his sins to get right with God, yet he already felt right and accepted by God through his personal experience. He remembers feeling like the beautiful, clear water from God was becoming muddy, and he started to feel fear and judgment.

Steve would eventually move to a more grace-based church, but sadly, he found that although they weren't as legalistic, they still focused on some traditional doctrines that place much of salvation on man. He got more involved, began to attend Bible school, moved up the church ladder, and started to preach. He recalls preparing for a specific message one day on a much-taught principle about the 10% tithe. In the preparation, he remembers feeling a real check in his spirit about the doctrine that if we don't tithe 10% of our income to the church, we are robbing God.

As he began to study, he learned that the 10% tithing is not a new covenant principle but, instead, is a doctrine of the church. Steve's denomination wasn't happy with his understanding, and the leaders attempted to stop him from questioning their doctrines. But Steve felt God impressing within his spirit a freedom to question doctrines. He learned that God not only enjoys our questions, but He can handle them! And he learned that Jesus, The Living Word of God in us, encourages us to ask questions and loves to give us His wisdom.

Steve very much enjoys his awakening to grace!

Grace I AM #36

Has anyone ever asked you if you're 'saved'?

Have you ever been told you have to pray a certain prayer a certain way to 'get saved'?

Have you ever been told that unless you are a baptized member of 'this' particular church, you're not 'saved'?

Have you ever been told that you have to 'do' something, 'receive' something, or 'ask' for something to get 'saved'?

Have you ever thought you were 'saved' but worried that maybe you 'did it wrong,' and it didn't 'take'?

Have you ever been told that maybe you were once 'saved,' but you have backslidden and are no longer 'saved'?

Have you ever wondered what you are 'saved from'?

Did you know that the contemporary religious understanding of 'saved' is not what Jesus and His friends meant in their language? They used a word that means to heal someone suffering from disease, to make well, heal, and restore to health (physical, mental, emotional, spiritual). Jesus did that, and scripture writers then said, "Jesus is The Savior of ALL people!"

You, and ALL people, ARE saved from the Doctrinal System of Darkness's lies about its fictitious angry, list-keeping, punitive, wrathful bi-polar *god*. Most people simply don't know that yet! The Really Good News is that your Teammates have included you in Their continual, ongoing joyful work of revealing this great Truth to ALL people!

Take a few minutes in your secret place with your primary Teammates, Jesus, Papa, and Grace, and say (out loud if you can) several times slowly, "I AM saved! I was saved by Grace through the Faith of Jesus and the Love of Papa! The Doctrinal System of Darkness has no power or effect on me!"

C. BAXTER KRUGER
Calm Insides

"I don't think the gospel is the news that we can receive Jesus into our life. I think the gospel is the news that Jesus has received us into His life.

"Been there (religion) and got a closet full of tee shirts that are all stamped with DISAPPOINTED.

"In over fifty years, it hadn't crossed my mind that there was a difference between my Jesus and the real one." —Baxter Kruger (as Aiden) in "Patmos"

If you like to read and be challenged by the very deepest and most penetrating questions and thoughts about God (Papa, Jesus, and Holy Spirit), you'll find Baxter Kruger in a league of his own! He is the preeminent Trinitarian theologian of our age. More than that, he's a very rare entity, a theologian with a great sense of humor, who is never boring and is delightfully relatable!

Baxter is a prolific author and the Director of Perichoresis Ministries, an international ministry proclaiming the gospel of the Triune God. A life-long student of psychology, Baxter has a degree in political science, and his Doctor of Philosophy degree from King's College, Aberdeen, Scotland. He is the author of nine books, including the international bestseller *The Shack Revisited* and, most recently, *Patmos*. Baxter and his wife, Beth, have been married for thirty-five years and have four children and three grandchildren. He teaches around the world in person and online.

Baxter explains Perichoresis as: "Genuine acceptance removes fear and hiding and creates freedom to know and be known. In this freedom arises a fellowship and sharing so honest and open and real that the persons involved dwell in one another. There is union without loss of individual identity. When one weeps, the other tastes salt. It is only in the Triune relationship of Father, Son, and Spirit that personal relationship of this order exists, and the early Church used the word 'perichoresis' to describe it. The good news is that Jesus Christ has drawn us within this relationship, and its fullness and life are to be played out in each of us and in all creation."

Baxter frequently speaks and does seminars and retreats with Paul Young, John Crowder, Steve McVey, and others. Their presentations are full of humor, good news, spiritual understanding, and insight formed not just in the libraries and classrooms of the world's greatest theological universities but also very much in the woof and warp of daily lives filled with tragedy and triumph, love and loss, hurtful rejection and blessed acceptance.

I have given away hundreds of copies of Baxter Kruger's thirty-one-page booklet *Parable of the Dancing God*, which presents Jesus' picture of God as Father in the most compelling way possible. One of my favorite memories is of reading it to a friend (who is blind) while he was in prison. My friend had suffered fifty years of spiritual, verbal, and physical abuse from both family and others. At the time I read the Parable to him, he had been attending a weekly 'jail Bible study,' where he was told every week that he was a 'wretched sinner' whom God detested, but if he 'said the magic words' and then proceeded to keep himself holy, he could escape eternal conscious torment after he died in jail!

My friend listened intently to me reading the parable with an ever-increasing smile on his weathered face. When I finished and paused, he said, "I knew it! I knew God had to be good and not be like the religious people told me!" My friend is still behind bars, but now, only brick and mortar bars. Inside, he's free, free indeed! I've heard numerous similar stories from people all around the world!

Baxter encourages, teaches, and loves people around the world both in person and via Zoom courses, Q & A, videos, interviews, books, and other media. He especially loves groups of thirty to fifty people, where he can entertain questions and interact personally with everyone.

He's one of a handful of people of whom almost everyone who is on the journey of Unconditional Love, Grace, and Inclusion says, "He's had a tremendous influence on my life." Baxter Kruger is truly an "agent of truth and witness of the Really Good News!"

From Notes From Papa, a 366-day devotional by Paul Gray:

A Note From Papa to you!

To My child, whom I would never hurt in any way,

I want you to absolutely know to the core of your being that I love you unconditionally and always will. You are My own child, My offspring. You carry My DNA. We are family. We are actually one, in union together.

All of that is because I am love, and I love you with no conditions, no limits, no restraints. There is nothing you, nor anyone, could ever do to separate you from Me and My love.

Knowing that, knowing My perfect love, dispels and casts out any fear of punishment that religion, evil, and the world ever throws at you. My perfect love casts out any ounce of fear of punishment from Me. I have never punished you. I will never punish you, ever!

Religion's crazed misunderstanding of Me and My love and goodness will try to convince you that I am bound (by Myself) to have to punish you forever in endless torment if you don't believe right, live right, ask right, confess right, on and on. That is a crazed lie that evil sends to people's darkened and confused minds. It absolutely is not true and never has been.

Some people mistake loving correction for punishment. They are not the same. When you encounter My white-hot consuming fiery love revealing to you the wrong beliefs that you have embraced and even cherished, it's not pleasant for you. It hurts emotionally. But that is not punishment. That is My love refining and purifying you, ridding you of impurities, and restoring you to My original, perfect intent.

My love and actions are always restorative, never punitive. My love never fails. My love never ends. My love has already won! I have wrapped you in My loving embrace, and I won't let go; nothing can force Me to!

I'm asking you to discard any thought or idea of punishment ever coming from Me and, instead, continually bask in My unconditional love for you and everyone!

~Love, Papa

STAN TYRA

If it is not scandalous love, it is not God's love!

Stan Tyra, from Lancaster, Pennsylvania, is the author of two books: *Let My People Go, Releasing the Church* from *Bondage and Awakened to Love: The Journey from Beliefs to Awareness.*

Stan has been a businessman in food sales, marketing, and manufacturing for over thirty years. He started two churches and has hosted annual Men's Encounter weekends for over thirteen years. He continues to write a daily Facebook blog, which started in 2009. It is reflective of his journey and is intended to encourage others in the uniqueness of their journey. Stan and his wife of forty-two years, Debi, have two children and four grandchildren. His purpose is always to invite people to look, without telling them what to see.

Stan knows that many people who are deconstructing religious fundamentalism experience great pain in their process. They often experience loss of relationships and find the people whom they once thought really loved them now relate in an adversarial manner. Sadly, people come to realize that what they thought was love and friendship was conditional on your agreement with others. Stan then muses, "Who knew awakening to a God of all love would reveal so many people who did not love you?"

Stan has found that as rejection begins, and you hear your former friends disparage you, your initial reaction may be to run or fight. However, he has developed the perspective of encouraging people who disparage him, loving them and trusting that God truly knows what He is doing, and He will work it all for good.

Stan says that while he was still involved in the fundamentalist Southern Baptist denomination, he found himself awakening and being saturated with the scandalous gospel of all-inclusive grace. He says, "If it is not scandalous love, it is not God's love." In the dismantling of religion, he was not only seeing the truth that Jesus Christ was inside of him but that He is also in all people! Stan relates that the transformation results in you becoming more patient, less judgmental, and you treat people through a lens of redemption because you see them now accepted and in the family.

Stan has changed in how he 'spends time with Jesus.' Rather than following his former fundamentalist way of trying to change from the outside in through reading the Bible and keeping the rules of religious duty, he now rests in the love, grace, and inclusion of God's embrace.

Stan Tyra realized that he had made the Bible his *god*, so he put his Bible down for a season.

He came to understand that the Bible contains words written about God, but Jesus Himself is the Living Word. Stan began to meet Him one-on-one in what he calls the 'secret place'—within, where the Spirit is waiting for us to fellowship with God.

As he began to process all this new revelation, Stan began to hear God from a place of intimacy. He believes we need to be patient as we wait on God's revelation. He has learned that the Spirit speaks to us the deeper things of Jesus, but if we are hasty, we can process it through all our old paradigms. God wants us to contemplate, let it incubate, and allow Him to develop the word within us.

Stan excitedly says, "God is doing so much in the world right now! We are carrying a new manifestation of God. We see so many across the globe awakening to radical grace and inclusion."

Stan encourages us by sharing, "Jesus has snuck into all our darkness like a thief, and He's stealing it away bit by bit. The Holy Spirit in us will awaken us from any spiritual slumber without even knowing we've been in one. That's the scandalous love and grace of Jesus!"

Grace I AM #50

Where is Jesus right now?

You got it! He's IN you, where He's been since before creation! What's he doing there? Have you ever thought about that?

Here's what Jesus' friend Paul wrote to you: "I possess an inward certainty about you, confident that Grace who is the initiator of the good work within you is also the One who is completing that good work by helping you live more and more like who you really are—the image and likeness of Christ!"

Paul was confident, and your Teammates want you to have absolute confidence that they are continually revealing every good thing in you to you so you can experience and enjoy LIFE on and in your TEAM!

Take a few minutes in your secret place with your primary Teammates, Jesus, Papa, and Grace, and say (out loud if you can) several times slowly, "I AM joyfully experiencing Grace continuing God's good work in me today!"

RYAN COKER

The Gospel is not an elevator ride but the light that shines within all men

Ryan and Mary Ellen Coker have been married for over twenty-five years and live with their children Christopher, Wyatt, and Morgan in Greenville, South Carolina. Ryan has lived in the upstate part of South Carolina his entire life, except for the four years he served in the US Navy (1985–1989) onboard the USS IOWA. He is the founder and head minister at Raised 'n Christ Freedom Ministries, in Travelers Rest, South Carolina. Their once-a-week meeting is live-streamed at 10:20 am EST. He considers himself an Ecumenical minister of the radical grace of Jesus.

A key verse for Ryan is John 1:2–4, which says, "He was in the beginning with God. All things were made through Him, and without Him nothing was made that was made. In Him was life, and the life was the light of all mankind." He says, "As Christians, we know this passage well. It is about the incarnation of Jesus Christ. And how God became a man and entered the darkness of mankind, to save all and restore us to the Father."

Ryan relates that religion taught him that salvation is only for a select few. He was deeply passionate about his faith, but his passion led him to become more of a self-righteous religious zealot as he looked down at people. He believed in the literalism of all scripture and something he named 'the elevator gospel,' believing some people were going up to heaven, but many were going down to hell.

However, in 2007, God used a provocative question from a friend at a funeral service eulogy to unveil and awaken Ryan to the all-inclusive gospel of Jesus Christ. His good friend and co-worker, whom Ryan had been trying to get 'saved,' asked, "Ryan, didn't Jesus say to love your enemies? If Jesus said this, why are you saying if I do not accept Him, I am going straight to a place called hell?" The question left him speechless. He looked at his coworker and said, "Brother, I don't know how to answer that."

He wrestled with that question, as it set him on a journey that would eventually rock his theological world. Over the next few years, Ryan saw his theology getting uprooted and one fundamental belief after another falling away. He wondered if it could really be true that the light of Jesus was in ALL people? He knew that if he believed it, he wouldn't have the freedom to talk about it, and it would probably get him kicked out of churches.

In 2010, tragedy struck his family when his sixteen-year-old nephew was hit and killed by an automobile while walking home from a party. The funeral service was packed with many people, including hundreds of his nephew's high school friends. During the service, one of his eighteen-year-old friends asked if he could come up and share a word. Ryan remembers feeling mad cause this boy was at the party, and he felt like he contributed to the death of his nephew. He inwardly questioned why the pastor would let this boy speak since he was never in church and had a bedroom covered in cannabis posters. He said, "I was self-righteously judging him."

But then the boy began to speak, and it was as if Jesus Christ Himself was giving the eulogy. The love of Jesus resonated with every word from this boy as he read his tribute letter. Ryan was seeing the answer to his question unveiled before him. He saw the witness of the life of Christ shine through that unbelieving boy standing in front of him. When he finished, the pastor rose but could not speak. It was that powerful. The Spirit of Christ moved so powerfully that many of the young students there said that they wanted to know Jesus! Ryan questioned, "How could this be?"

God used an unlikely young man to show Ryan that no matter who it is or how dark they may appear, Jesus is the light shining from within them. Ryan now sees everyone with such value that it has improved the love he has for his wife and family and all those he connects with, including those who may think differently. He now sees all through the lens of Christ's acceptance and His indwelling ALL people!

Grace I AM #51

Most of us put a high premium on our Freedom, and we don't want anyone to mess with it or take it away. The United States was founded, in great part, on the concept of 'religious freedom,' which meant that the people didn't want to be told or forced by the government to believe or adhere to a state-mandated religious system.

Our forefathers fought and died for religious freedom. Ironically, that has morphed into having the freedom to choose which variation of the Doctrinal System of Darkness we want to be enslaved to!

But the really good news is still Really Good News!

Jesus point-blank told the religious leaders of His day (and you) that as they hung out with Him, got to know Him and Papa—the Only True God—that He, Truth, would MAKE them free. He followed that up by clarifying that His Freedom made them (and you) free indeed. A very special kind of ultimate freedom!

Take a few minutes in your secret place with your primary Teammates, Jesus, Papa, and Grace, and say (out loud if you can) several times slowly, "I AM truly free! The Doctrinal System of Darkness's fictitious *god* and its demands and rules has no power over me. I AM Free Indeed!"

KEITH STANTON
The Refuge

Keith Stanton lives in Clearwater, Florida, with his wife, Marjorie, and their dog Rosie, where they are involved in leading a wonderful church called The Refuge, which is not your traditional church in any way.

The Apostle Paul wrote to a church that he started, "Bear one another's burdens, and thereby fulfill the law of Christ." Loving people very much involves sharing in their burdens. Keith and others at The Refuge had a vision. They dreamt of having a place one day that would be hope for the homeless community of North Clearwater. They wanted to provide a place where they could love people with the kind of love God loves them with.

They wanted church to be a refuge for those who need to get out of the weather, relax, get something to eat, fill their need for spiritual nourishment, take a shower, do their laundry, get some clothes, and get a hug. The heart behind The Refuge is to share the unconditional love of Jesus with people seen as marginalized.

Keith knows that God has reconciled all of mankind, and sharing that message with those who come to the Refuge brings him great joy. Many guests at The Refuge are loved in and sometimes lifted out of their situations to subsequently live their life more abundantly. The Refuge team helps people get their proper VA benefits, obtain social service benefits and citizenship, and they partner with guests to remodel houses the guests can then live in themselves!

The team at The Refuge simply loves people. Motivated by grace that includes everyone, the team wants to be a part of sharing this with a community that often feels rejected. They meet people where they are at, no questions asked, just like Jesus. Since ALL people are made in God's image, ALL deserve to be treated with integrity, dignity, and respect and be shown they are loved, valued, and accepted.

The Refuge is open daily and provides breakfast and lunch almost every day. Besides being a place to rest and eat, people can take showers, do their laundry, and once a week participate in a Bible study as well as experience 'church' Sunday mornings. A normal day at The

Refuge includes guests being involved in the day-to-day operation. That gives people a sense of value and worth as they participate in a variety of ways, including picking up donated food, cooking, cleaning, and serving each other.

The Refuge has a Sunday morning meeting that's full of joy, love, fun, and encouragement. Keith explains that there is great freedom in how the service goes; people are free to speak, and there is no judgment. People share their needs and their success stories with one another to lift each other's spirits and give hope. People who have gotten jobs, reunited with their families, and got connected back into a more permanent support system get to share their victories. After such transitions, many return to The Refuge to serve and fellowship.

The Refuge is a nonprofit that receives many of their needed supplies from different local businesses. Places like Publix, Wawa, and Panera Bread provide food as do local school cafeterias. Sometimes, they unexpectedly have trucks arrive and drop off needed things. It seems like there is always someone who is giving, and sometimes, just like when Jesus multiplied a few loaves of bread and then fed thousands of people, they will have an overflow. This enables them to turn that around to other food banks and churches, providing a perfect picture of the community coming together to love one another.

A part of the mission there is "The homeless have taken ownership of The Refuge as their church." And they have. Thanks to Keith and many others who pour into this place of refuge; a greater number have taken back their life in victory!

I have had the blessing of being hosted by my friends Keith and Margorie (and Rosie) in their home, meeting with The Refuge leaders, and hanging out and speaking at The Refuge. It's addictive! Having started and led a medical outreach for those without insurance for ten years, I know first-hand the sweet joy of becoming friends with and serving those who can be considered 'marginalized.' I'm thrilled to offer you the opportunity to connect with Keith and Marjorie Stanton and The Refuge!

From Grace Is … by Paul Gray:

Deep Love

Ephesians 3:16–19, "I pray that out of His glorious riches He may strengthen you with power through His Spirit in your inner being, so that Christ may dwell in your hearts through faith. And I pray that you, being rooted and established in love, may have power, together with all the Lord's holy people, to grasp how wide and long and high and deep is the love of Christ, and to know this love that surpasses knowledge—that you may be filled to the measure of all the fullness of God."

When Jesus became our sin at the cross, He (and we with Him) died to sin. He went to the very depth of our sin with us and met us there. He took it all, experienced it all, took it all away, and died to it all.

Saul of Tarsus was, in his own words, the worst sinner there was. Think of someone who hates Jesus; who hates Christians; who participated in the murder of Christians; who had authority and went around, arresting Christians, taking them away from their family and livelihood and kept them in prison just for being Christians. Sounds like ISIS today.

God's love for Saul was so deep that He stopped him in his tracks and revealed that Jesus had always been in him since his birth.

Galatians 1:15–16 (MIRROR), "God's eternal love dream separated me from my mother's womb; His grace became my identity. This is the heart of the gospel that I proclaim; it began with an unveiling of sonship in me, freeing me to announce the same sonship in the masses of non-Jewish people." (Translator's note: 'The Greek text is quite clear: "It pleased the Father to reveal His Son in me in order that I may proclaim Him in the nations!" Not "among" the Gentiles as most translations have it.')

The love of Christ can't be comprehended with human knowledge; it has to be revealed to us (that you may be filled with all the fullness of God). What enables us to realize, experience, enjoy, and use all the fullness of God that we are already filled with is comprehending God's love!

Ask God to reveal His love to you today!

RON WRIGHT
A Mystical Union with Christ

> *"God is the great collector and restorer of LOST things. This was the mission of Christ: to seek and save everything 'lost' from its original design and divine Wholeness. For anything to be lost, it had to first BELONG—and all things belong to God. He is the Great Wholeness in which all things find their completion and fullness. We are at the deepest levels of being, one infinite frolic in the perfect wholeness of God's delight."*
> *~Ron Wright*

Ron Wright was born and raised in a small farming community in Ontario, Canada, and had deep spiritual interests and aspirations as a young teenager. He says that even as a child, he sensed a presence with him, continually comforting and watching over him.

At age eighteen, he had a personal encounter with Christ that changed the direction of his life. He had plans to be a wildlife biologist, but after this awakening experience, he turned to seminary instead and was ordained to the Christian ministry when he was twenty-three. He spent about twenty years with Castle Assemblies of Canada and pastored for twenty-eight years throughout southwestern Ontario with seven different churches.

In 2009, he left the ministry to pursue an exciting and meaningful career working in social services, providing safe and affordable housing to low-income families. Today, he writes and speaks on spiritual matters, helping people to navigate their inner search for a deeper and more fulfilling experience with God. He labels himself an ontological mystic and helps people find the reality of God's life within their own spirit.

Wright did not grow up in a Christian home. Religion was not part of his upbringing. At about eighteen years old, he began to research spiritual things, including religions, at his local library. He was looking for purpose and meaning in his life. He researched Hinduism, Buddhism, Zen, and everything he could get his hands on. When it came to Christianity, he was not sure what to use for a book but remembered that he got confirmed as a teenager at a United church and received a Bible.

He left the library, went home, found his Bible, and blew the dust off it. He opened to Matthew chapter five and the Beatitudes. What happened next would change his life. As he was reading, the white in the pages of the Bible began to move and became translucent. It began to lift off the page and form into what he described as a presence flooded with light. As the room filled up with this intense light, he felt love, and it moved and stood at the head of his bed. It did not speak or form any distinct image, but he remembers he was overtaken and began to feel this overwhelming love for the first time in his life. It felt clean and pure, but it was overwhelming as well, overwhelming enough that it caused him to throw his Bible up in the air and run out of the room. Ron's room was invaded by a presence, and all he could feel was tremendous acceptance and love. When Ron returned to his room and opened his Bible, he began to experience the supernatural presence of God again.

The next morning, he woke up to what he says was a whole new world. He said that it was like he was floating to school that day. Everything was different. The colors were brighter. Everything looked pure and radiant to Ron. Cats, dogs, even the blades of grass had more vibrant colors. Ron knew that in all his research and reading in Hinduism and Buddhism, nothing like that happened, and those gods were all dead.

When he got to school, he recalls looking for some Christians he knew to share and ask about what had happened to him in this mystical experience. They told him what happened was a born-again experience. Ron experienced the Lord without ever knowing a single thing about Christianity.

This encounter with God then provoked an interesting conversation with his mom about destiny. She began to tell him something he did not know about himself. She said, "I always knew this day was coming" and went on to explain to Ron that he was a miracle. About a month before he was born, all his fetal movement had stopped in her womb. The doctors told her they believed he was dead; they could not detect any heartbeat. But then, when he was born, he was very much alive!

They took him away quickly, and tests showed he had birth defects. But none of that ever manifested, and he is healthy and very much alive!

Life's 'purpose' for Ron has been found in the mystical union with Christ. Today, he can be found teaching and writing from the flow of this union. He wants others to know they, too, can experience God deeply and are included.

Ron's frequent online posts are in a league of their own; my words can't adequately describe them or do them justice. I invite you to connect with Ron Wright yourself. Be prepared to experience the mystical presence in a way you may never have dreamed was possible!

Grace I AM #52

Have you ever thought about how much your Teammates love you?

Have you ever thought about the scope of your Teammate's love for you?

God's love for you is PERFECT!

God's love for you never fails; it never ends!

God's Perfect Love for you casts away any fear you ever could have of *god's* punishment or torture for you or anyone! We have no scientific (or other) instruments to measure God's Perfect Love; it's infinite and can't be measured. God's love for you has no conditions, no limits, no contingencies, no caveats, no 'buts,' no trace of darkness (from the Doctrinal System of Darkness)!

2,000 years ago, Jesus' friend Paul wrote this to you, "God's LOVE is higher, wider, deeper, and longer than we can imagine! Nothing, including yourself, can ever separate you from God's love for you!"

Take a few minutes in your secret place with your primary Teammates, Jesus, Papa, and Grace, and say (out loud if you can) several times slowly, "I AM loved by Papa, Jesus, and Grace, and Their Love is higher, wider, deeper, and longer than I can even imagine!"

MARTIN BROOKS
Following Jesus, Waging Peace

Martin Brooks is the president of Peace Catalyst International, located in fifteen cities in three countries, and whose focus is on creating an environment of greater understanding between Muslims and Christians. They describe their work in four words "Following Jesus, Waging Peace," drawing on the teachings of Jesus.

Martin has worked with local churches and mosques to create safe spaces to break bread and build greater trust between Christians and Muslims. He has organized service projects, iftar meals, and peace feasts with Palestinians, Syrians, Turks, Pakistanis, Somalians, Kurds, and Iranians. He works with city officials, refugee agencies, local clergy, and interfaith groups to seek peace in the city.

He recently helped organize "The Big Table," a community potluck dinner in Louisville, Kentucky, that attracted people from across the city, bridging ethnic, religious, racial, and socio-economic divides. This Big Table event was held in a local park and attracted 1,800 people. Martin has been with Peace Catalyst since 2011. Prior to that, he and his wife, Susan, and their family lived in Turkey, Portugal, Mozambique, and many other countries. His wife, Susan, uses her artistic skills as a visual peacemaker, and they now live in Louisville with their three children and nine grandchildren nearby.

Martin, Susan, and their group at Peace Catalyst International take special heed to Jesus' words from the sermon on the Mount: "Blessed are the peacemakers, for they shall be called Sons of God" (Matthew 5:9).

Martin Brooks started his mission work with the intention to get numbers of Muslims converted to Jesus. As this journey progressed, he no longer saw an 'us-them' relationship but began to see that Muslims are real people just like him! Martin knew that in America, the focus in the church is almost predominantly evangelism, which usually means "We set out with this underlying mission to do what Christians call 'friendship evangelism,' but to be honest, we often end up treating people as targets, without any friendship. God's love is all-inclusive, and when you know this, you will begin to see the image of God in everyone you meet, including our Muslim brothers and sisters.

"We also have found in our mission work that once you let Muslim people share their own core beliefs about Jesus, you validate who they are. Allowing this space to voice their differences often opens the door, and you move into real dialogue. Relationships form, and the gap begins to bridge between two faiths that have been known more for war than peace for thousands of years. We do not have an agenda to convert these people. We do speak the love of Jesus very freely, though. That never changes."

In America, Martin has often experienced resistance in getting Peace Catalyst started in local churches. Martin says, "Many individuals was to be involved, but leadership is not supportive because they fear that half the church will be upset.

"We want to be known for being Ambassadors of Peace and bringing together the divide between Muslims and Christians. Jesus was the prince of peace. Christians need to learn to interact face to face with our Muslim brothers across the table, where we are willing to set aside our preconceived notions and break bread with them. This is what Jesus did, and this is love."

When a person expresses an interest in being a part of Peace Catalyst, to break them in, Martin may say, "Great! Let's go to what the Muslims call a Jummah prayer service. It is simply their equivalent of our Sunday morning service. They gather in a Mosque, hear a sermon, pray, and experience community. We are asked to take our shoes off when we enter, but it is simply a hygiene thing because they are going to be bowing down and putting their face to the ground."

Often, Martin will get pushback from Christians who claim that

Muslims are not worshipping the same God and don't believe in Jesus. However, Martin has learned that most Muslims believe in the patriarchs of the Old Testament and in Jesus, although they don't (yet) see Him as God. "But we are acting in peace and simply bridging relationships," he says. "We are forming friendships and keeping conversations open. And Jesus is always talked about. We have nothing to be afraid of.

"I learned myself that so many of the claims people have made about

Muslims as a people are simply untrue. They make up only about 3% of the American population, and when it gets right down to it, they are very much like Christians, just people trying to live their life. We hope, if anything, our mission will change the mindsets of many people, and peace will prevail."

Grace I AM #53

Do you have any idea how God really feels about you? Your Divine Teammates, Papa, Jesus, and Grace delight in you. That's right; God DELIGHTS in YOU!

We can't understand that because the Doctrinal System of Darkness has lied to us that its *god* is really bummed with us because of our behavior ... bummed so much that it can't even stand to look at us or be around us.

But you've had the revelation and are starting to enjoy and experience the truth that the Doctrinal System of Darkness is a house of cards that is collapsing all around us. Thank God!

Jesus wrote to you (via some of His friends who were inspired by Grace) that They literally sing and dance and rejoice over you and delight in you, not because of your behavior or anything you do; it's because they LOVE you unconditionally!

Because of lies we've been taught, that's hard for us to understand, Jesus urges us to "Trust in Them completely, and do not rely on your own opinions."

Take a few minutes in your secret place with your primary Teammates, Jesus, Papa, and Grace, and say (out loud if you can) several times slowly, "I AM rejoicing because Jesus, Papa, and Grace continually delight in me!"

DR. DARREL D. PROFFITT
A fundamental re-working of an Episcopal Priest's theology

"Pops, it's all about love!" Those words changed the theology and life of a Ph.D. Episcopal Reverend as he heard them from his unchurched, non-religious adult son, Joseph. Darrel Proffitt's subsequent decision to leave full-time congregational leadership emerged from Joseph's tragic death. He describes his grief work as a "fundamental re-working of his theology." He says, "Grief is the price of love."

Darrel describes what has emerged from this journey as an "inclusive view of God's love and mercy." A most meaningful quote to him is from Paul Tillich: "Genuine belief is maintained 'in spite of' circumstances that would undermine belief and not simply because of circumstance that would confirm it. It does not take a great deal of imagination or courage to believe that God is on your side when you are prospering or winning; it takes a great deal of courage and imagination to believe that God is on your side when you are suffering and losing." Darrel says, "Paul Tillich puts in words what I have experienced in spite of and even to death."

An acclaimed Episcopal priest, ordained in June 1991, Darrel has served churches, from Chicago to Houston. Under his leadership, St. Margaret's Church in Lawrence Kansas was recognized as the second fastest-growing Episcopal Church in the United States. He was also awarded the 'Merit Award' from his seminary, Seabury-Western Theological Seminary, in 2004 as an outstanding leader in the Episcopal Church for his innovative approach to church leadership.

He served the Church of the Holy Apostles in Katy, Texas, from November 2007 to February 2018 before his decision to step down from full-time ministry to focus on writing and helping other congregations. Currently, Darrel is working on his first book, reflecting on his time in congregational leadership, while serving as Interim Rector at Holy Comforter Episcopal Church, Spring, TX.

When not doing interim ministry, he continues to preach from time to time at a local Lawrence Kansas non-denominational church.

As Darrel continues to read avidly, study continually, and grow in grace daily, he's anything but a 'party-line' regurgitator of centuries-old platitudes and unquestionable doctrines. You'll often hear him ask questions like this one that he posted recently:

"Too often Christianity is viewed as being concerned with a set of beliefs concerning the world. What if it's more than that? What if it's more of a call to enter into a different way of existing in the world? Maybe there is a way of celebrating life that is more authentic, enriching, and healing than just being part of some tribal, exclusive club?"

From Notes From Papa, a 366-day devotional by Paul Gray:

A Note From Papa to you!

To My much-loved child, whom I continually delight in,

People have always wondered what I'm like, and their imaginations have come up with some pretty bizarre ideas! When I wanted you all to see the truth about Me and My love for you, Jesus came in the flesh to give you the exact picture of Me. He could do that because We are of the same essence. So, when you read about Jesus' earthly life, you find that He and I always have your best interests at heart.

Jesus came to serve you all, and He did. Every miracle He performed was to help benefit those in need, never for His own selfish gain. When Jesus encountered people whose lives were a mess because of their poor decisions, He never condemned them. He forgave them, loved them, encouraged them, and gave them grace, just like Me!

Jesus never punished a single person, ever; Me neither! The only people Jesus forcefully corrected were the proud religious leaders—people who taught others lies about Us, Our love, compassion, mercy, and grace. He wanted everyone to know the truth about Me—that I am love, and I am for you, not against you!

There is no dark side of Me that Jesus hid from you. He demonstrated with His finished work at the cross how We have saved you from the disastrous effects of your own sin. We have forgiven and taken away all your sin (past, present, and future) and never hold it against you. We have reconciled you to Us and made you right to be with Us now and forever.

Grace is the face love wears when it comes in contact with imperfection. Grace is Jesus, and He is grace. I am grace. Please, never listen to or believe anything you hear that seems to indicate that I am angry with you, not pleased with you, against you, or want to punish you. I love you and am for you yesterday, today, and forever. You can believe Jesus and Me!

~Love, Papa

MIKE ROUGH
Law-less Grace Fellowship

Grace got ahold of Mike Rough in a BIG way in 1975 and has been revealing more and more about God's Unconditional Love, Pure Light, Perfect Goodness, and Inclusion to him ever since!

Mike Rough is a business graduate from Illinois State Normal University, who was mostly self-employed until retirement in 2002. He likes to say that God blessed him financially through his business so that he now doesn't have to 'charge' for ministering grace!

When he was in his mid-thirties, Mike had a dramatic Grace encounter and a subsequent dramatic awakening when The Holy Spirit revealed to him Christ's Universal Salvation and 'hyper-grace' for and to ALL people.

As is true with many 'Grace Restoration Team' members, Mike doesn't have any 'formal religious training,' but he exudes God's love and Grace to all he's with! His contagious joyful attitude draws people to him like a divine magnet, and they're never disappointed in the time they spend with him.

Mike has mentored and continues to teach numerous people around the country and overseas via social media and personal contact. For decades, he has led a weekly group called the Lawless Grace Fellowship—he co-hosts a weekly radio program and has a weekly Wednesday evening 'Bible class' called Law-less Grace Fellowship. He has provided scores of books at no cost to his group and loves to go through them at their meetings. He and his group were the 'Beta Test' group for Paul Gray's PURE LIGHT WALKER course, and they provided tremendously valuable input and help in coming up with the 'final product.'

Mike says that he loves sharing the gospel that the love and grace of the Trinity is infinitely greater than all of everything, including sin, death, hell, the grave, and people!"

Grace I AM #54

Did you know that Papa, Jesus, and Grace created you 'In Christ' and on Their team before they created the universe for a specific reason? The main reason is so you could experience Their Love, and They could experience the joy of loving you! But wait; there's more!

Jesus revealed to His friend Paul, who wrote to you: "We are His own masterwork, a work of art, created in Christ Jesus for good works, which God prepared for us before we were born, so that we would live the good life which He prearranged and made ready for us!"

They created you as Their Teammate so that as They love you, you can do specific good things that they prepared for you to do as you live the Good Life They made ready for you!

Yeah, I know, it may not seem at all like you are living the good life, let alone doing good things. Been there.

But I've learned that since I've left the Doctrinal System of Darkness and begun seeing who God really is, who I really am, and who ALL people really are, my Divine Teammates not only delight IN me, but They also delight in giving me the desires of my heart (after all, they put the desires of my heart in me, to begin with).

Experiencing the desires of our heart, living 'the good life,' and changing our situation can seem impossible.

Jesus tells us that in our own strength, it is impossible. BUT with our Team, ALL things are possible!

I'm not going to throw cheap platitudes or a myriad of Bible verses at you. I do want you to know that with the help of Jesus, Papa, and Grace, and with the encouragement, inspiration, and help of The Grace Restoration Team, you will see your life change, and you will start to experience 'the Good Life.'

Take a few minutes in your secret place with your primary Teammates, Jesus, Papa, and Grace, and say (out loud if you can) several times slowly, "I AM expecting to do the good God created me to do as I live the Good Life!"

BILL CARPENTER
A Dreamer Again!

> *"The moment you put expectations and conditions on love, you become a judge. God is NOT a judge! He is our Loving Father!"*

Bill Carpenter exudes God's Unconditional Love, Grace, Goodness, Inclusion, Acceptance, and Joy so much that when you're with him, you feel like you're with Jesus, and you are! Bill knows that Christ lives in him and as him, and he loves being a catalyst for people to meet the Really Good God.

Raised on a farm in Ohio where he milked cows by hand before riding the bus to school every day and hitchhiking 13 miles home so he could participate in athletics, Bill has since instilled his 'Country Boy' values in his ten children and scores of grand- and great-grandkids. He and Jennifer have been married for well over fifty years, and together, their message is "God Loves YOU!"

Amongst many other talents, abilities, and accomplishments, Bill is a gifted poet, whose verses seem to flow from the very mouth of God. He's amazed to find that people have shared his poems and reshared them without his knowledge, with the result of a myriad of people being eternally touched by God's love. Some groups have had special meetings at their churches to read, ponder, meditate, and discuss Bill's wonderful words.

He hasn't written books (yet) and doesn't have a podcast or make videos, but he loves to connect with people online, where you can see his poems and stories like this one, titled *Courage to Live.*

Six years ago, I had the privilege of watching a young man live his life as we all should.

I attended a high school wrestling match at Washington Courthouse in Ohio. I watched a young man that obviously had Cerebral Palsy walk very unsteadily to the mat to compete with another wrestler that was seemingly unimpaired. No 'special' consideration was asked for, and none was given. The young man lost, but you could tell that his physical handicap in no way hindered his desire to LIVE life as he wanted to.

I asked my grandson, who, himself, was wrestling at this tournament, about this young man, and he told me that he thought this was his third-year wrestling at this tournament. He said, "You should have been here when he won his first match. I thought the gym was going to explode."

I was embarrassed as I watched this young man wrestle, not because of his condition but because of his COURAGE, as he continued to live his dream.

It doesn't take courage to die; our LORD JESUS CHRIST took that FEAR away at the CROSS. Physical death is something we will all face one day, whether we have the courage or not.

BUT IT DOES TAKE COURAGE TO REALLY LIVE LIFE ON OUR TERMS!

In 79 years, I have met many people (myself included) that have survived many life-altering situations. But just surviving is not living our dreams. I realized with his disability that he was more alive than I was at that moment.

His COURAGE to live his dream condemned my excuses for not living my life to the fullest. The excuse of being too old or "you must be careful" are all just survival mode words.

LIVING is LOVING and DREAMING and letting the world adjust to you like this wrestler did yesterday. He was comfortable with his condition; I was not.

I have thought about this for the last six years and realize that I have watched this same scenario take place at every girls' basketball game I have attended this past 6 years.

Although not physically seen, one of our players plays with a condition that is and, in some ways, even more serious than the wrestler I spoke of. But she pursues her dreams with the same fervor and dedication and COURAGE.

Six years ago, while in High School, she was told she had a condition that was life-threatening and that she would not be able to play sports or any strenuous activity because of a heart problem.

But she didn't take that as the only answer. Her parents and she sought different opinions from other doctors, and they found that if she followed a strict set of procedures, she could play and ENJOY the game that she loved.

She not only found a way to play the game she loved, but she found that the condition she had was and does affect many young people, and because they don't know they have it, it has taken the lives of many unsuspecting girls and boys.

This condition can only be detected by a doctor running certain tests, so this young lady started a charity while in High School called KATE'S KAUSE. You can find out about what the condition is through KATE'S KAUSE.

The reason I'm writing this is that on the 29th of January this year (2022), I went to Marietta College and watched this same girl I have followed since her High School days PLAY for the 16th ranked Ladies Pioneers Basketball team of Marietta College.

The question was never "COULD she?" it was "WOULD she?" and the answer was "YES."

I talk about the ABUNDANT LIFE we have in CHRIST. The question is, do I have the courage to LIVE it?

The ABUNDANT LIFE is FREE, and it's by GRACE.

Do I want to ENJOY it or just talk about it?

It is important that I know there are people that have LIVED and are LIVING their DREAMS and that are experiencing the ABUNDANT LIFE in this world of mostly SURVIVORS. The ABUNDANT LIFE has nothing to do with HEALTH or WEALTH; it's made up of PEACE, JOY, and the FULFILLMENT of the HEART'S DREAM.

At 79, they are my heroes. I thank them ALL very much.

A DREAMER again … Bill Carpenter.

Bill Carpenter is so much fun to be with. His humor is as infectious as his joy and love for life and God. You will be inspired, blessed, touched, and encouraged by his wonderful poems and posts!

From Notes From Papa, a 366-day devotional by Paul Gray:

A Note From Papa to you!

To My dear child, whom I love with all My consuming, fiery, white-hot passion,

I am more than able to fulfill all of My promises to you. In My economy, they are finished already!

You tend to worry, doubt, think 'lack' and fear the worst. You unnecessarily imagine the worst-case scenario of future situations in your life. Here's what I really want you to do: focus on Me, My abundance, and know that I am infinitely good. I am always for you!

Use your sanctified imagination and see Me, the ultimate provider, pouring out My grace on you and making all your 'crooked paths' straight!

Don't even entertain 'what if' thoughts about My blessings drying up and going away. (That's Diabolos thinking.) Know, believe, and trust that I am for you, I am faithful in fulfilling My promises, and I will give you the desires that I placed in your heart.

Expect Me to lavish blessings and provision on you in such an unexpected, out-of-the-ordinary way that you and everyone will know beyond a shadow of a doubt that it's Me providing what I promised. When it looks like things are going down-hill, and I'm not involved, others may say, "What bad luck," but I want you to say boldly and confidently, "No, it's an opportunity to trust and wait on God, who is for Me and loves Me and keeps His promises, and He's for you too. I'm excited about what He's in the process of doing as we wait!"

Every second that you spend thinking 'lack' and worrying about worst-case scenarios is an opportunity missed to rejoice in Me and My promised provision and lavish blessing. Believe Me! Trust Me! Expect Me to provide.

Lovingly, gently, and compassionately encourage one another and remind each other of Me and My goodness. Excitedly anticipate My exceedingly abundant blessings. Enjoy them. Enjoy Me!

You know I love you, and I am for you. My love never fails!

~Love, Papa

JONATHAN JONES (THE WHY GUY)
Is God bi-polar?

> *"Why do I believe what I believe? That would be important to know, wouldn't it?" ~Jonathan Jones*

Johnathon Jones (the Avatar name for a man who is also known as The Why Guy on social media) is well known for his video teachings that dismantle many western evangelical church doctrines that until recently have gone unchallenged. His meticulous research has exposed doctrines that contradict God's unconditional love. He's become a prolific author, and his books are as challenging as are their titles: I*n Defense of God's Love, Is God Bi-polar?* and *Know Love No Fear, No Love Know Fear.*

Johnathon lives in the northwest in a house he and his friends built on the side of a mountain. He has his leather-working shop there, where he masterfully repairs leather-made treasures. He describes his rebellious teen years and loves to relate how a friend invited him to a youth group that met in the adult leaders' home. He was drawn to the music, loved to sing, and had a strong desire to play the guitar. He prayed to own one and promised God that if He would teach him how to play the guitar, he would worship Him for the rest of his life.

One night, at youth group, Johnathon was approached by an older woman who he felt intimidated by because of her talent. She spontaneously handed him a guitar. She looked at him and said, "God told me to give this to you." It was clearly a beautiful 'God' moment and answer to prayer. Johnathan had never held a guitar before! He took home his cherished treasure, went to bed, and woke up the next morning able to play wonderfully well!

He never took lessons but ended up teaching guitar, banjo, and other stringed instruments that he was supernaturally able to play. He developed a love for worship music, and he recalls a foundational moment one Sunday while singing a song titled "I Love You, Lord." He realized that he didn't love God because he had been taught that God was going to torment a good portion of people on the planet in a place called hell. He knew he couldn't really love or trust a *god* like that.

He felt a stirring in his heart to discover "Why do I believe what I believe? Is what I believe about God true? How can God, who says He is Love and who asks us to love our enemies, at the same time torment his enemies forever?" He decided to research religion's doctrinal teachings that present a bipolar *god* of anger and vengeance and sometimes love. He was experiencing cognitive dissonance as have many on the Grace Restoration Team.

Johnathon shares a fond memory of what he believes a picture of the true church looks like. He remembers when he was building his home in the mountains with a wonderful community of friends helping him. He noticed that there were 5 different denominations represented. He thought, *What a beautiful picture of unity when we take our denominational walls down and all our 'goofy beliefs' that only separate us and come together as friends!*

Johnathon named himself the Why Guy because of his desire to question what he believed. He has spent long hours researching doctrines, digging into the original languages and early church history. He found that The Truth points to a God who is good and whose plan is to reconcile all things.

Much to his delight, he discovered that this Truth is backed by Scripture, Acts 3:23, and other places, and it's what the early church believed and called 'Apokatastasis'—the Greek word meaning "the restoration of all things." Everybody was included in Christ at the cross. God has included all mankind in Christ.

As do virtually all those on the Grace Restoration Team, Johnathan has found that rather than the pressure-filled, angst-inducing fear of treating people like an agenda to get saved, he now has joyful freedom to simply love all people without judgment and tell them the good news of who they already are in Christ as the opportunity comes.

The Why Guy is refreshingly unconventional, delightfully honest, suffers no fools, and has a unique style of showing us how we've been duped by religion's con game. Check him out!

Grace I AM #55

Acrostics can be an excellent memory tool for us. You will most likely come up with one more meaningful to you than the following—but here's mine for the TEAM concept:

Teacher— Jesus/Mind of Christ

Encourager— HS Grace Amore— Papa Me— Me!

While we can't accurately describe The infinite God of the Universe, who is Spirit, with human words, they are the best we have, so Teacher, encourager, and Amore ('love' in Italian) are helpful to me.

For me, remembering that my TEAM consists of three other very real entities with personalities, names, and specialized areas of expertise, who are all contributing to help me and continually work all things for my good, is very beneficial.

Of course, They have an infinite number of other descriptors, adjectives, character traits, and ways They help us. You may want to compose your own TEAM acrostic.

Take a few minutes in your secret place with your primary Teammates, Jesus, Papa, and Grace, and say (out loud if you can) several times slowly, "I AM so grateful that I have the BEST Teammates in the universe constantly and lovingly helping me in every way!"

MARK VENABLE
The prison door is open

Mark Venable is Texas-born, New Mexico-raised, and currently lives in West Tennessee. Mark is on an amazing journey from destructive legalistic religion to basking in God's Unconditional Love and Grace!

Mark is humble, kind, and generous. He's a 'straight shooter' guy who is sincere when he says that he has been through hell and back in his journey from legalism to grace. He started his journey in a very religious environment. Hell, fire, and brimstone was the consistent message. In his church, he was taught that you needed to 'pray it through' when you had a problem. He was told that if you did not pray it through with persistent ongoing effort, that meant you were not even saved. This teaching left Mark in a constant state of fear and anxiety.

Like all of us, Mark just wanted to know that God loved him. Instead, what he heard about God left him with a ton of guilt and shame. He was taught that if you broke any rules and regulations, you needed to fear "God's wrath and punishment." He says, "The threat of hell dangled over you unless you kept up with reading your Bible, tithing, praying, and of course consistently repenting. You would be at the altar on a regular basis, making for a very insecure walk with God."

Mark says he tried to walk away from God. Instead, The Only True God led him straight into His arms! His journey started with a well-known teacher of grace, Joseph Prince. His message helped Mark unravel the confusion between the old and new covenant. He learned for the first time that we live under the new, better covenant of grace and are no longer bound to the law. For the first time in his life, Mark started to see the true nature of the Father whom Jesus came to reveal.

Often, as we unravel legalism, we begin to see God through a more familial relationship. God begins to show us comparisons in our own family. Mark remembers thinking how deeply he loves his children. He knew that religion teaches that you must 'do something' to become a son of God, but Mark realized that his kids were his kids without them having to do anything to be accepted. He says, "They did not have to 'make a decision' to be my kids."

Mark talks about how Paul wrote that God is the Father of every family on earth; no one has to do anything to be His child. He knows that God is now awakening us all to this wonderful truth!

Mark expresses gratitude for the many pastors that he has been connected to through social media that have helped him grow in grace. He especially credits Global Grace Seminary's founder Don Keathley, Gracewalk's Steve McVey, *Grace to ALL's* Paul Gray and Freedom Ministries' Mike Popovich. Mark says that all of these men have taught him so much about "the God that he always longed to know, the One who loves him as he is and without condition, the One who is all-consuming love and grace.

Although Mark says he is very much still in the process, he is patient in the process. He is learning a new sense of rest, despite the occasional struggles of guilt and shame from remembering his past in the depths of legalism. Now he spends time meditating on the love God and the truth that we have never been separated from Him. Mark confidently says, "I'm never going back. The prison door is open, and I am never going back again."

From Grace Is … by Paul Gray:

No Fear with This Love

When we grasp how God really loves us (which can't be understood humanly, it must be supernaturally revealed by God to our spirit and then believed by our mind), we need never be afraid of God for anything, including judgment! That's a new, and much better, way of living!

1 John 3:1, "Behold what manner of love the Father has bestowed on us, that we should be called children of God!"

Jesus calls us to love others with agape love, whether they are fellow believers (John 13:34) or bitter enemies (Matthew 5:44).

"This is how we know what love is: Jesus Christ laid down His life for us. And we ought to lay down our lives for our brothers and sisters" (1 John 3:16).

The opposite of unconditional love is when you think you are not loved unconditionally, and the result of that is fear.

1 John 4:16–19, "We have come to know and have believed the love which God has for us. God is love, and the one who abides in love abides in God, and God abides in him.

"By this, love is perfected in us, so that we may have confidence in the day of judgment; because as He is, so also are we in this world.

There is no fear in love; but perfect love casts out fear because fear involves punishment, and the one who fears is not perfected in love. We love because He first loved."

1 John 4:18 (AMP), "There is no fear in love [dread does not exist], but full-grown (complete, perfect) love turns fear out of doors and expels every trace of terror! For fear brings with it the thought of punishment, and [so] he who is afraid has not reached the full maturity of love [is not yet grown into love's complete perfection]."

MELISSA DENYCE
The world is starving for love

Melissa Denyce, born into a family of strong Judeo-Christian faith in Grand Rapids, Michigan, has always had an incessant and desperate thirst to know God. She deeply values the faith passed on to her by her parents which gave her a solid structure from which to understand spiritual things. Ultimately, though, almost three decades within fundamentalism did not provide the answers she was seeking.

At the age of twenty-nine, Melissa had a spiritual awakening that upended her entire life and pointed her to answers so simple and satisfying that she found it impossible to keep them to herself. She has now made it her life's mission to share these truths with others in a way that is easy for them to understand and experience.

Melissa and her husband live in Montana, where she homeschools their three children. She reaches people via her YouTube channel, where her main areas of focus are Universalism, Christian Mysticism, and Non-Duality. In her "Course in Miracles" and sharing "Near-death Experiences," she gets great joy from helping people know and experience that God is love and that God is within them.

Melissa Denyce grew up in a strict fundamental branch of Christianity where she was taught about a *god* of religion, who predestined some to heaven and some to hell. She was taught that you had to love Him, or He'd hate you. This led to cognitive dissonance, being told God loves people but not all people. She awaked to the reality that this teaching was fear-based control that was used to manipulate people.

She also discovered the opposite side of the world's doctrinal system of darkness that says "'God' loves you, but you have free will to reject that love, and He permissively lets you live how you want, letting you control your eternal destiny." She saw that version of God as being powerless. Neither traditional doctrine seemed right to her, which led to a crisis in her faith.

Melissa then describes a season where she and her husband began experiencing many hardships—a cycle of job losses and rough marital issues. She says that she reached rock bottom. To find help from God, she began to look beyond the religious boundaries that once guided her. She began to study near-death experiences and began to listen to testimonies from people who experienced them.

These testimonies repeatedly spoke of experiencing a bright light and a God who is different than what religious doctrines had ever taught. There seemed to be a common theme about a God who is so much more loving and wiser and certainly more capable than we have ever imagined.

She came to realize that God does give us limited free will in this life, but it is because He knows that He is continually working all things for good and bringing about ultimate restoration for ALL! She embraced the revelation that His love is the unchanging reality of all that exists, and we are all expressions of His love. She quotes Richard Rohr, who says, "Love is the unifying principle and that which pulls everything back toward God. It is powerful like gravity."

Melissa found it challenging to find homeschool resources that teach that God has included all, and love is in all. So, she creatively came up with her own resources to help young people experience and demonstrate God's love. She says, "I think that is the most important thing to walk children through their actions and model the love of God themselves and other people."

One of the exercises she developed starts in the morning when she asks her children to pick five ways that they will show people love as they go about their day. Melissa has learned that doing this fosters a heart that thinks of others. At bath time, she teaches by having her kids drop pebbles in the tub and watch the ripples, then seeing how our actions, thoughts, feelings, and words will affect the world around us. Melissa's goal is to raise her kids to walk in compassionate love because she knows that every action of love affects the world. She says, "This world is starving for love, and we have it to give!" Melissa posted this great advice:

> *Things parents should not teach their children: that they are sinners, undeserving of mercy and grace, and deserving of punishment in eternal hellfire.*
>
> *Instead, teach your children that they are magnificent.*

Teach them that they are powerful, courageous, and inspired.

Teach them that they are kind, empathetic, patient, and good.

Teach them that they are capable, funny, intuitive, and intelligent.

Teach them that they are strong of heart, mind, and spirit.

Teach them that they are magic. Teach them that they are divine.

Teach them not only that they are deserving of love, but that they are a living, breathing, manifestation of love.

And teach them that everyone else is this too.

But also, teach them that they are having a human life, which involves making mistakes.

Teach them that they are perfection experiencing imperfection.

That they are limitless experiencing limitation.

That they are abundance experiencing lack.

Teach them the beauty of those imperfections. Of their emotions, their scars, their flaws, and their missteps. Teach them to embrace every human aspect of themselves and of others.

Teach them to have both compassion and boundaries with those who have lost their way.

Teach them to clean up their messes, not to hurt others, and to take responsibility if they do.

Teach them when they make mistakes to remember who they are and rise to that.

Children don't need to be guilted and manipulated into doing right. They are already more enlightened than the rest of us.

They need gentle guidance to fully step into who they are.

Grace I AM #56

Once we start really grasping these wonderful truths of the Really Good News, many of us want to share them with our friends, but what do we say? Something like this may be helpful:

God is NOT like you may have thought or been taught! Here's Good News!

God is totally GOOD—pure goodness! Anything you hear about God that is not good is simply not true!

God has always LOVED YOU, LOVES YOU NOW, AND WILL ALWAYS LOVE YOU! God's Love is unconditional—no limits or conditions!

You have never been separated from God. God has always been in you. You never had to be 'saved.' Jesus 'saved' you from being afraid that you weren't saved or had to do the right thing to 'get saved!'

God is PURE LIGHT with no trace of darkness. Anything dark that you hear about God is not true!

God's GRACE made you forever right with God before you were born! That's true, no matter what you think, believe, or do. It's

AMAZING GRACE!

God is always FOR YOU!

God is always working out all things, even your screw-ups, for good!

Take a few minutes in your secret place with your primary Teammates, Jesus, Papa, and Grace, and say (out loud if you can) several times slowly, "I AM ecstatic to know that God is totally good and always loves me. I can never be separated from God. God is pure light with no darkness. God's Amazing Grace keeps me right with God, no matter what. God is always for me, and God is always working out all things for my good!"

MICHAEL MCELYEA
Standing before Jesus!

Michael McElyea is a mystic whose encounters with God have opened his eyes to the richer, inclusive gospel. He says that the key to revelation is in being humble and having an open, teachable heart. He's found that God will freely give what you are open for. Mystics are people who experience God deeply, and Michael's experiences have radically changed his life. He describes a wilderness-like season when he felt like Moses; when the goodness of God passed before him, and he saw the glory of the Lord for the first time with unveiled eyes. He started to go on contemplative walks through quiet woods, where he began to hear the Lord speak.

Prior to his awakening to the Truth, Michael believed, as many do, that all people are wretched sinners who are separated from God. But on one of his walks, he describes a powerful encounter when God opened his eyes and caused him to see that Christ is in ALL.

During that encounter, he saw the scene when Jesus was on the cross, and the earth shook as He gave up His spirit. At that time, the veil in the temple was torn. Michael wondered, *What was behind that veil?* God showed him that He is behind the veil and has always been; most just don't yet see what really is! Then Papa revealed to him that each of us is the temple of God, where the very presence of God is!

This experience altered how Michael sees everything, including the way he looks at people in life's 'bad' situations. His old religious self would look differently, but now he can see past all of it and look into the eyes of people and see Jesus. He describes locking eyes with people and realizing, "Oh my gosh; I'm standing before Jesus."

He began to see Scripture in a whole new light. He saw things he could not see before, including the myriad of passages that say ALL are included. One such passage dramatically affected Michael—it was when The Apostle Paul was in Athens (Acts 17), and he told pagan people who were worshipping false gods that they were worshipping Jesus without even knowing it. Paul told them, "In Him you live and move and have your being, as you too are God's offspring." Michael has had many profound moments of seeing Jesus in other people. He has seen Jesus as an older man cleaning stalls in the bathroom. He has seen Jesus at the barbershop watching a man meticulously cut a little boy's hair. He sees Jesus dropping the trash off, Jesus delivering the mail. He says, "We live in a Christ-soaked world."

He now loves to study the incarnation and the early church. He often muses about how far we have drifted from the beliefs of those closest to the disciples such as Athanasius, Clement of Alexandria, Gregory of Nissa, and Maximus the Confessor.

Today, his teachers of influence are Paul Young, C. Baxter Kruger, Francois Du Toit, Brian Zahn, John Crowder, Andre Raabe, and Brad Jersak. He has learned that they, like the early church fathers, walk and live this same message.

He quotes Brian Zahnd: "We had a beautiful gospel the apostles delivered, and instead of deconstructing faith today, it is more like a Rembrandt painting that got dirty, and we are restoring it. We are getting all the dirt off it and getting back to the beautiful, glorious faith that was given to us."

Michael shares his experience with great passion. He says that while he is still learning, he has a continual euphoric sense of God's unfailing holy love, which has caused his heart to explode within. It brings joy, and for the rest of his life, he wants to marinate on God's goodness. He believes that love is the essence of the gospel, and love is really the essence of all things. He lives his life now walking in that ever-increasing love.

From Notes From Papa, a 366-day devotional by Paul Gray:

A Note From Papa to you!

To My dear child, who is the object of My affection,

I want you to know why I am so very much for you—I specifically created you to be with Me! You're not an accident, not an afterthought, not an insignificant pebble of sand on a beach covered with billions of sand pebbles. No! Never!

I dreamed you up. When humans have a baby, they never know what it will be like. But I planned you! I knew you before you were conceived. I formed you in your mother's womb! I designed you and made you just as I planned! You have always been the object of My affection!

I created you for one purpose—to be with and enjoy Jesus, the Holy Spirit, and I in Our Divine Triune circle dance of love, joy, peace, and everything good now and for all eternity! You are the desire of My heart! I would rather die than live without you, and I did! I was in Christ at the cross, reconciling you to Me. I did that!

I made you into a new creation, in Christ, one with Us, fit to be with Us, just right for Us, set apart for Us. That's what pure, holy, righteous, and innocent mean! I saved you from sin, death, and darkness and gave you new life. I transferred you into My Kingdom of Light in Christ Jesus. I did all that!

Now, as you see what We have already done and how We love you and are for you, you can relax and enjoy new life with Us—which is why we created you, saved you, and included you! Remember this always; We do!

~Love, Papa

NICOLE JANSEN
Believe in people's greatness ... not their weakness!

Nicole Jansen is a business breakthrough coach and human behavior specialist. She is a keynote speaker who has a gift to captivate and inspire audiences of all sizes. She has also been a business owner and entrepreneur for over thirty years and has helped thousands of leaders and organizations earn millions of dollars by bringing massive value to the marketplace. She has a deep passion for helping people discover their greatness and to live life at the next level. She has become an in-demand speaker and coach in her region with a message of empowerment, focus, and relentless commitment to teaching people to be the best that they can be. She believes that the road to success is paved with a blend of conscious awareness and inspired action that fosters meaningful connections with others.

Nicole's journey began when she was in her twenties, already in business successfully with her parents. She has always been a very driven person, so it would take something very powerful that she calls a 'divine download' from God to change the direction she was in and lead her to leave that business and begin to coach others and launch her own podcast. She described hearing from God that He wanted her to allow Him to lead her and bless her in her life. She did not have a desire to do this, but she knew to let go of the need to control and trusted God and let Him lead her to a new and more fulfilling career.

While Nicole believed in the unconditional love and grace of God and that He absolutely loves all of us, she soon found herself tested by circumstances that showed her what loving without conditions really looks like. She began to face severe marital problems and learned her husband wanted out of their marriage. He said that he just needed to find himself.

Nicole became confused and fearful. She believed when she got married that marriage was for life. She remembered the vows: "in sickness and in health until death do us part." However, her life wasn't turning out that way. As difficult as it was during this trial, Nicole said that God began to do an inner work of healing, and she began to grow deeper in her understanding of what His grace and unconditional love really is.

During her initial time of unbelief and disillusionment, she remembers crying out to God and asking why this was happening. Feeling victimized by the circumstances, she was also questioning herself and her own worthiness. In all the shakiness and chaos of what was happening, she remembers going to the beach one day for seven hours to sit, think, and try to hear from God. As the sun begin to go down, she began to drive back to Malibu. She then describes the moment when God began to speak. She pulled over to the side of the road and began to journal. It was then that she heard God say, "I want you to love him."

Thinking it would be impossible to love a person who wants out of their marriage, Nicole began to do just that. She made the decision she would love and accept her husband in the middle of the messy circumstances. However, despite her efforts, things went from bad to worse. He decided to move out of the home and start divorce proceedings.

Through it all, Nicole remained loving and forgiving toward him. He even said to her at the courthouse, "I hope one day you forgive me," and she told him, "I've already forgiven you." Nicole sees how, in the midst of all the hurt, God was healing something in her. She was experiencing Him in a much deeper way and learning a deeper level of His grace and forgiveness. Nicole believes she was learning how to love like God loves.

To her, the important kingdom lesson became: "Unconditional love is not just loving people who do things the way you think they should, but it is loving them for who they truly are but can't yet see." Although her marriage ended, much of what she learned about the value of love and forgiveness, she now integrates into the coaching of others.

The very happy ending to this story is that on May 14, 2022, Nicole and her former husband celebrated their wedding day! Nicole really does practice what she preaches.

Nicole's a delightful, encouraging, and inspiring person who has a tremendous heart especially for helping women succeed in life. She's the host of the Leaders Of Transformation Podcast, and co-author of the book *Power Up, Super Women*. Nicole has developed her own unique brand of mentorship, which focuses on unleashing your authentic self while integrating business and life mastery for holistic success.

Grace I AM #57

Jesus' friend Paul wrote to you that Jesus revealed to him the Whole Creation is eagerly waiting for the sons and daughters of God to MANIFEST! Manifest: to display or show (a quality or feeling) by one's acts or appearance; demonstrate

Now that you know who you really are, take a few minutes in your secret place with your primary Teammates, Jesus, Papa, and Grace, and say (out loud if you can) several times slowly:

"I AM manifesting as God's son/daughter today!"

"I AM aware and grateful that I AM a son/daughter of God! I AM God's son/daughter incarnate!"

"I AM aware that Christ is in me, one with me and living AS Me!"

"I AM aware that Papa is MY Father!"

"I AM aware that Grace is my Friend, Teacher, Encourager, Inspirer, Counselor, Comforter, Power infuser, Wisdom, Guide, Live Giver, and Energizer!"

"I AM aware that I AM loved unconditionally, included unconditionally, accepted and forgiven unconditionally, cherished unconditionally, valued highly, delighted in and One with Papa, Jesus, and Grace, who are Pure Light, Love, Joy, Peace, Grace, and Goodness!"

"I AM aware that Christ is living AS me! I AM delightfully expecting the effortless manifestation of Christ's Life today!"

"I AM aware that I AM on The Greatest TEAM ever! I AM aware that Christ in me is more than able to accomplish everything He wants to do today!"

"I AM aware that Christ in me is achieving infinitely more than my greatest requests, my most unbelievable dreams, and exceeding my wildest imagination. He is outdoing them all, for His miraculous power constantly and effortlessly energizes me!"

"I AM aware that I AM continually manifesting pure Life, Light, and Grace to everyone I'm with!"

TOM BASSFORD
Significant Matters

> *"I believe God cares about the 'here and now' as much as the hereafter and would have His church be a tangible and redemptive expression of that care in every realm of creation."*
> *~ Tom Bassford*

Tom Bassford is the founder and executive director of Significant Matters, Inc., based in Kansas City. Prior to leading Significant Matters, he pastored for thirty-plus years in the Midwest.

Tom's passion and mission is to help churches reframe their missions work around sustainable solutions and create room for the kind of business-minded people who can help that happen. His experience includes the U.S. and international ministry, where he has helped churches, businesses, city governments, and various other organizations move their charitable work and missional efforts toward more sustainable solutions.

In 2014, under his leadership, Significant Matters launched SATtalks, a TED talk-type of gathering and video website, to explore and demonstrate ways to move beyond 'helping that hurts' in church missions. They also launched the Missions 3.0 Network and Peer Learning Communities for churches wanting to move their mission work beyond 'helping that hurts.'

Consuming Fire: The Inexorable Power of God's Love: A Devotional Version of Unspoken Sermons by George Macdonald continues to be a source from which Tom (and many others) are inspired.

Tom has the unique ability and leadership skills to help people look at old problems through a new (and more beneficial) paradigm. His infectious personality, ready humor, deep love for and relationship with Jesus, and willingness to serve have coalesced multiple teams of people who have made significant differences in people's lives all over the world!

Tom and the board of Significant Matters have recently embarked upon the Reg CF Funding portal called EquityVest, which brings together entrepreneurs and investors who believe it is possible to run a business that both fuels the enterprise and evidences the virtues and vision of our Christian faith. We mean to leverage both the passion and compassion of the faith-driven community to support business as a God-ordained means of overcoming poverty, extending the gospel, and creating a free and virtuous society.

He also developed and provides a unique Equity Crowdfunding Portal for Christian entrepreneurs and investors.

Tom, as well as virtually all those featured in *Grace to ALL*, has undergone significant transformations in his spiritual understanding and is delightful to connect with and dialogue about his continually evolving grace journey.

I became good friends with Tom Bassford in my first ministry job in 1989. He counseled and mentored me through a very dark time in my 'religious' life, and I'm forever grateful! We have remained friends, as we have each experienced dramatic spiritual transformations and the highs and lows of 'doing life.' Oh, the stories we can tell (just not in this book).

Grace I AM #58

As you move ahead in living the 'GOOD-GOD Life,' your teammates want you to know and remember that You never do anything by yourself!

You never go anywhere by yourself!

You never feel anything by yourself!

You never think anything by yourself!

You never see anything by yourself!

You never hear anything by yourself!

You never taste anything by yourself!

You never love anything by yourself!

You never like anything by yourself!

You never delight in anything by yourself!

You never plan anything by yourself!

You never write anything by yourself!

You never read anything by yourself!

You never relate to anyone by yourself!

You never play by yourself!

You never celebrate by yourself!

You are never alone!

Take a few minutes in your secret place with your primary Teammates, Jesus, Papa, and Grace, and say (out loud if you can) several times slowly, "I AM always with my TEAMMATES! I AM never alone! They never leave me or forsake me!"

EAMON MCMULLEN
The whole world is starving for the goodness and love of God

Eamon McMullan is an Irishman living in the UK who has been so captivated by the goodness and grace of God that he lives much of his life intentionally sharing it. You will find him teaching about Jesus through YouTube and Facebook as well as on the streets of London. He says that the love of God compels him to tell people and help bring them into the truth of their already being in Christ.

His method is not the classical fear-based coercion and subsequent trying to get someone to say a sinner's prayer. Instead, he leads people to the Christ that is within them already! He introduces them to the love of God as he explains the mystery that has been hidden for ages and is now being revealed to ALL.

Eamon's story is about the goodness of God in his own life. He joyfully lives life and simply relates to people. He knows that many people think an 'evangelist' is going to tell them about an angry judgmental, wrathful *god* and are justifiably quick to reject pushy religious encounters.

Eamon is anything but pushy and simply wants people to have hope in this world by knowing the One who created us all to be loved. Like the God he knows, he's very creative in getting his message to people. He decided to compose a letter to share his own testimony of when he encountered Jesus Christ. He doesn't try to tell people what to believe, but instead wants to be a witness to 'grace for all' and only hopes his story will provoke a personal encounter with those who read it.

He says, "It is just being friendly and loving the people in front of you." Sometimes, he will go to the park and see a group of men playing football and, when they finish playing, engage with them to share his letter. He always leaves it and gives people space to read it on their own. In the same day, he may do the same while waiting at the bus stop or with people while riding the train.

Eamon simply hands out his letters of grace wherever he goes and engages in conversations where there is freedom. This is a way of life for him, and by the end of the day, he often has handed out 300 to 400 letters!

He knows our world is saturated with the grace of God, but most don't experience it. People simply need someone to point them to it. As Eamon says, "We have got this amazing Grace and goodness and the whole world is really starving; people are starving for the goodness and love of God. We are a witness to His life and resurrection because we have experienced it, and walking in the spirit, we want to give it away. We have this glorious Life Source flowing through us, and we are not to lock it up but in generosity give it away. God has been super generous to all of us, and when you experience this, you want to be generous to others. We should never grow weary in doing good."

Early in his Christian experience, he was involved in a church that had a good deal of strife and whose leaders seemed to force 'supernatural experiences.' Fortunately, he soon met two special people that would bring a revival to his heart at a weekend retreat. Feeling a bit disillusioned by his church, he remembers sitting there and kind of challenging God to 'show up.' Then, in an auditorium filled with 500 people, the speaker on stage, Charles Slagle, called Eamon out from the back row and began to prophesy over him. It was with such accuracy he knew it could only be from God. The prophecy and the details would impact Eamon in more ways than he expected. What impacted him even more was Charles and his wife Paula's character. They both exuded the love and grace of Abba. This is the same love and grace that Eamon has been possessed by, and he now lives his life sharing with others daily.

I, too, have been wonderfully impacted by the Grace of God via Charlie and Paula Slagle, and I encourage you to connect with them and Eamon as well!

From Convertible Conversations, a novel by Paul Gray

Both grace and truth are Jesus personified. When you see what really is (truth), then Christ, who is in you, will set you free from trying to get back in God's good graces, trying to get in, because you will know the truth that you are already in!

You will then be able to experience and enjoy a new and better way of living new life in Christ. You will be:

- free from feeling like you have to perform to please God.
- free from fear, doubt, and anxiety.
- free from fear of being punished by an angry *god*.
- free from guilt, condemnation, and shame.
- free from fear of death.
- free from wondering which denomination or doctrine is right.
- free from *god's* judgment.
- free from judging others.
- free from excluding others.
- free to enjoy life.
- free to love.

In this new and better way of living, every day you find out that God is better than you thought the day before!

Take a few minutes in your secret place with your primary Teammates, Jesus, Papa, and Grace, and say (out loud if you can) several times slowly, "I AM enjoying a new and better way of life. I AM Free!"

WENDY FRANCISCO
Love Heretic

Wendy Francisco is a widely acclaimed Artist, Recording Artist, Graphic Artist, Nature Photographer (especially with snowflakes) singer, songwriter, and guitarist. In 2003, Wendy and her Dove award-winning husband, Don Francisco, collaborated to release "The Promises," an album that consists almost entirely of selected and paraphrased readings from the Bible. Don has won two Dove awards: 1980 song of the year (for "He's Alive"), and 1980 Songwriter of the year.

Wendy raises and nurtures a wide variety of animals at their mountain home in Colorado. She hosts and facilitates a Facebook group Love Heretic, which is a fellowship of people who are in various stages of moving beyond religion's angry, judgmental, exclusive retributive *god* to experiencing the Only True God of Love, Grace, and Inclusion of ALL. Members of this group include those who are just beginning the process, ministers who are preparing to present it to their congregations, authors who are writing about their experience, and even theologians who are struggling with cognitive dissonance in their religious belief.

A major part of Love Heretic is about helping people restore their lives after being negatively affected by destructive religion. Wendy often shares many of her own insights, and she loves to discuss God's Unconditional love and grace, especially how it has facilitated changes in her and Don's lives for the better.

Wendy describes her journey through her personal deconstruction as painful. She says, "You cannot escape it. When you begin to walk out of the grave of religious indoctrination and a retributive punishing *god*, despite your newfound freedom, there will often be inner turmoil." She recommends great patience as you walk each phase out and into the arms of an all-loving God. This process, in part, motivated her to begin Love Heretic.

"It certainly can be tough wrestling and untangling everything you were ever taught. We learned a lot of fear and doctrines that taught a message of 'us vs. them.' It was all rooted in separation." She continues, "We were told of this *god*, who is going to torment most of mankind, including many of your own family members. All these beliefs bring fear." One fear Wendy had was of dying and meeting *god* for the first time. In her younger days, she often lay in bed at night, staring up at her ceiling paralyzed in fear. Her ever-present fear was "Am I really saved? Have I done enough and believed the right things?"

She wrestled with the question: "If Jesus is the Savior of the whole world, why are there so many outsiders who are going to 'hell?' If we have to do something to accomplish our own destiny, doesn't that make US our own savior?"

Wendy and Don were aware in their itinerant music ministry that there were many different beliefs about God and Salvation. In part, this led her to realize that "God is not about formulas and protection plans. He is about including all of mankind in His family and rescuing all who are in darkness."

Wendy says, "I think people who don't believe in *god* simply don't believe in the fictitious concept of a *god* who remembers sin, keeps account of sin, and needs sacrifice to pay for sin. I don't believe in that *god* either!"

She says, "Regarding the word 'Christian,' I think it means 'like Christ,' and I am pretty sure I don't always do a great minute-to-minute job of that. To me, it isn't something you print on a shirt you wear and then think you are one. Most 'Christians' think you aren't one unless you believe in hell. Let that sink in. A Christian is one who believes in Christ; that's what I thought, but apparently, a Christian must believe that Christ failed, hell claims more people than Jesus, and it's up to Bible thumpers to complete the work of converting everyone who is vulnerable. I mean, we do know that there are many specific Christian denominations who believe that only their denomination goes to heaven and that all other Christians go to hell, right? The problem might not be getting your doctrine correct so you don't go to hell. The problem might be the hell doctrines in the foundation of retributive religion in the first place! Maybe realizing that that is the problem is what gets you out. That, sure, is how it worked for me.

"I went all over the world to many different fellowships. Which one was I supposed to choose? Each with their many sets of sacred cows? It's ironic that in people's attempt to get those who have never heard about hell 'saved,' they actually put people in a state of fear, thus creating a'hell right here, right now' in their minds."

Check out "Love Heretic" on Facebook—here's the description:

WELCOME TO LOVE HERETIC!

This is a group to discuss inclusion, the idea that God does not either send or allow people to remain in a Dante-style hell. The group name comes from the irony we feel when we get called heretics and rejected, not for some heinous sin but for having too big of a view of God's love. There is no Greek word for hell, as we have been taught. The group is not here to debate this; this is a group to facilitate the change that millions are making away from the spiritual abuse of hell doctrines, a place where we can heal and rebuild.

"Our rules— We are LGBTQ+ affirming, and we're not debating that in this group. No group or racial profiling. Things that include the words 'white evangelicals' will likely be booted. And the people will too. No political recruiting.

"We're not deconstructing from the right to the left. That is not deconstructing; it is doing a geographic. I try to make deconstruction about ridding myself of all the hate-based narratives, be it the religious indoctrinations or political convert-making, and make it about myself, about taking my own life back.

"Some ground rules: No using of laugh icons derisively, please. If a comment disagrees with you, please don't laugh at the person; express yourself intelligently.

"We don't do hostile politics or shame culture. We have people here from all ends of the political spectrum because inclusion is not a progressive concept or a conservative one—it comes from ancient church history. This is not a progressive page, and not a conservative one. Christianity should not have these two factions.

"You can be booted for harassment of another member. The group is not secret, but it is closed, so please don't share comments until you get an okay from the person who posted."

Grace I AM– Re #1

Having troubles today? Are there things you are worried about? Are you anxious? Angry? Troubled? Don't be surprised—your Teammate Jesus knew you would. He said, "In this world you will have troubles. But! Take heart, be of good cheer, I have overcome the world!"

How do we actually do that? There are a number of 'REs' that help us immensely! When you experience troubling thoughts, immediately ask your Teammates to help you RECOGNIZE something's wrong.

We can stew and worry and get angry or depressed very quickly when troubles come, so it's imperative that we immediately RECOGNIZE what it is that's affecting us negatively. Otherwise, we become victims of the doctrinal system of darkness and fall prey to the devastating results of believing lies.

You can learn to do this instantly. The moment you experience trouble, STOP!

RECOGNIZE that something's not right.

That's your starting place.

Take a few minutes in your secret place with your primary Teammates, Jesus, Papa, and Grace, and say (out loud if you can) several times slowly, "I AM learning to STOP the moment I experience trouble and RECOGNIZE that something's not right."

BRETT NEIL
Have a Grand and Glorious Day!

Brett Neil was born in a small farming community in Missouri. Growing up on a farm allowed him to learn the value of hard work and hard play. He had a successful sales career and then went on to operate his own businesses. He has learned the value of family, friends, living life to the fullest, and figuring out his purpose. For Brett, that is best done when helping other people find their purpose in life.

Brett is not a well-known speaker, author, or entrepreneur. You haven't seen him on TV or in People Magazine. He is simply a real, no-nonsense, down-to-earth person who is tired of politically correct mumbo jumbo that leaves people frustrated and confused.

His book *Have A Grand and Glorious Day* was written for anyone on any level to be able to understand a few basic facts of life and, when followed, will help them experience joy, peace, and fulfillment.

Brett is the youngest of seven children, with twenty-one years age difference between him and the oldest. Their father, a hardworking farmer, avid hunter and fisherman, and top-notch semi-pro baseball player died of cancer when Brett was three years old. Brett credits his older brothers and their spouses, along with a farming neighbor, for helping through the very hard experience of growing up without a father.

After some rebellious teen years, Brett married a beautiful farm girl whom he grew up with. He and Linda have raised two wonderful sons, Josh and Caleb, and have enjoyed successful careers (Linda as a Cardiac Nurse and Brett as the owner of a construction company).

Initially, Brett followed in his father and other family members' Baptist religious tradition, then moved to different non-denominational congregations. He has always been faithfully involved and serving in a wide variety of capacities and always being very generous both to the church and to family and friends.

Evangelism was a priority in Brett's life until this last decade. He 'witnessed' to family and friends alike, including those whom he and Linda met on their many fun vacations around the world. Being a likable, fun, knowledgeable, and genuine guy, people often responded positively to his 'presenting the gospel' to them.

In that period of his life, he told people that God loved them but would have to burn them in 'hell' unless they asked for God's forgiveness, repented, sincerely prayed, and "asked Jesus to save them and come into their heart." When he was rebuffed, he believed those people were damned to hell.

Then Brett started experiencing the cognitive dissonance of impossibly trying to reconcile a 'God who is Love' with an angry, punitive, wrath-filled *god* who would lock people in an eternal fiery torture chamber just because they never heard of 'it' or rejected 'it.'

Through a series of 'God-incidences,' he discovered and started reading books and listening to teaching by many of the people featured in this book. Jesus used Paul Young, Baxter Kruger, Peter Hiett, and others to reveal The Only True God (as Jesus refers to His Father and Our Father) to Brett.

He discovered, much to his delight and relief, that God is not at all like religion taught him. In fact, he's now learned that the Real God is virtually the opposite of religion's dark, angry, punitive, list-keeping, vindictive, and wrathful *god.*

Brett continues to have a passion for 'evangelism' but now with a 180-degree twist! He loves to help people come to the joyous revelations that God is pure goodness, pure light, pure love, pure grace, completely inclusive, is for everyone, keeps no list of wrongs, and likes being with us so much that He lives IN each of us and always has. He's found non-religious people to joyfully embrace that Really Good News!

Like many of us, he's also found that religious people are the most defensive and adamant defenders of 'hell' and *god's* wrath for those who "aren't like them and haven't jumped through the hoops that they have." One of Brett's favorite authors is the early 20th-century Scottish pastor/author George McDonald who wrote, "Good souls many will one day be horrified at the things they now believe of God."

Brett has found that it's easier to brainwash people than to convince people they have been brainwashed!

Now, Brett is able to leave people in God's hand, trusting that the One whose love never ends and never fails—and whose will is for all to subjectively know what is already true objectively, that God loves them and has always been in them and is working all things for the good—will see to it that ALL people come to know him!

I am particularly fond of and proud of my first cousin, Brett Neil. We share the same fond memories of our mothers and grandparents and the same love and joy of the eternal embrace of the God of Perfect Love, Light, Grace, Acceptance, Joy, and Goodness of Jesus, Papa, and Grace. Mammy and Pappy are especially rejoicing in our mutual great cloud of witnesses!

Grace I AM Re #2

As soon as you RECOGNIZE that something's not right in your mind and emotions, REALIZE that whatever it is is harming you, and something needs to be done.

Once we RECOGNIZE trouble, if we don't immediately do something, we subject ourselves to the strong possibility of not having a pleasant experience, but more importantly, missing the abundant life that our Team made possible and wants us to have!

REALIZING that the trouble we're experiencing is harmful to us and that we have two different possibilities then prompts us to listen to our Teammates and take appropriate action. As we practice this, it will soon become almost automatic, and the process will quickly flow.

Take a few minutes in your secret place with your primary Teammates, Jesus, Papa, and Grace, and say (out loud if you can) several times slowly, "I AM realizing that this troubling situation is harming me, and something needs to be done."

ANISSA ZUCKER
God is the God of Now!

Anissa Zucker is an adult educator who has a master's degree in literacy education and a bachelor's degree in psychology and elementary education. Her life-long interest in writing drew her toward groups that especially provide inspiration and encouragement. Her poetry book F*earless Expressions: A Time for Us* and *The True Story of Santa Claus* is about the true meaning of Christmas and the spirit of giving. It was inspired by a friend of Anissa's, the clown doctor, Patch Adams.

Ever since Anissa was a little girl attending a congregational church, the mystical experience was being formed within her as she felt the deeper things about God. She even remembers at a young age always loving the 'mischievous ones' and believes that that was Christ in her loving them. Her inquisitive nature provoked her to ask questions about various traditional beliefs. She has never believed in eternal conscious torment and found to her surprise that anyone who would ever question that doctrine or many other religious traditions would be met with opposition and eventually treated with separation.

Anissa has always loved the things of the supernatural and never walked away from God, but she could not get away from feeling guilt and shame. Eventually, she got on her knees and said the sinners' prayer. But Anissa recalls that it still did not cause her to feel close to God. That didn't happen until the day she came home from work, entered her kitchen, saw a bright light, and had a powerful encounter with Jesus.

It was after this deep experience that she began getting what she would call 'downloads' in the spirit. She says, "For Christian Mystics, it is just natural to experience God's oneness." She began to hear specific things to do, and she knew they were from God. She loved experiencing the things of the Holy Spirit and noticed how it was bringing her an inner transformation. She found how tremendously exciting it was when she heard God tell her, "You can do this."

These experiences confirmed to her that God is real, and He is tangible. She says, "He is not a big mystery. He wants us to walk in close relationship with Him. This is all that mysticism is: a contemplative walk that connects to our oneness with God. We can know Him; even when you are having a bad day, you can turn within where Jesus lives and ask Him to help!"

Anissa remembers a very real and special moment when she, her husband, and her daughter were at a lake, and a little girl wanted to swim with them. She remembers being prompted to invite her to join them, and she immediately heard the Father say, "Anissa, this is what I want for all mankind." She felt the Father's love and inclusion for all of mankind in that moment. She now feels this love deeply for others. It has especially changed her relationships.

Because of the revelation of God's inclusion, Anissa often feels a drunken joy and freely loves all people, even friends of different faiths. She has a best friend who lives in NY, who is an orthodox Jew. Anissa used to feel pressure to proselytize her friends, but she now knows Christ is in her friend, as Christ is in all. In Hebrews, the Bible says that all will know Him, from the greatest to the least--thus leaving Anissa the freedom to just love her friend.

Anissa says that we are living in an incredible age. She feels so blessed to be a part of it all. She knows the closeness of God and what it is like to be experiencing Him mystically and wants everyone to know that it is not spooky but natural. Her journey is now more authentic and genuine, and there is more fruit of the Spirit being experienced in her personal life. She wants to share all that she knows with our youth.

She recently started a new school, Kainos Education & Youth Services (KEYS). With her background and education in teaching, she is passionate that our young people know the all-inclusive love of the Father. She helps them see that their creativity comes from their creative Father! She helps them experience God in a very real way in all they do. "As a mystic, you live in the here and now because God is the God of now!"

Grace I AM Re #3

Now that we've RECOGNIZED troubling thoughts and REALIZED that they are harmful to us, our TEAMMATES want us to immediately REJECT THEM!

Papa, Jesus, and Grace live in us, are for us, empower us, continually help us, and work all things for our good. Knowing this enables us to REJECT the harmful thoughts; simply give them to Grace. Jesus tells us to not take those thoughts. They will come, but we have His power and ability to not take them. REJECT them!

Jesus' friend Paul learned this well, and he wrote to you that you have Grace's power to reject harmful thoughts. That's the same power that raised Jesus from the dead. Pretty powerful, right?

He takes them hostage and never condemns or shames or berates you for having them. You don't need to feel bad or beat yourself up or ask for forgiveness! There's NEVER any condemnation from your Teammates!

Take a few minutes in your secret place with your primary Teammates, Jesus, Papa, and Grace, and say (out loud if you can) several times slowly, "I AM REJECTING these harmful thoughts by the power of Grace!

DR. ROY RICHMOND
A Contemporary Messenger of the Really Good News

"Scripture teaches us we each exist as the Face of God."
~Roy Richmond

Dr. Roy Richmond is a scribe, theologian, teacher, author and president of Tree of Life Ministries International, Inc. He began ministry in 1988 and has pastored several fellowships. He resides in Oklahoma City, Oklahoma, with his wife of fifty years, Donna, and ministers around the world in person and online, including a live stream on Facebook Sunday mornings at 10:00 a.m. CST. He focuses on man's eternal Oneness with Father God.

Dr. Roy also serves as a professor and academic dean at Global Grace Seminary in Houston, Texas. Since 1988, he has written sixty-eight books pertaining to the Bible. Additionally, he has translated Romans, Galatians, Colossians, half of Revelation, and hundreds of chapters in various books of the Bible as well as several thousand sections of verses.

Roy Richmond is a passionate lover of God and people and is continually pursuing a deeper understanding of the scripture. He studies Hebrew, Aramaic, and Greek, along with learning about the cultural, historical, parabolic, and allegorical influences of the text. This journey has led him to a richer revelation of Christ. He started his journey learning what he calls "the unfortunate western view of the doctrine of separation."

In 1988, Dr. Roy felt prompted by the Holy Spirit to begin to question church doctrines that did not line up with the Father he knew. He remembers challenging friends about what was being preached concerning condemnation by a supposedly loving God. His study led him to realize that Scripture does not teach us to preach condemnation; rather, the Bible tells us to preach the good news to ALL people that Jesus revealed.

Roy teaches that the Good News is a proclamation. Jesus was the perfect revelation of Father God, and prior to His coming to earth, no person ever had a clear revelation of God. Jesus came to set the record straight and show us that God was never mad at us. He has always been with us, and He included all of us in reconciliation. Roy's studies and relationship with The Teacher in him have equipped him well to teach and share the truth that Jesus said makes us all free.

Roy believes one of his callings is to be a contemporary messenger of the Really Good News. It was while he was reading Jeremiah that he was reminded of how Jeremiah would continually bring messages to the people in his day, and how time and time again he would face rejection, even to the point of being beaten.

As Roy continued reading, he remembers hearing the voice of the Father speak to him that like Jeremiah, many people were going to initially reject the Really Good News that Roy would proclaim, but God would ultimately restore them. Seeing the joy of truth resonate in a person whose face lights up because they are getting it for the first time compels Roy to continue. He knows his listeners are ALL one with the Father, and as Roy learned from a study in Hosea, they exist as the face of God.

Roy wants to remind us that Holy Spirit is not out there in the sky, separate from humanity. He reminds us that even though we were erroneously taught by religion to seek God from without, the truth is that God is Spirit, and He lives within us!

He has found that as we proclaim the truth to people, their spirit will resonate with the Holy Spirit within them. God himself knows the end from the beginning with everyone, and He sees them as He made and keeps them: righteous, blameless, and holy. Like many others in the Grace Restoration Team, Roy gets to be the one to watch people's faces light up at the really good news!

Grace I AM Re #4

Recognizing troubling thoughts, realizing they are harmful, not taking them, and rejecting them is the beginning of the 'Re Process.' We also need to be aware that those thoughts are persistently nasty! Our memory is tempted to think them again or even beat ourselves up for thinking them in the first place! Insidious, I know!

So, we RELEASE them.

Many Hebrew and Greek words have had their original scriptural meaning corrupted by the Doctrinal System of Darkness. Both the word in the Hebrew Scripture ('Old Testament') and the Greek word in the New Testament that are translated into English as 'forgive' actually mean to "lift up, release, and send away!"

Contrary to the lie of the Doctrinal System of Darkness, Jesus didn't come to make it possible for you to get divine 'forgiveness'; He literally lifted up, sent away, and RELEASED any and all things that we thought God was holding against us! That's good news!

And similarly, we can take harmful thoughts, even the recurring memory of them, lift them up, send them away, and RELEASE them!

Take a few minutes in your secret place with your primary Teammates, Jesus, Papa, and Grace, and say (out loud if you can) several times slowly, "I AM RELEASING any and all harmful thoughts. I AM sending them away!"

CAPREE GREEN
A Child's Ladder to the Light of the Sky House

Capree Green is a happily married, stay-at-home mom, who had her theological world turned upside down by her own children. She has two boys—Jedidiah, eight, and Solomon, five. Rather than learn from religious teachers, her boys are the ones who helped unveil God's unconditional love and grace to Capree through a series of supernatural meetings they experienced.

It began when her four-year-old son, Jedidiah, said he met Jesus. He described an encounter and a ladder to heaven. He and Jesus would go up the ladder to a door at the top where it opened, and they stepped into heaven. He has since told her about countless experiences in heaven, where he has also met God the Father.

Capree also shares how her youngest, Solomon, is engaging with God in much the same way. He talks about a 'sky house' where he goes with God and sees the 'light.' These boys and their mystical encounters are what Capree says eventually led her and her husband out of religion. They left the church and religious setting they were in and set aside everything they had been taught so they could start all over again like infants in their faith, realizing that "God is not found in buildings or religious doctrine." Indeed, she is learning from her little children about The Only True God, who is unconditional inclusive love!

Capree began to ask Jedidiah questions as he opened up more about his visits with Jesus. His experiences on the ladder to heaven sparked great curiosity. At first, she asked about specifics and tried to connect them to the Bible. But what he was saying was quite different from things she had been taught Scripture meant. For example, Jedidiah told her God is in everybody's heart, and He sings inside of everyone's heart.

When people begin to discover that God loves all mankind and included everyone in salvation, their religious people and family members can tend to reject their new beliefs, sometimes even to the point of rejecting them. Capree considers herself blessed to have a husband who is also on board on this new journey of discovering the

God of inclusive grace. "We are both seers and have keen discernment," she says. "We can see things nearly the same way." She says he was by her side through all that they were wrestling with in change and transformation and was a very encouraging part of her journey. She also shares the desire to meet more people outside of her family who walk through grace and the inclusionary love of God.

Capree and her husband realized there were so many similar events, details, and revelations in what they were each experiencing that it was hard to deny. That prompted her to begin to write and keep journals. One such entry is of when Jedidiah told her of a time when God took him back to being a baby. God put him in His backpack and went up a mountain. She was amazed at how a four-year-old could know and remember specific details of his encounters. He continually explained all the details of his adventures with God. One day, she asked him to draw a picture of the ladder he climbed with Jesus. And he drew the picture of the ladder; he called it the ‚eight ladder.' What he drew formed an eight with lines, and it was a picture of a DNA strand!

Capree laments that in the four years since they left their former church, no one even sought them out or questioned where they were. However, they love where they now are with God, and they enjoy becoming like little children and learning who God is in the discovery. She says that she always knew there had to be more than what she was learning about life and about God. She found that He is much greater, and life is much grander than anything she ever learned in church.

Capree Green is now beginning to get deeper downloads of her own revelation. She shares with us about having a dream where her son Jedediah was speaking, and she was presented with two glowing doors—one red, and one blue. In the dream, she heard God's voice say, "I need you to choose a door." She chose the blue door. Then her son Jedediah woke her up from the dream, and God has been pouring revelation into her ever since!

Capree joyfully says, "God is real. He is definitely better than we have been taught. Our family has learned we must truly become like children to see Him!"

Grace I AM Re #5

The next part of the 'Re Process' includes the awful religious word 'repent.' I don't like to even use the heinous intentionally incorrectly translated word, but its original meaning fits the 'Re Process.'

The Greek word metanoia means "to change one's mind." Jesus and the New Testament writers used it specifically regarding to no longer believing the Doctrinal System of Darkness's deceitful caricature of *god* and changing our minds to believe in The Only True God (Jesus, Papa, and Grace) who are Perfect Love, Pure Light, Abundant Grace, and the Savior of ALL).

We now have irrefutable documents that show that in the 4th Century, the Catholic pope commissioned his personal secretary, Jerome, to translate the Hebrew Scripture into Latin. In addition to many other mistranslations, Jerome substituted the Latin word 'Penance' for the Hebrew 'change your mind.' The concept of 'penance' was used by priests to require payment rendered to the church for certain 'sins' that were confessed.

After a while, in order to raise even more money to build huge cathedrals and fund an ever-growing paid clergy who promoted the Doctrinal System of Darkness's lies, the prefix 're' was added to extort even more money!

While Protestant translators knew better, they continued to use the Latin word 'repent' in the King James and subsequent translations. Of course, today it carries the unfortunate meaning of begging and attempting to wrest favor from an unwilling, angry, offended *god.*

In our 'Re Process,' after recognizing troubling thoughts, realizing they are harmful, rejecting and releasing them, we 'repent' or completely change our minds from what we were previously thinking about and replace them with thoughts from our Teammates.

Take a few minutes in your secret place with your primary Teammates, Jesus, Papa, and Grace, and say (out loud if you can) several times slowly, "I AM changing my mind about any and all harmful thoughts and their potential negative repercussions and choosing to replace them with thoughts that are pure, lovely, admirable, honorable, and worthy of praise!"

RONEL LONZER
Where focus goes, energy flows

Ronel Lonzer and her husband of twenty-two years have two teenage boys and live in the northern part of Germany, where they own and operate an Aluminum business. When COVID first started, rather than worry, she listened and asked God what He wanted her to do. As a result, Manifest Coaching was born. Part of her coaching includes weekly podcasts where she shares tips, testimonies, and interviews on her YouTube channel. She has a Facebook group and incorporates both groups in her private coaching.

Ronel Lonzer is living a lifestyle of spiritual manifestation. When she was a little girl living in South Africa and first introduced to Jesus, she remembers she could not stop talking about Him. She was drawn to and loved the supernatural. She saw food multiply and legs grow out, and these 'miracles' made deep impressions on her heart that God was real, and He could do anything.

As her relationship with Christ deepened, she says that she naturally saw God's goodness. She believes the key to all spiritual manifestation is in both knowing and believing and says, "We have to understand the goodness of God and that we can be in constant ongoing dialogue with heaven Himself. We can know that He really wants to be good to us and our families."

She says, "Spiritual manifestation is a new concept to 'Western-minded Christians' who haven't heard the term before, but it is not a foreign concept to God. He, Himself, is the One who brings the dead to life and who creates new things out of nothing. Manifestation is simply an unveiling and manifesting of what is already true. When the Spirit of God awakens people to see who they really are and that there is no separation from Him who created all things, they come alive to the powerful truth that we have a full inheritance waiting for them to experience."

Ronel teaches that we are co-laborers in Christ. We get to be co-creators with Him. In Him, we live and move and have our being, and He has given us all power to live our lives out of abundance. Jesus said,

"I have come to give life and life more abundantly." She helps those whom she coaches realize that their thoughts are immensely powerful and can cause them to miss God's truth because they often get stuck in ruts of negativity.

Her 'heart to help people' influenced her to become a manifestation coach, where she simply helps 'people get unstuck.' She guides people to shift their focus and to move from a mindset of negative cycles to the truth that all things are possible with God. She believes strongly that we will release what we have in us. She says, "Where focus goes, energy flows."

Ronel helps people shift their focus from a negative cycle to an attitude of gratitude for God's goodness, grace, and abundance. She helps them see that God has placed within each of us the desires of our heart. He has given us each unique dreams and visions to live out. She helps people to shift their focus from a place of lack to, instead, focus on what is true, pure, and lovely and to foster a lifestyle of thankfulness. She says, "God has given us creative imaginations so we can begin to imagine and experience our dreams as if they already were true. Every good gift comes from God's abundant goodness, and we get to see our dreams brought to life."

One extremely powerful testimony is of a friend who began to experience heavy internal bleeding as she delivered her baby. The bleeding was so serious that her friend was placed on life support. The doctors told everyone she would not live. Ronel tells of how she and her husband and family began to see her friend not as she was; rather, as healed. They envisioned her off life support and joyfully relating to people. They visualized going to visit her at the hospital and rejoicing as they sang praises for her recovery. Three days later, her friend woke up, and while the medical staff was amazed at her awakening, they gave the prognosis that she would not be able to live a functional life.

However, Ronel and her family continued to see her up and out of the hospital, imagining and visualizing her completely healed. After three more days, her friend was recovering so well that the doctors dismissed her! They also said she had 'religious insanity' because she was so happy! Ronel says that's what manifestation looks like, and she reiterates, "ALL things are possible with God."

At the beginning of this year, Ronel posted: "This year we really have a choice to blossom and start living from rest ... seeing the effect we have on those around us by loving the unlovable, loving the irritating, letting people be who they are choosing to be, being aware of the flowers, animals, hot water, coffee, friendship, relationships, running water, flushing toilets, arms and legs and all the many things available for us to enjoy.

"This year we would really like to inspire YOU to live from the 'overflow' of the NOW ... the place of gratitude and thankfulness ... the place of observation without assessment ... the place of looking at things objectively ... letting it go ... Allowing it to be the here, now ... for now ... allowing love and allowing effortlessness ... allowing for change ... from within.

"This year we would like to keep on inspiring you to see the unseen manifest in your life as the seen. Not by striving to change anything, trying to, pushing to, but by the awareness of this intimate and oneness you have with GOD, that allows you to be all that HE is in this beautiful dance of equality.

"Awaken to the fact that there is more to you ... more than fate, more than a destined path ... a path you get to walk by your choices ... A path you get to plan ... a path you get to manifest in the way you apply whatever is going on in your life."

Grace I AM Re #6

Now that we have changed our minds about any and all harmful thoughts and their potential negative repercussions and chosen to replace them with thoughts that are pure, lovely, admirable, honorable, and worthy of praise, we are in an unhindered position to 'RECEIVE' thoughts from our Teammates via the 'Mind of Christ!'

Jesus' friend Paul wrote to you that you actually HAVE the Mind of Christ! I don't think that means we can instantly morph into a calculus whiz or be able to do brain surgery, but it does mean we have information and wisdom for whatever we need at the moment!

Paul also wrote to you that in addition to having the Mind of Christ, "you are partners with Christ Jesus because of God. Jesus has become your wisdom sent from God, your approval, and your holiness!"

Take a few minutes in your secret place with your primary Teammates, Jesus, Papa, and Grace, and say (out loud if you can) several times slowly, "I AM continually RECEIVING thoughts, wisdom, and reminders of God's approval of my holiness from my Teammate, Grace!"

CAROLYN SMITH AND LILA COOK
Religious Rebels

Carolyn Smith and Lila Cook are delightful ladies who ooze God's unconditional love and grace! They are co-founders and leaders of the New Covenant Grace Family on Facebook, which is a wonderful place where over 1,200 people gather and share in the Oneness and Unity of the Trinity.

Their mission is to see broken hearts mended; share testimonies, faith, and God-inspired messages. Lila and Carolyn desire to acknowledge every good thing within us in Christ Jesus; exhort and build up one another; flow together in the spirit of unity as a response to the love, peace, and joy of Jesus in us all.

Carolyn grew up in a religious family. Don Keathley, who's featured in this book, is her brother. After years of striving to appease and measure up to religion and its fictitious angry *god's* demands, she received the Holy Spirit's revelation that God is indeed pure light with NO trace of darkness!

Lila grew up in an abusive and highly dysfunctional family. She says, "This affected me mentally, emotionally, and physically. However, during my childhood, Papa was always near me, always protected and comforted me, and I learned early on that He was my friend, and somehow, I knew God intrinsically before I ever began to attend church."

When she was six, her family started their 'church experience,' and Lila endured religious and family abuse for many years before leaving their family's legalistic church, being set free, and becoming overwhelmed with God's unconditional love and grace. She says, "I finally came to terms that I really was a rebel, a rebel against religion! Despite the pain I experienced, Papa was within me! Soon, I reconnected with Carolyn Smith, who left the same church. We became best friends! It was surely God's plan!"

Lila relates, "As heartbroken as I was over leaving family and friends, Papa began to shower me with His love. Scriptures came alive to me. I had never known this love since my early childhood relationship with

God before we started going to church! My life had meaning again, and I knew on a deep level that I had made the decision Papa wanted for me. I began to see that I had lived my life in an illusion. My new life began. My life changed, and I made amends to all those I had offended with my stiff-necked religion."

Upon reconnecting with Lila, Carolyn related how grace had changed her life. She knew exactly what Lila had been experiencing since her exodus from the church. God's grace!

Lila said, "Papa spoke to both Carolyn and me about ministering to those whose eyes were still blinded, and we felt led to begin a group of pure grace. At New Covenant Grace Family, we minister to people who are hurting over religion in their lives. Under the direction of the Holy Spirit, we help in mending the broken hearted. In our group, we lift one another up and give encouragement to both the hurting and to those who are living in grace. We help others to pass through the deconstruction process by assisting them to reconstruct under Papa's love and grace. Basically, we are helpers. We help others by exposing religion and directing them to love and Grace!"

I love New Covenant Grace Family and enjoy the posts and stories from their ever-growing group of people who are coming into the light of Papa's perfect unconditional love for all, grace, and inclusion of all! Carolyn and Lila nurture their family well, and I'm grateful to be a part of it!

Grace I AM Re #7 and #8

Most people with religious backgrounds have heard the term or read the scripture that says, "Do not be conformed to the patterns of this world, instead, renew our minds." And most of us have no idea what that means or how to do it!

The 'patterns of this world' are anything that comes from the 'Doctrinal System of Darkness.' It's any teaching that has even a trace of darkness about God's perfection, your perfection, and everyone's perfection.

In our 'Re Process,' after recognizing troubling thoughts, realizing they are harmful, rejecting and releasing them, changing our minds ('repenting'), replacing harmful thoughts with thoughts from our Teammates; continually receiving positive, encouraging thoughts from Them; we then RENEW our minds by listening to Grace in us remind us of our original origin—WHO WE HAVE ALWAYS BEEN!

Most of us would like to have a do-over—a second chance—and the opportunity to run the tape back and start over with a clean slate, wouldn't we?

If you're like me, you'd like to have a plethora of do-overs! Renew means to be the same as when new. It's returning to our original state of perfection. We've actually never left that original state of perfection, but the 'Doctrinal System of Darkness,' in its insidious propagation of lies, tells us we were never perfect, to begin with. That's one of those harmful thoughts that we need to apply our 'Re process' to.

When you were 'new,' before you were even born, before creation, you were pure, perfect, right with God, one with your Teammates, without fault, blameless, a beloved child of Papa!

Renewing our mind simply means to not listen to the 'Doctrinal System of Darkness' and to listen to what Grace tells our heart and believe (in our mind) what has always been true!

Take a few minutes in your secret place with your primary Teammates, Jesus, Papa, and Grace, and say (out loud if you can) several times slowly, "I AM continually RENEWING my mind with the truth I hear from Grace in me and returning to my original genesis of perfection!"

GARY MATTHEWS
ALL means ALL

Gary Matthews and his wife, Carole, have been married for fifty-one years. They met in Bible college in Nyack, New York, when they were twenty-one and nineteen. They have lived in Stockton, California for almost thirty years and have been a part of every church they have attended their entire marriage, hook, line, and sinker. But they never knew Grace to be anything other than "God's riches at Christ's expense" and the hymn "Grace, greater than all our sin."

The Shack, by Paul Young, was the catalyst that introduced Gary to the love of God in a bigger way than he ever imagined.

Although Gary is a Bible college graduate, he was surprised to find out the real meaning and scope of God's unconditional love and grace when he was in his late sixties!

Listening to Mike Zenker's message "All Means All" and Francois Du Toit's message "Known and Loved" started Gary on his grace walk. Then Carolyn Smith and Lila Cook's Facebook group Grace Covenant Fellowship introduced him to like-minded folk. The Mirror Bible was also a great resource for Gary.

Gary is a kind, sensitive, good listener who has the gift of encouraging others and rephrasing or expanding their words to reveal even deeper meaning and insight. He doesn't often post things of his own on social media, but I'm continually blessed by his comments on other people's posts.

Gary is a retired barber/hairstylist, who now styles words about God's unconditional love, grace, goodness, and inclusion!. Look for his always-encouraging posts on the New Covenant Grace Community, Grace to All, and other wonderful social media communities.

Grace I AM Re #9

In our 'Re Process,' after recognizing troubling thoughts, realizing they are harmful, rejecting and releasing them, changing our minds ('repenting'), replacing harmful thoughts with thoughts from our Teammates, continually receiving positive, encouraging thoughts from Them, thus renewing our minds by listening to the Mind of Christ in us, we then replenish our positive thoughts as often as necessary.

We not only have the Mind of Christ, but the wisdom of Grace has filled us to overflowing like a gushing river inside us that not only fills us but overflows to replenish any dry spots that might be needing more help.

Papa, Jesus, and Grace delight in helping us, providing for us, and replenishing us with whatever we need for the moment.

Peter wrote you that you have already been given ALL things for God's kind of abundant, joyful, meaningful life. Your spiritual warehouse is bursting and overflowing with whatever you need!

Take a few minutes in your secret place with your primary Teammates, Jesus, Papa, and Grace, and say (out loud if you can) several times slowly, "I AM replenishing myself with whatever I need from my spiritual warehouse!"

RANNIE CHILDRESS
Set free from religion but still behind bars ... for a while!

My friend Rannie Childress should definitely write a book about his adventurous life; then my friend Dominick Domasky should make a movie of it; then we should all give copies of both to all our friends!

Rannie has had a long and wonderful journey since his early days as a bartender and ordinance man in the USA Navy, and his journey includes fifteen years behind bars (Texas & Alabama combined). As you listen to his podcast interviews, you'll hear how much of his prison time sounds like a Barney Fife fantasy story, but it's true.

He has a very powerful and captivating testimony! A kind of prison rags-to-riches story. It is a story of many twists and turns that ultimately would take Rannie from prison to pastor. He spent fifteen years in a maximum-security prison where he witnessed what he refers to as a lot of darkness and jailhouse perversion. Facing the very real possibility of never getting out, he says that as dark as it felt, he was too afraid to kill himself.

Rannie talks about a turning point for him when prison authorities began to allow a rehabilitative program called Kairos into the prison. The volunteer counselors were people who Rannie says were different. They treated the prisoners with unconditional love and refused to label them. He had not experienced this type of love and grace before, and it had a real impact on him. Subsequently, Rannie began changing, and he experienced a multitude of things unfolding within the four walls of his prison life.

Opportunities would often arise in perfect timing and situations that would require just the right people to be in the right place. This led to Rannie being transferred to a minimum-security prison on a work-release program, where the warden of the canning plant where he worked would eventually recommend that he be released from prison. So much fell so neatly into place that it was beyond coincidental. He knew it was God's divine hand on his life lighting the path out of prison. He even shares how the commissioner who signed his actual release would tell him, "I don't even know why I am signing this."

Rannie came out of prison eager to begin a new life. His path would now include getting married, new job opportunities, new ministries, and eventually becoming a pastor. Then, in 2009, he tells of a near-death experience he had while in the hospital for a surgery to repair heart problems.

Rannie says that he died. He remembers in this experience that he was laying on the bed and could hear the people around him discussing his funeral. But he was in another realm, having a conversation with God. He remembers that even after all that he had witnessed of God's goodness in his life, he was still afraid.

He wondered, if it was time for him to go, had he done enough to be OK? And then he felt supernatural warmth flood him like a warm shower going down his body. The next thing he remembers is waking up with a multitude of tubes attached to him. Having just encountered God and realizing he was brought back, he told them to pull the tubes, and he was going home. Rannie was discharged thirty days later.

After this life-altering experience of resurrection, Rannie reconnected with an old pastor and began learning about the teachings of the Trinity, the divine dance, being entangled by love with the Father, Son, and Holy Spirit. He started helping other men on a regular basis and eventually bought a building to start his own church.

He read *The Shack*, connected to the Author, William Paul Young, and they subsequently became friends. He also connected to and learned from Baxter Krueger, Steve McVey, and Mike Zenker. He has grown in the grace of God and of His all-inclusive love. Rannie says,

"The God we call Abba Father took this prisoner and set him free!"

Rannie was eventually ordained as a pastor, has his own prison ministry, and now helps men who struggle with addictions see and be who they really are. He says. "This is the power of the gospel that saves. God takes all our messes and sets us free to then go help others do the same."

Today, Rannie and his team at Grace Ministries at Rapha have an ever-expanding online ministry, with teammates leading groups in several countries on multiple continents!

Sometimes, when Rannie is teaching online, it requires two

translators: one to translate his heave deep southern accent into understandable English, and another to then translate to Spanish or one of several African dialects!

Grace I AM Re #10 & #11

In our 'Re Process,' after recognizing troubling thoughts, realizing they are harmful, rejecting and releasing them, we 'repent' or completely change our minds from what we were previously thinking about and replace them with thoughts from our Teammates. But wait; there's more!

As we continually replenish ourselves with whatever we need, it's very REFRESHING to simply savor the blessing and REJOICE! Take a little time to thank your Teammates for abundantly blessing you.

They have just taken you from recognizing a potentially harmful problem to joyfully replenishing you with abundant blessings. That's called Grace!

The more you avail yourselves of the 'Re Process,' the quicker you will go from the initial recognition of what you're experiencing to being refreshed, as you know that your teammates enjoy, savor, and delight in you.

Contrary to the lies of the Doctrinal System of Darkness, we don't GAIN Their delight by doing things. They delight in us simply because Papa is our Father, Jesus is our brother, Grace is our Friend, and it's Their nature to delight in us!

Take a few minutes in your secret place with your primary Teammates, Jesus, Papa, and Grace, and say (out loud if you can) several times slowly, "I AM REFRESHING myself and REJOICING as I thank my Teammates for Their continual blessings to me!"

REX GASKEY
Forget all the things religious people have taught you!

Rex Gaskey is a 'good old southern boy!' When you hear him talk, you can picture him sitting on a porch in western Tennessee, talking until the sun comes up. When you speak to Rex, you will feel like you've known him your whole life. He has a southern drawl; he is kind, funny, and down to earth. You will also detect beautiful freedom in every word he speaks.

Rex grew up in Birmingham, Alabama, and went to a private 'Christian' school from third to twelfth grade, where he says, "I learned a LOT about the Bible, and virtually NOTHING about God."

Rex earned a Bachelor of Mechanical Engineering degree from Auburn University and worked as a design engineer at Power Plants and foundries before he started his current career in industrial sales.

He is married to Tommie Gaskey and says, "She is my right hand!" He loves to play chess and research things on the internet. He loves the music of the 60s and is a self-described 'flower child.'

Rex explains that when he attended Christian school, he was taught a lot of information but virtually nothing about God relationally. He says that he has always loved God, but in his Christian education setting, he quickly learned how his picture of a good and loving God would go as far south as his accent. It was there that he learned of a doctrinal teaching referred to as hell, the concept that God will keep people alive supernaturally and torment them forever for not saying a prayer or as, Christians often put it, 'accepting Jesus.' Rex says he never could line up that teaching to the God he knew.

Rex believes it was the very nature of God and His Spirit in him that would cause him to ask, "How can a loving God send someone to a place of eternal conscious torment?" The fear that this doctrine might be true ended up affecting his mental health, and he became severely depressed. The mental health issues changed his brain chemistry and landed him in mental hospitals four times. Much of this dark time, he also lived life dangerously. When his first marriage ended in divorce, things got even darker, and he eventually attempted suicide.

By the grace of God, his attempt failed because the gun jammed. Rex survived the suicide attempt. He says it was soon after that that he heard the tender voice of the God he knew speak to his heart, saying, "Rex, you need to forget all the things religious people have taught you, and you need to do your own research."

This launched Rex into researching the Christian doctrine of eternal conscious torment. He would learn that it is a man-made western doctrine that is not believed in other parts of the world. He would soon connect to Julie Ferwerda, author of the book *Raising Hell.* Julie heavily researched the doctrine and found where it originated—the English mistranslations of the word hell in the Bible, and the actual context of the scriptures that are so often used to defend it. Rex and Julie have now become good friends through social media, and her book has helped many people get free from a doctrine that causes so much fear and torment that it often turns people away from the faith.

Before Rex learned the truth, he hated sharing the gospel with people because, in the back of his mind, he realized how dark the threat of hell was. He recalls one day in the middle of this journey, he went into a store and decided to buy himself a gift. He saw this plaque that read, "Love endures all things, love bears all things, love never fails." He thought, *THIS is the exact God that I have always known.* This is the God his research would reveal, a God who IS all LOVE.

Rex says that the three most destructive things that man has ever created are: nuclear weapons, eternal conscious torment, and credit cards. Rex also believes, "You have to let go of hell to deepen your relationship with God."

He has found freedom. He has moved through healing in his struggles with mental illness to wholeness. He knows peace and joy and unconditional love. He's happy that he has connected via Facebook to many friends who are on the same journey of discovering the all-inclusive grace of God.

Grace I AM Re #12 & #13

Congratulations! You are learning and benefitting from your Team's 'Re Process' and are enjoying and experiencing the abundant Reservoir of the lavish riches that your Teammates continually provide for you.

Contrary to what the 'Doctrinal System of Darkness' teaches you, instead of working and striving to achieve these riches, we simply REST!

The writer of the scripture book of Hebrews tells us, "The promise of entering into God's rest is still for us today. So, we must be extremely careful to ensure that we all embrace the fullness of that promise and not fail to experience it. For we have heard the good news of deliverance just as people before Christ did, yet they didn't join their faith with what they heard.

"Instead, what they heard didn't affect them deeply, for they doubted. Now we have the Faith of Christ which activates the promise and we experience the realm of confident rest!

"Those who first heard the good news of deliverance failed to enter into that realm of faith's rest because of their unbelieving hearts. Yet the fact remains that we still have the opportunity to enter into the faith-rest life and experience the fulfillment of the promise Today! For God still has ordained a day for us to enter into called today …

"There is still a full and complete REST waiting for us to experience. As we enter into God's faith-rest life we cease from our own works, just as God celebrates his finished works and rests in them. So, then we must be eager to experience this faith-rest life, so that no one falls short by following the same old pattern of doubt and unbelief."

Today, our Teammates have revealed to us their 'Re Process,' which culminates with resting and experiencing peace.

Take a few minutes in your secret place with your primary Teammates, Jesus, Papa, and Grace, and say (out loud if you can) several times slowly, "Today, I AM RESTING in the reservoir of my TEAM's abundant blessings!"

DAVID CUBBEDGE
Eating popcorn and watching a movie with Jesus

Former Air Force Nuclear Missile Security Force Member David Cubbege is a Certified welding inspector and purveyor of God's unconditional love, grace, and inclusion. He lives in Colorado with his wife and daughter and is a humble, blue-collar guy who has a deep love for our country, family, and the simpler things of life. In the past several years, David has been on a journey into a beautiful awakening—a deeper knowing of Jesus Christ and His all-inclusive love.

David grew up Pentecostal and was taught that God was distant, was up in heaven, sitting on a throne, and looking down upon everybody with distaste. He was an angry, vengeful, wrathful *god* that looked more like Zeus. This *god* was about performance. The idea of watching a baseball game that he loves and not having a passing thought about this *god* brought him feelings of condemnation. He was taught that this vengeful *god* is separated from us, and it is up to us to become good enough to be acceptable to him.

He experienced heavy pressure to keep his life on the 'straight and narrow' while at the same time knowing that he could never do it. Many of his own family who grew up in the same way left religion because of feeling constant rejection, condemnation, and fear. The idea that someone David loved—but who did not make the active choice for God—would end up in a place of eternal suffering weighed heavily on him. It didn't make sense to him that it is all up to us to be in a relationship with God. Reflecting on that experience of cognitive dissonance, "It doesn't seem like unmerited favor or unconditional love if we have to do something to get back to God."

An unveiling of the truth began while he was working on a job in India. His father was his boss, and David walked in to see his stepmother reading a book in the office. He noticed her close the cover and lower her head in prayer. When she looked up, there were tears in her eyes. David felt such an impression he asked her what she was reading and what was so moving. The book was *The Shack* by William Paul Young. It was about a man named Mack and his healing journey of meeting the Trinity face to face. David learned it was a best-seller, got a copy, and began to read. The story moved him greatly, and as a result, he began to search out the Truth about God.

Through a conversation with a former pastor about his journey, he was connected to a stranger named Andrew Mack via Facebook. The two began dialoguing and soon became friends. They talked about Jesus. One day, David shared with Andrew how he would just love to share popcorn with Jesus and watch a movie together. He wanted to know Him that way and to experience His nearness. Andrew's response to this desire was a simple question, "Have you ever watched a movie with another person? Then you watched a movie with Jesus, as he lives inside of that person." In fact, Andrew told David that Jesus lived inside of him and told him that Jesus is not a far-off, distant *god*. He told him that Christ is all and in all. These Facebook conversations were becoming the soil where the garden of greater unveiling would grow. David says that he saved his messages with Andrew and often listens to them because they are precious to his journey. He gets choked up every time he does.

David is a reader and has many books in queue on his kindle. Through a 'must-read' suggestion, he began to read *The Great Dance* by Baxter Kruger, which would change his life and his lens of the Trinity and of who we are in Christ. It took David a year to read because he spent considerable time researching what Baxter wrote. He now says that this is the book that woke him up to the inclusion of all in Christ, the same 'all in all' that Andrew had told him about.

David says, "Once God brings you to see it, you cannot unsee." His favorite scripture is 2 Corinthians 5:19: "God was in Christ reconciling the entire cosmos/world, not holding sin against us." He rejoices in knowing that all people were forever reconciled at the cross in Christ!

David muses that the tiniest blade of grass is inside the Trinity. He knows that God is not at all distant anymore; He lives within us all!

I've had the wonderful privilege of connecting with David via Zoom—many times while he's in his truck on the way from one job site to another. Each of those encounters leaves me better, fuller of joy, and more excited than before!

Grace I AM Re #14

From time to time, often many times a day, we continue to experience things that would have taken us down before we started employing the 'Re Process.'

We can get tired, burned out, and the Doctrinal System of Darkness attacks us again. The lying voices of religion whisper (OR SHOUT), "You are not! You are not right with God. You are separate from God. God is really mad at you. You have to do what we tell you to get back in *god's* good graces, or it will torment and punish you forever in 'hell.'"

Your Teammate, Jesus, continually lovingly offers His help. He says to you, "Are you tired? Worn out? Burned out on religion (the Doctrinal System of Darkness)? Come to me. Get away with me, and you'll recover your life. I'll show you how to take a real rest. Walk with me and work with me—watch how I do it. Learn the unforced rhythms of grace. I won't lay anything heavy or ill-fitting on you. Keep company with me, and you'll learn to live freely and lightly."

You now have access to the best Recovery Group that exists! Whenever you need to, take a few minutes in your secret place with your primary Teammates, Jesus, Papa, and Grace, and say (out loud if you can) several times slowly, "I AM coming to You, Jesus, Papa, and Grace because I'm tired, worn out, and burned out. I need to RECOVER the Abundant Life you gave me. Thank you for continually teaching me the unforced rhythms of grace!"

SYLVIA ELIZONDO
Daddy's baby girl is home!

It only takes a few seconds of listening to Sylvia Elizondo, a mom of two in Houston, Texas, to realize you're hearing someone who is truly excited about the Love of God and the way it has impacted her life! Her joy is infectious, and there's no doubt that the encounter she describes is genuine.

In her own words, she says, before she was awakened or transferred from darkness into light, "I used to judge a lot. I used to be very angry, and the way that I saw people, especially my family, was so different. It was conditional love. 'I'll do something for you when you do something for me.' And if they did something bad to me, I'd repay them by not speaking to them." Bitterness, strife, resentment, and unforgiveness were rampant in her life.

"Now, I just love people! I really do love them. That's the biggest difference I've noticed since the light of Jesus has shone into my heart. I mean, how much more can someone show us their love than by dying for us?"

In describing her life-changing encounter with Jesus, Sylvia relates that she wasn't involved in a church at that time. She considered herself Catholic because of her upbringing, but she also had several family members who were Jehovah's Witnesses, who told her that if she didn't become a Jehovah's Witness, she would perish in Armageddon. "So, I had this vision of God being an angry *god* just ready to zap me," she said.

Oddly enough, her encounter with the real God started while watching an episode of Oprah. Something told her to watch it, and she found that they were featuring a story about a single mother who was abducted by a man who was wanted for several murders. During the seven hours the mom was held, she told her captor her life story and read to him from a famous Christian book. She told him how God could use him if he surrendered and set her free. He did so the following morning!

As Sylvia watched this compelling story, she was focused on the woman and the light that seemed to be emanating from her. She thought, *I want what she's got!* Not sure how to go about that, she went to a local bookstore, bought the book, and began listening to some teachers online.

The book was full of Scriptures she hadn't been familiar with that made her think, *Wow. It sounds like He's an awesome God!* Her focus began to change, and she began to view Him and herself very differently! She realized that God made her and loved her.

By the twenty-third chapter of the book, she knew. She got down on her knees and prayed to a God she had never known before. At first, she wanted some sort of proof or sign. She wanted to know that it was real. She tried bargaining with God. "If you change my husband, then I'll change." She said the same thing about her son and her daughter. But she heard an inner voice in reply that said, "It's you that I'm here to change, child." Sylvia, astonished, asked, "Me? Is that you, God?" The answer that followed was, "Yes, child. This is Jesus. You have to change."

Sylvia describes a sense of Pure Love coming over her then, and she saw her life clearly. She realized that she was allowing people to dictate the way she felt. She wasn't happy or joyful and depended on the people around her to make her happy.

Now Sylvia knows that only Jesus can give us joy. He put HIS joy inside of us. She felt the Love of God overshadow her that day, a kind of love that she didn't even know existed. She realized that Heaven is within us, along with all the fullness of God. She described seeing Heaven all around her. Everything seemed brighter and greener; the birds were singing louder; she could now see God's glory. "Now, I can hear it," she said. "Everything that has breath is praising God. The trees, the birds chirping; they're all praising God." She went outside, looked up at the sky, and said, "Daddy, your baby girl is home."

She detailed other changes that have taken place—her heart softening and being able to forgive people and not hold onto resentment toward them. God's Word became alive to her, much more than words on a page. She saw Jesus as the Living Word. Instead of an angry deity to be feared, she now saw God as Daddy.

She knew immediately after this encounter that she no longer wanted Catholicism in her life, although she did have an urge to seek out like-minded people who believed in the awesome God she had so recently met. She briefly tried a church, but it wasn't a good experience. They didn't teach about the God she'd met in her living room. She soon recognized that religion wasn't the answer. None of the religious experiences in her life matched the Jesus she was coming to know.

Sylvia longs to see her family experience the enlightening that she's had, but she knows that God knows exactly when each person is ready and that she just needs to love them. "Not that everything around me is perfect, but this perfect love is inside of me now, and I'm able to handle the imperfections around me."

Grace I AM Re #15

As you become more and more aware that your Teammates are with you and for you 24/7, you will hear Grace lovingly and gently remind you to repeat your 'Re Process.' You may want to 'dog-ear' this page or photocopy it and keep it in an easily accessible place. Here's the entire 'Re Process':

"I AM learning to STOP the moment I experience trouble and RECOGNIZE that something's not right."

"I AM REALIZING that this troubling situation is harming me, and something needs to be done."

"I AM REJECTING these harmful thoughts by the power of Grace!"

"I AM RELEASING any and all harmful thoughts. I AM sending them away!"

"I AM changing my mind about any and all harmful thoughts and their potential negative repercussions and choosing to replace them with thoughts that are pure, lovely, admirable, honorable, and worthy of praise!" (REPENT)

"I AM continually RECEIVING thoughts, wisdom reminders of God's approval of my holiness from my Teammate, Grace!"

"I AM continually RENEWING my mind with the truth I hear from Grace in me and returning to my original genesis of perfection!"

"I AM REPLENISHING myself with whatever I need from my spiritual warehouse!"

"I AM REFRESHING myself and REJOICING as I thank my

Teammates for Their continual blessings to me!"

"Today, I AM RESTING in the RESERVOIR of my TEAM's abundant blessings!"

"I AM coming to You, Jesus, Papa, and Grace because I'm tired, worn out, and burned out. I need to RECOVER the Abundant Life you gave me. Thank you for continually teaching me the unforced rhythms of grace! I AM going to REPEAT the 'Re process' whenever I need to!"

This concludes the short inspirational 'Grace I AMs,' *Notes From Papa* pages, 'Grace Is …,' 'Convertible Conversations,' and fifteen Grace 'Re' pages in this book. I encourage you to refer to them often to refresh and reinforce your growing understanding of the Only True

God!

“While not having ‘Grace Restoration Team’ type ministries, the following ‘Grace with Paul Gray’ interview guests have wonderful encouraging books, videos, non-profits, or are prolific social media commenters and writers that you may resonate with. I’m delighted to include them in this book!” ~Paul Gray

DOMINICK DOMASKY
Feeding the Spirit

Dominick Domasky inspires, motivates, and encourages people to be champions in what they do. His inspiration-sharing company, Motivation Champs, works with a wide range of inspirational authors in a variety of fields. He is a best-selling author himself, a YouTube show producer and host, actor, and continual student of life.

Dominick states, "I believe inspiration is like medicine; we each take and receive it differently. My ultimate goal is to share inspiration, positivity, and grace in as many ways and places as possible."

(As someone who has been working with Dom for the past several years, I, Paul Gray, can attest that every day he makes great progress with his ultimate goal!)

Dom arrived at inspirational story writing and storytelling with a unique background. As a boy, he learned the value of hard work by pulling weeds and doing odd jobs in the fields of his father's landscape company. He took those lessons of hard work, incorporated them into his passions, and carried them throughout every aspect of his life from basketball to business.

In addition to writing, publishing, acting, and inspiring, Dominick is vice-president and an active leader of Feeding the Spirit, a ministry in the Pittsburgh, Pa., suburb of Greensburg, Pa., where amazing things transpire on a daily basis!

The idea for Feeding the Spirit was born on an early January morning when Dom's friend Deb Thackrah, an avid runner, altered her running route, only to come face-to-face with a segment of our community that few knew existed. On this trail, generally used for walking and bicycling, she encountered people sleeping on benches and in tents nearby. She found people of all ages, some huddled in blankets, others covered in cardboard. Deb's heart exploded with compassion and a strong commitment to DO something. That 'something' has grown into Feeding the Spirit.

Feeding the Spirit's mission is: Helping people break through barriers of poverty, homelessness, and hunger through crisis management and transitional resources while instilling hope and dignity.

Each week, guests gather to receive nourishment—in mind, body, and spirit. Volunteers join to serve everyone in an atmosphere of perpetual grace, fellowship, and acceptance.

At the heart of their mission is an atmosphere of unconditional acceptance and respect for each individual. Within that environment, they work to nourish not just the body but also the mind and spirit of those in their midst.

Last year, they served approximately 11,000 meals, provided over $36,003 to house 476 displaced families and individuals in need of overnight shelter for 646 nights, and provided $35,818 in assisting 179 families facing rent problems and/or eviction. They have served over 50,000 meals since their inception in November of 2011.

In addition to providing leadership, organization, communication, fundraising, and inspiration to Feeding the Spirit's team and their guests, Dominick can be found preparing and serving meals, providing rides, delivering meals, collecting clothing, handing out gloves and scarfs, and in a variety of other ways. Dom is a board member of the organization, as is Lynn Wagner, who does the layout for my books, maintains and updates my website, and designed the logo for Grace to All and the Grace Restoration Team! I love how Grace has brought us together as like-minded spirits!

In Dom's spare time, he recently wrote and published his newest book *My Name is Sharon*, which is a unique and timeless love story. There is no bond more unbreakable than the unconditional love between a mother and child. *My Name is Sharon* chronicles the pain a family feels when their mother's advanced memory loss collides with a global pandemic. This timeless love story attempts to put a face on Alzheimer's disease and explain the grief and guilt felt by the families quietly mourning the loss of the living. The loss of a loved one is never easy; however, we attempt to find comfort in the special memories we shared together. *My Name Is Sharon* is a journey through a collection of precious family memories where we uncover the deep bond between Dominick and his mother and learn she will be remembered as far more than a victim of disease.

HARRY SPAIGHT
Selling with Dignity

Harry Spaight was a missionary for over a decade, but a nagging sense that God was better than his religious organization believed led him to question how a supposedly 'good *god*' could torture people forever for any reason, let alone because they never heard about him. Harry's struggles with spiritual cognitive dissonance and the inability to get satisfactory answers to his questions led him to leave missionary work and organized religion.

Today, Harry is a keynote speaker, author, and coach. He grew up in a small New England town and inherited 'old school values.' He became involved in mission work as a young adult, supporting himself with his small janitorial/office cleaning business. Mission work is what gave Harry the most joy and purpose. That work led him to spend years in the Dominican Republic working with the local population to improve their life skills and spiritual growth.

Upon returning to the States, Harry transferred his skills, working with people, to sales. With very little business acumen, Harry applied the principles from the Bible as a guide on how to treat people. Those principles that were two thousand years old or more still proved to be practical.

To Harry, life was all about serving others. Harry believed that people would buy from him if he had a servant's mindset. The principles worked. Harry eventually moved and was leading a team of sales professionals in downtown Washington, D.C., just a few blocks from 1600 Pennsylvania Ave. Harry wondered if the principles would work in such a competitive market as Washington, D.C. The answer is "Yes!" The principles are indeed timeless.

Now, after spending over twenty years as an award-winning multi-million dollar sales producer and sales leader in the extremely competitive arena of corporate sales, Harry knows firsthand how to be successful in sales and lead winning teams. While many sales leaders choose the cozy corner office, Harry preferred to be in the street, sleeves rolled up so to speak, with his team.

Harry is one who leads by example, knowing it is better to get in the trenches with his people than to bark commands at them. He spearheaded sales teams to achieve the amazing success that resulted in over a hundred million dollars in business. Harry has a 'serve others first' mindset, which is largely due to having served for over a decade as a missionary.

Harry's understanding of clients, sales professionals, and sales leaders in building trusting relationships gives people the confidence in putting his knowledge and experience into practice.

Harry is the co-host of a top 20 podcast "Lead Sell Grow, The Human Experience," and his inspirational book *Selling With Dignity* is now available. Harry is on a mission to take the sleaze out of sales and show success in sales can be achieved with honor. Harry works with sales teams and executives to elevate their craft of selling and leading with dignity.

TRINA L. MARTIN
Pursuing Your Wildest Dreams

Trina L. Martin is a motivational speaker who inspires emerging leaders to pursue their wildest dreams with heart and grit. An accomplished and dedicated member of the U.S. military for nearly thirty years, she has broken barriers and made strides in her career that many said weren't possible. Her new mission is to show others how they, too, can achieve the impossible and define success on their own terms.

A native of Chicago, IL, Trina grew up watching her mother struggle financially to take care of the family. She dreamed of attending college one day but knew she'd have to find a way to achieve that goal on her own due to the lack of support and resources at home. With unwavering determination, she enlisted in the U.S. Army and served in the reserves to put herself through school at Alabama A&M University. Both of these choices fueled Trina's desire to succeed and revealed the depths of her resiliency.

After several years in the Army, Trina transferred to the Navy and earned an MBA degree from Western International University. Naturally skilled at finding the harmony between technology, science, and data, she has led a stellar career in the Information Technology field and as an Intelligence Officer in the U.S. Navy. Trina has pierced the glass ceiling and excelled in positions typically held by men. As a speaker, she takes a refreshingly honest and relatable approach to teaching student leaders, new professionals, and women how to develop the confidence they need to do the same. Based in Houston, TX, when she's not helping others realize their full potential in the office or on a stage, the role she values most is that of a mother to her two children.

CHRISTINA DENT
End it for Good

Christina Dent is a writer, TEDx speaker, and perpetual question asker. She grew up in a conservative Christian home and earned a degree in Biblical Studies with an emphasis in Christian Ministry from Belhaven University. As a young adult, Christina assumed she had a solid understanding of how the world works. That changed when she and her husband became foster parents in 2014. The neat bow she had tied around her mental box of how the world works began to unravel. What had previously been a category of people in her mind, people addicted to drugs, now had a name, face, and an infant son that was sleeping in the extra bedroom down the hall. Her foster care experience gave her an up-close look at the realities of addiction, drug use, and the far-reaching impact of our drug laws.

This became the catalyst for months of reading, questions, and listening as she tried to reconcile her beliefs as a Christian with the pain and suffering she was seeing first-hand. What she learned changed her mind. The laws she thought were the answer to keep people from using drugs she now saw as causing more harm than help to people made in God's image. Christina founded End It For Good out of her desire to invite others to listen to the voices directly impacted by our drug laws. Her hope is that more people will explore the root causes of drug-related harm and consider a different approach. She is currently writing a book on the research and experiences that changed her mind about the best path forward to help people thrive, even in a world where harmful drugs exist.

In 2017, she began hosting book discussions in her home state of Mississippi using Johann Hari's book *Chasing The Scream: The First and Last Days of the War on Drugs*. Those discussions grew to hundreds of people and continue today as Christina invites people to explore how addressing drugs and drug use as a complex health issue could dramatically reduce crime, overdose deaths, and the destabilization of families.

Christina founded End It For Good from the same passion that led her to foster care—helping children, families, and communities thrive. She isn't advocating drug use. She's advocating approaches to drugs that prioritize life and the opportunity to thrive.

End It For Good Core Values:

- We do not celebrate, encourage, or trivialize drug use. We value life – We support approaches to drugs that protect life.
- We value health – We support approaches to drugs that encourage better health.
- We value strong families – We support approaches to drugs that strengthen families instead of destabilizing them.
- We value safe communities – We support approaches to drugs that reduce crime and violence.
- We value respect – We treat everyone with dignity and respect, whether they agree with us or not. We don't use anger or shame to silence other perspectives.
- We value integrity – We win support with truth and reason, not fear or manipulation.
- We value open dialogue - We calmly invite people to learn, ask questions, and consider a health-centered approach to drugs.

JOHN GRDINA
Freedom to Ascend

John Grdina is a special education teacher, podcast host, leadership coach, and so much more! He has taught in public education for the past seventeen years, starting with career and technical education before moving to Special Education. He has also coached baseball and golf and teaches a leadership class at the high school—the very school he graduated from on the east side of Cleveland, Ohio. John graduated from John Carroll University in 2004 with a Bachelor of Arts degree, earned his Master's in Education degree in 2009 from Notre Dame College, and his Education Innovation and Leadership endorsement in 2019 from Fort Hays State University in Kansas.

In his spare time, he is an ultra-endurance athlete who helps train other athletes across the United States, the owner of a True Supporter Group that prays for those in need, and founder of 40 Days of Deliverance—a program to improve individuals' mind, body, and spirit.

John enjoys nature walks with his family, coaching and supporting his children's local sports teams, and spending time with his extended family. He loves helping others grow and wants everyone to "exhaust all their gifts" that God has given them in this life.

In talking about John's first book, *Freedom to Ascend*, he says: "When outlining what I thought would be my first book, the focus was on telling the story of molding the minds of young adults. As I discerned what my mission was for writing a book, I understood that there was a greater purpose, one that touched more than just the mind. What I have discovered in my life is the power of the influence of the Holy Spirit, Christ, and the Father. The true source of my strength in my success is given to me every day by the Trinity. So, the beginning of my journey of wisdom was understanding that it began once I opened up to having a relationship with the Lord. This understanding—I call it an awakening—about how I can live with confidence and make an impact was not always there.

"Growing up, I was a churchgoer and was raised Catholic, but I knew there had to be a deeper meaning to my faith than just showing up to the church. I had to experience the presence of the Holy Spirit to help guide me and help in all the activities of my life. Once I realized that I cannot do life alone and that I needed guidance, support, encouragement, and enrichment from the word of God, then I truly understood the righteous path for my life.

"Understanding why I exist and my mission is where the seed is planted to live my life to the fullest. My mission in life is to serve the Lord and imitate His ways while exhausting my gifts for His kingdom. All of us have gifts given to us, which along with our free will are reservoirs for making decisions and positively using our potential.

"For example, if a man is given a million dollars, and he just buries it in the ground, he has wasted his resources. On the other hand, if a man who is given a million dollars uses it to live a life of influence and experience and to help others, then he has truly made use of this opportunity to have a major impact during his life.

"This book is meant to tell the story of how I became who I am today, how my belief system guides my decisions daily, and the specific strategies I use to have an impact on others' lives. I hope that you learn how you can have the confidence and freedom to make decisions that positively impact you, your family, and your future family so that when you die, you know you lived a fulfilled life that is truly rich with experiences and meaningful relationships.

"The stories in this book derive from my experiences as a parent, educator, coach, leadership coordinator, ultra-runner, and podcaster. I include stories of students who had given up on themselves and thought they could not make a difference in their own lives, let alone someone else's. I believe by being positive, loving, and truly caring about those who walk into our lives, we can give them hope. These testimonies and stories serve as examples and inspiration for all readers to learn to build more positive and impactful relationships.

"Each chapter was written with a specific message, and I believe these can be driving principles for good when implemented. At the end of each chapter, the Action Steps will give concrete and practical ways to incorporate these principles into your life and your relationships.

"Putting all of these pieces together has been quite a process, but

I hope that you will enjoy reading this book and that its message will help you impact others by being able to shine your light and influence in others' lives."

TRACEY YANG
Entertainment has the ability to change countries

Tracey S. Yang is a thought leader, business owner, and author. Her desire to influence positive change in the lives of others is the reason why she currently writes, and her written work has appeared in the People Development Network, The Odyssey, Thrive Global, Medium, and more. Her past experiences, including having a debilitating illness for two years and also experiencing severe bullying, have combined with her Christian background as inspirations for her work.

Tracey's first book was as a co-author: *Power Up, Super Women: Stories of Courage and Empowerment*, which was released in February of 2019 by the publication company Motivation Champs. She has also appeared in several podcasts, television shows, and other forms of press. Some of these include The Japan Times, The Northport Gazette, and the television show The Talk of Alabama.

She decided to follow a career path in entrepreneurship at twelve years old, and she dreamed of one day owning her own entertainment company. Tracey carries the belief that entertainment has the ability to create a much-needed positive change for the world. This desire to influence positive change can be found in all of her work. One day, as a child, Tracey watched a television show that featured a speaker who spoke about his belief on entertainment and change. He said, "Entertainment has the ability to change countries." This statement encouraged Tracey to continue onward with her chosen career path. Due to her determination, passion, and persistence to make her dream a reality, today, Tracey owns the videography company, Kyo Production, along with her husband, John. They live in Alabama, along with their duck child, Woody.

ROSS KNOWLTON
No one is excluded

Ross Knowlton loves people, life, and God. Apart from organized religion or Scripture, God revealed to Ross that ALL people have always been included in Papa's family, and no one is excluded! This multi-talented Christ follower and mountain lover is also a reggae/hip-hop musician and behavior technician who serves children who have autism and other special needs.

Ross has followed in his parent's footsteps as a gifted teacher, leader, and mentor in the field of Special Education. Ross initially started teaching and serving children with special needs and their families, and as he continues, he also trains other teachers and navigates the myriad of governmental regulations that are ever-present in attempting to protect and ensure care and understanding for those who often can't care for or advocate for themselves.

Ross's heart for the vulnerable is a gift from God, and he stewards this gift admirably.

He loves all things Jayhawk and has a very unique 'secret' room in his home that is a Jayhawk man-cave that's featured on YouTube at Ross Knowlton.

EVAN MONEY
The World Needs More People Living Their Dreams

Evan Money is a self-described happily married, #1 bestselling author, Ph.D., and Global Entrepreneur. Evan and his bride remarry in a different state or country every year and just celebrated wedding #28 on top of one of the tallest buildings in the world in Dubai. They homeschool their two amazing children and live in Rancho Palos Verdes, a quiet enclave in Los Angeles. Evan and his bride have been interviewed by and featured on ABC, NBC, CBS, The Wall Street Journal, SUCCESS, and Fast Company magazine.

Evan says: "Along our journey as husband and wife and now mom and dad, we realized that in order for things to get better, we had to get better, and in order for things to grow (like our marriage and our finances), we had to grow.

"This meant we had to stop blaming everyone else, like the government, the traffic, and the economy, and start taking full responsibility for our lives.

"Our mission is to bring your dreams to life because the world needs more people living their dreams.

"It's time to trade in your OLD life for the GOLD life, and it all starts with putting God first."

Evan and Susan host marriage conferences and provide business and personal coaching.

Evan is the producer of the film "Words of Art (success is one thing, Impact is another)," featuring his interviews with Joel Osteen, Darren Hardy, and Denis Waitley and stories about Evan's friend, Jim Rohn.

He is also the producer of the film 2Miracles In Action," starring Angela Alexander.

RASHEED SAMI

Think about your thinking

Rasheed is a motivational speaker and counselor of B.A.M: Chicago's Becoming a Man. This is a school-based social-emotional support program that helps at-risk young men in middle and high school navigate the difficult circumstances that threaten their futures. The foundation of B.A.M.'s model is the creation of a safe space in which boys are free to explore the challenges in their lives.

By teaching young people to 'think about their thinking,' B.A.M. participants develop a future orientation and the skills necessary to resolve conflicts, express themselves positively, practice integrity in their daily interactions, and set ambitious goals for their futures. B.A.M. 'circles' are one-hour clinically-based group sessions that meet as a twelve to fifteen student cohort once per week over a two-year period and work through a curriculum that incorporates aspects of cognitive-behavioral therapy, youth development, and mentoring.

Rasheed is an engaging young man who mentors, helps, and encourages youth like himself who grew up in inner-city Chicago. He relates well to them, and they respond well to his leadership!

RENEE GALLOWAY
Done!

Dr. Renée Galloway is ardent about assisting individuals and groups to achieve and maintain solid, personal, and professional growth. Through her training and development programs, she endeavors to empower others to pursue their goals and dreams while embracing tools and principles to make positive change a way of life.

For over ten years, Dr. Galloway has developed and facilitated workshops in personal and professional development, financial principles, and Biblical economics at conferences, churches, and small group settings with proven results. She has completed extensive leadership and financial-related training programs, including those of Les Brown, Stephen Covey, John Maxwell, Larry Burkett, and Dave Ramsey.

Renee is the author of *Done! Prioritize, Plan and Perform to Accomplish Your Goals*. Having used the tools described in *Done!* to complete personal and professional goals, Dr. Galloway has firsthand insight and experience with the path to personal success. Preview

Done! at www.sweetinspirationsllc.com.*

Dr. Galloway earned her doctoral degree in Higher Education Administration from the University of Pittsburgh, her MBA from Point Park University, and her BS in Business Administration from Robert Morris University.

CHRIS WIRTH
Positivity, Persistence, and Prosperity

Chris Wirth is the founder and president of No Quit Living. They motivate and inspire their clients to never give up on themselves or their goals. Chris is also the host of the No Quit Living Podcast, which has been rated as a top 50 business podcast on iTunes. He's a sought-after keynote speaker who has coached AAU, high school, and college basketball.

Chris lives in Greenwich, CT, with his three children—Zachary, Emily, and Mason, and they enjoy spending time playing sports, traveling, reading, and working out.

He's the author of *The Positivity Tribe*, where he takes you on a journey that demonstrates how life doesn't happen to you; it happens for you! Chris states that his goal is to 'Pay It Forward' by positively motivating others to never give up on themselves, their goals, or their dreams. Through sharing his 'No Quit' mission, he wants to help people succeed in life and concentrate on his three Ps: Positivity, Persistence, and Prosperity. With accountability and self-accountability, he aims to inspire people to take action.

FRED QUARTLEBAUM
The Positivity Tribe in the Locker Room

Fred Quartlebaum is the most positive person you'll ever encounter! (Full disclosure—he's tied with many others in this book!)

Coach 'Q' has been a division 1 basketball coach for more than twenty-five years and is currently on the coaching staff at the University of Kansas. He's had coaching stops at North Carolina, St. John's, and Notre Dame, among others. While at Kansas, Fred has been a part of six Big 12 regular-season championships, two Big 12 Tournament titles, three NCAA Championship Elite Eights, and one Final Four in 2018.

Coinciding with the publishing of this book, Fred's University of Kansas Jayhawks won the 2022 NCAA Basketball National Championship! Behind by 15 points at halftime to North Carolina, Fred and the other coach's positivity in the locker room was a big part of Kansas erasing that largest-ever NACC championship deficit and storming back to win the title.

Fred played college basketball at Fordham University, where he was a four-year letter winner from 1985 to 1989. He helped the Rams to an NIT appearance in 1988 and was co-captain his senior season. He graduated with a degree in communications and is a member of Kappa Alpha Psi Fraternity, Inc.

Fred has teamed up with his close friend, inspirational author, coach, trainer, and top podcaster Christopher J. Wirth to coauthor book two in *The Positivity Tribe* series. Their new book, *The Positivity Tribe in the Locker Room*, tackles culture, kindness, overcoming adversity, and the importance of teamwork.

Catch up with Coach Q on Instagram or contact The Positivity Tribe for more information.

BRIAN P. SWIFT
Getting up is the key to life!

Brian P. Swift, J.D., has over twenty years of corporate training, sales, and marketing experience. He has been instrumental in the marketing and leadership of three successful start-up companies. He has developed and implemented many new employee-training initiatives to enhance people's skills for the achievement of organizational goals. He has also created strategic alliances to achieve aggressive sales objectives in the organizations.

Brian developed his own strategy of success, which he refers to as CIA (Commitment, Integrity, and Attitude). His success comes from his ability to share his vision, motivate, and inspire people to become uncommon. As a motivational speaker, he has been asked to speak at one of the leading rehabilitation institutes as well as numerous educational institutions. He received his Juris Doctor from DePaul College of Law and was a National Negations finalist. He has spent over twenty years motivating, inspiring, and coaching football and basketball.

He is a father of three adopted children. His wife teaches in a suburban school. He is excited to be taking his talents into the writing arena and had his first book published in October 2013. All of these accomplishments have come after he broke his neck at the age of seventeen.

Up: Getting Up is the Key to Life is the first book by Brian, in which he shares his personal paradigm for mental, emotional, and spiritual recovery and facing the challenges of life as a quadriplegic. It is the author's hope to inspire those with similar injuries and give hope to their medical caregivers, family, and loved ones. He instructs that recovery consists of healing the mind, not just the body, and that recovery is a journey, not a destination. In 2015, he started a nonprofit called Swift Outdoor Accessible Recreation (SOAR) and has two other books published.

Swift Outdoor Accessible Recreation (SOAR) is a 501 C (3) nonprofit organization dedicated to helping people with disabilities participate in outdoor recreational activities. The mission of SOAR is to provide hope in the form of programs, services, and equipment to improve the emotional and physical quality of life for people with disabilities along with their families.

The 'Grace Restoration Team' Ministry

Together, Everyone Accomplishes More

We're inviting YOU to help provide MUCH MORE!

One of the first people featured in this book is Mike Popovich, and you may recall reading about his 'Inspire 100' ministry that helps solo parents and their children.

Our 'Grace Restoration Team' is a subsidiary of our 501 c 3 nonprofit ministry. Mike Popovich's 'Inspire 100' ministry has been our inspiration. People from around the United States and the world are part of this team. 100 % of all profits from the sale of this book, *Grace to ALL*, and all donations to The Grace Restoration Team are given to solo parents (single moms and dads) who need help.

Single parents and their kids are among the most vulnerable people in society, and many can seemingly be without hope. James, Jesus' half-brother (their mother, Mary, was a single mom) wrote this: "True spirituality (true ministry) that is pure in the eyes of our Father God is to make a difference in the lives of the *orphans*, and *widows* in their troubles."

The Greek word James used 'orhpanos' means 'the fatherless' or 'the comfortless.'

In those days, being a single dad didn't generally cause financial problems, and single moms were usually taken care of by family or the church, but not always. Today, solo parents generally have 24-7 solo responsibility for their children—who sometimes are children with special needs—physical, psychological, emotional, mental, and certainly financial.

Only 43.5 % of single parents receive the child support their former spouse is obligated to pay them. Due to death and other circumstances, many aren't even eligible for child support.

Those who have jobs work all day, spending a substantial amount of their income on child care, and then are the only person available to care for their kids when they are home. Many single parents lose their jobs because they've had to miss too much work in order to take care of their kids. Some have family, a network of friends, or church support. Some don't. We can't help every single parent, but we can help some! YOU can help us help many more! The more people who are part of our team, the more single parents and their kids we can help.

Like our friend Mike Popovich, we are Delightfully Expecting Effortless Manifestation (DEEM) 100 people from around the country who donate $100 each month, providing a total of $10,000 every month, which we then give away to single parents in need. Some people can do that. Some can do less. Some can do more. Some of you know friends who are interested in helping single parents.

Following are some recent examples. (Note: these are not their real names.)

Marie found herself and her six-year-old son, James, alone in their apartment when her (now former) husband moved out. Suddenly, she had the sole financial responsibility of paying their rent. Within a few months, she was able to move into a small rental home, but it had no appliances. We provided her funds to purchase every appliance she needed. Imagine not knowing how you'd get a stove, fridge, washer, dryer, and other small appliances and suddenly being given a check for MUCH MORE than you imagined!

Autumn and her three children escaped a very abusive situation, which meant temporarily moving in with relatives in a distant city. While she looked for a new job, we provided her with funds for temporary housing.

Kaye's deteriorating health, coupled with Covid-19 circumstances, left her unemployed and with no income while she started the process of applying for disability. She had less than $10 to her name, was behind in rent and utilities, needed to pay taxes and insurance to renew her car tags, needed medicine, and was seemingly without hope. The Grace Restoration Team provided funds to get her current on all her bills, take care of her car and medicine needs, and covered ALL her monthly expenses for three months while helping her get available government assistance and work on her disability application. It was MUCH MORE than she expected!

Rita and her two elementary school-aged children had dug out of a financial hole after her husband left. She was working full time (and going to school to get an advanced degree to provide a better-paying job). Her job was in a city 30 minutes away. Then her seventeen-year-old car stopped running. She was on the third day of renting a car and waiting to see if her car was repairable when she was referred to us. She got the call that for $2,500, it could be fixed and expected to provide reliable transportation for a couple of years until she finished her schooling and could afford a car payment. We provided all the funds to repair her car and MUCH MORE to cover her rental vehicle costs and more.

These are just a few recent instances of helping single parents and their families.

In addition to no-strings-attached financial help, we help single parents learn about The Only True God (as Jesus calls His Father and Our Father), and we help them connect with people in the Grace to ALL Team. We provide free copies of this book, complimentary membership to the PURE LIGHT WALKER online course, and a variety of other gratis resources.

You can start your own similar ministry to solo parents in your area or check out 'Inspire 100' at www.inspire100.org.

To learn more about The Grace Restoration Team and how we help solo parents and their children, please go to www.gracewithpaulgray.com/singleparenthelp. You can also email Paul Gray at gracerestorationteam@gmail.com All contributions are tax-deductible and go 100% to help those in need. Giving can be done through PayPal to gracerestorationteam@gmail.com.

You are FREE to Connect!

Jesus' friend Peter finished his first book with these words: "Grow in the grace and knowledge of our Lord and Savior Jesus Christ. To him be glory both now and forever! Amen."

Growing in Grace is, of course, a lifelong project—it even continues into eternity!

Jesus' friend Paul wrote this to you: "Throughout the coming ages you will be the visible display of the infinite riches of his grace and kindness, which was showered upon us in Jesus Christ."

A great way to continue growing in grace and to be encouraged and inspired by the revelations you've received and become aware of in this book is to connect with some of the Grace Restoration Team members you've been reading about. Following is a list of their contact information, podcasts, books, courses, meetings, etc.

Teammate Information

David Adams

Located: Lakeland, Florida

Facebook: www.facebook.com/profile.php?id=100021788262158

Podcast Episodes 234 & 236 - Proving Them Wrong Parts 1 & 2

Paul Anderson-Walsh

Located: London, UK

Email: info@thecentreforinclusiveleadership.com

Websites: www.thegraceproject.com, www.thecentreforinclusiveleadership.com

Twitter: @PawSight, @tcfil_official

Facebook: www.facebook.com/paul.andersonwalsh, www.facebook.com/thecentreforinclusiveleadership

LinkedIn: www.linkedin.com/in/paul-anderson-walsh-frsa-3617671b/

YouTube: www.youtube.com/user/paulandersonwalsh

Podcast Episode 62 - Love IS Unconditional – Adding Conditions Negates Love!

Tom Bassford

Located: Olathe, Kansas

Websites: www.SATtalks.org, www.significantmatters.com, www.satcatalyst.com

Email: tom@significantmatters.com

Twitter: @TomBassford @SignificantMtrs @SATtalks

SM Facebook: www.facebook.com/SignificantMatters

SATtalks Facebook: www.facebook.com/SATtalks

LinkedIn: www.linkedin.com/in/tom-bassford-3606568

YouTube: www.youtube.com/channel/UChsYAFNYfg1t5CANTww12Pg/

Podcast Episodes 40, 88, 90 – Significant Matters and Significant Matters with Tom & Wayne McDaniel Parts 1 & 2

Florian Berndt

Located: Germany

Blog: www.wadinginthemysticalflow.com

Ministry and publishing business Divine Embrace Ministries & Publications, "where we mostly translate English speaking books into German": www.divineembrace.net, www.divineembrace.de The German-speaking network of Perichoresis DACH (Germany, Austria,

and Switzerland), A resource center and community of believers in the Gospel of the Triune God of Grace: www.perichoesis.de
Email: Abbas_Child@gmx.net, AbbaCallingMinistries@gmail.com
Facebook: Abba Calling – www.facebook.com/groups/478339185903768
LinkedIn: www.linkedin.com/in/florian-berndt-289b4b90/
YouTube: www.youtube.com/channel/ UCo1qO4srzoD83FR8Ze1QE_w
Podcast Episode 30 – the Unfailing Love of God our Abba Father

Martin Brooks

Located: Louisville, Kentucky
President, Peace Catalyst International
Email: martin.brooks@peacecatalyst.org
Website: www.peacecatalyst.org
Twitter: @martinkbrooks
Facebook: www.facebook.com/martinkbrooks, www.facebook.com/peacecatalyst
Facebook Group: www.facebook.com/groups/christianpeacebuildingnetwork
LinkedIn: www.linkedin.com/in/martinkbrooks
YouTube: www.youtube.com/user/PeaceCatalystInt
Podcast Episodes 108 & 110 – Following Jesus, Waging Peace Parts 1 & 2

Dave Carringer

Located: Cleveland, Tennessee
Email: merhobyahpress@yahoo.com
Facebook: www.facebook.com/dave.carringer
Books: *Born From Above: Waking Up to Our Genesis*
Podcast Episode 130 – Born from Above & 132 Human Treasure Hunter

Andre Chiasson

Located: Kelowna, British Columbia, Canada
Facebook: www.facebook.com/andre.chaisson.39, www.facebook.com/groups/1819083404996753
Podcast Episodes 286, 288, 290 - On a Mission in a Street Mission!

Rannie Childress

Located: Springville, Alabama
Email: chaplain170@gmail.com
Websites: www.trinitariangraceinternational.com, www.graceministriesatrapha.com
Senior Pastor Grace Ministries at Rapha (AKA) Trinitarian Grace

International
Recovery Group: "Life More Abundant" (LMA) Facebook: www.facebook.com/Chaplain170, www.facebook.com/rannie.childress1
LinkedIn: www.linkedin.com/in/rannie-childress-554a2b36/
YouTube Channel: www.youtube.com/channel/UCdo9tKJ0gub_G2acVZ-8z0A
Podcast Episodes 180, 182 & 184 - From Prison to Setting People Free, Parts 1, 2 & 3

Michele Francesca Cohen
Located: Dallas, Texas
Email: www.michelefrancesca.com/contact
Website: www.michelefrancesca.com
YouTube: www.youtube.com/c/MicheleFrancesca www.paypal.com/paypalme/MicheleFrancesca
Website: www.michelefrancesca.com
Twitter: @MicheleFCohen
Facebook: www.facebook.com/michelefrancescacohen www.facebook.com/MicheleFCohen
LinkedIn: www.linkedin.com/in/michelefrancesca/
Books: *EdenSong, Arise, LoveSong*
Podcast Episodes: Episodes 248 & 250 – Inspiration for Life Part 1 & 2 and Episodes 344 & 346 Inspiration for Life and Arts

Ryan Coker
Located: Travelers Rest, South Carolina
Facebook: www.facebook.com/ryan.coker.319, www.facebook.com/RC-Freedom-459852377479254
LinkedIn: www.linkedin.com/in/r-c-freedom-ministries-inc-2b1668b4/
YouTube: www.youtube.com//user/rcoker66
Podcast Episode 146 – The Gospel is NOT an Elevator Ride!

Lila Cook
Located: Michigan
Facebook: New Covenant Grace Family private group: www.facebook.com/groups/236426860185745
Podcast Episode 44 – From Beaten Down to Lifting Others Up!

Lisa Wentworth Couture
Located: Salem, New Hampshire
Email: lisa.couture777@gmail.com

Twitter: @lcouture63
LinkedIn: www.linkedin.com/in/lisa-wentworth-couture-721b13a/
Patreon: www.patreon.com/user?u=54243960
YouTube: www.youtube.com/user/sxfnlc
Podcast Episode: Episode 134 - The Honey Love of God!

John Crotty

Located: Tyler, Texas
Facebook: www.facebook.com/john.crotty.967 Podcast Episode 28 - I died for 45 minutes!

David Cubbedge

Located: Johnstown, Colorado
Email: david.cubbedge@yahoo.com
Facebook: www.facebook.com/profile.php?id=100015472740103
LinkedIn: www.linkedin.com/in/david-cubbedge-31627469/
Podcast Episodes 154 & 156 – Loving as Jesus Loves Parts 1 & 2

Bill Carpenter

Located: Ohio
Email: dreamer4242@live.com Facebook www.facebook.com/bill.cee.566
Podcast Episode 316 - Love is THE Key!

Rob Decker

Located: Colorado Springs, Colorado
Facebook: www.facebook.com/rob.decker.589
LinkedIn: www.linkedin.com/in/rob-decker-61378680/, www.linkedin.com/in/rob-decker-a706b9143/
Podcast Episode 96 – In a Very Tough Place and Episode 98 – From Tragedy to Triumph

Christina Dent

Located: Ridgeland, Mississippi
Email: christina@enditforgood.com
Twitter: @EndItForGoodMS
Website: www.enditforgood.com
Facebook: www.facebook.com/christina.dent.142, www.facebook.com/EndItForGoodMS
LinkedIn: www.linkedin.com/in/christina-dent-5674b51a2/
Podcast Episodes 308 & 310 - End It For Good

Melissa Denyce

Located: Montana

Email: www.lovecovering.wordpress.com/contact/

Website: www.lovecovering.wordpress.com

Facebook: www.facebook.com/MelissaDenyce, www.facebook.com/ groups/1362898643777677

YouTube: www.youtube.com/c/LoveCoveredLifePodcast

Podcast Episodes 224 & 226 – Love Covered Life Parts 1 & 2

Dominick Domasky

Located: Pittsburgh, Pennsylvania

Email: motivationchamps@gmail.com

Twitter: @Motivationchamp

Website: www.motivationchamps.com

Facebook: www.facebook.com/dominick.domasky, www.facebook.com/Motivationchampsanddominickdomasky

LinkedIn: www.linkedin.com/in/dominick-domasky-997b5414/

YouTube: www.youtube.com/DominickDomaskymotivationchamps

Books: *My Name is Sharon*

How to Write a Book in 2020

The Journey of a Grunt

Go Ask Your Dad

The Unofficial Guide to Fatherhood

Don't Double Bread the Fish

Podcast Episode 32 – Inspiring Multitudes! and Episode 319 Feed the Spirit

Phil Drysdale

Located: England

Email: phil@phildrysdale.com

Websites: www.phildrysdale.com, www.thedeconstructionnetwork.com, www.thegracecourse.com

Twitter: @phildrysdale

Facebook: www.facebook.com/PhilDrysdaleMinistries

LinkedIn: www.linkedin.com/in/phil-drysdale-72242b1b/

Podcast: www.phildrysdale.com/theshow/ YouTube: www.youtube.com/phildrysdale

Course: www.thegracecourse.com

Podcast Episodes 138 & 140 – Across the Pond Parts 1 & 2

Lydia du Toit

Located: Hermanus, Western Cape, South Africa
Email: info@mirrorword.net
Website: www.mirrorword.net
Twitter: @francoislydia
Facebook: www.facebook.com/lydia.toit,
www.facebook.com/ groups/179109018883718
YouTube: www.youtube.com/channel/
UC63YHkpabON9nHgQqWeIPkA/featured
Podcast: www.open.spotify.com/show/3qsgRsf2SNDx1bubxngw0W?si=
e d189a572d0943d4
Podcast Episodes 198 & 200 – Unconditionally at Home Parts 1 & 2
Lydia is the wife of Francois du Toit, author of the *Mirror Bible Translation*

Sylvia Elizondo

Located: Houston, Texas
Email: sylnjav@hotmail.com
Facebook: www.facebook.com/sylvia.elizondo
YouTube: www.youtube.com/channel/UCir5TE5emHZ5ku-ROk7oZsg
Podcast Episode 266 – Agape Love Part 1, 268 – Agape Love Part 2

Jamie Englehart

Located: New Albany, Indiana
Email: heartmin@msn.com
Website: www.connectinternationalministries.com
Facebook: www.facebook.com/jamie.englehart.1
www.facebook.com/Connect-International-Ministries-119990561361772
LinkedIn: www.linkedin.com/in/jamie-englehart-60161645/
YouTube: www.youtube.com/channel/UCWm39B_
rdsN6UFZ53bU67XA
Podcast Episodes 256 –258 – Encountering the Liquid Love of Abba!
Episodes 331 & 332 From Pouting to Shouting!

Dr. Kay Fairchild

Located: Fort Wayne, Indiana
Facebook: www.facebook.com/Dr-Kay-Fairchild-New-LifeMinistri
es-173172069428171/, www.facebook.com/kay.fairchild.18
YouTube: www.youtube.com/channel/UCklA0A2PAVixCxoTg2UKbWg

Podcast: www.anchor.fm/dr-kay-fairchild
Books: *Revelation Revolution*
Living Out of Your Spiritual Resources Vol 1 & 2
No Penal Substitution Vol 1 & 2
Builders of the Tabernacle
What's in a Name
Sonship
Universal Reconciliation
The Calling and Making of the Kingdom Man of God
Podcast Episode 26 – The Father's Love Changes Everything!

Julie Ferwerda

Located: Puerto Rico
Email: jferwerd@gmail.com
Website: www.raisinghellbook.com, www.julieferwerda.com
Twitter: @julieferwerda
Facebook: www.facebook.com/ferwerda
Patreon: www.patreon.com/raisinghell
YouTube: www.youtube.com/raisinghell
Book: *Raising Hell*
Podcast Episode 220 – Raising Hell!

Dr. Paul Fitzgerald

Located: Olathe, Kansas
Website: www.HeartConnexion.org
Twitter: @drpaul
Facebook: www.facebook.com/drpaulfitzgerald
LinkedIn: www.linkedin.com/in/pauldfitzgerald/
YouTube: www.youtube.com/channel/UCP3ReZ6kY2CFNbP9n_xxtLg/
Podcast Episode 80 – Invincible Preciousness!

Wendy Francisco

Located: Livermore, Colorado
Websites: www.wendyfrancisco.com, www.godanddog.org
Twitter: @WendyFrancisco
Facebook: www.facebook.com/WendyWings
Facebook Group: Love Heretic - www.facebook.com/groups/309407729424607
LinkedIn: www.linkedin.com/in/wendy-francisco-20079728/
YouTube: www.youtube.com/user/crackonoon

Podcast Episode 12 – Love Heretic

Dr. Renee Galloway

Located: Pittsburgh, Pennsylvania
Email: info@sweetinspirationsllc.com
Website: www.sweetinspirationsllc.com
Twitter: @Rgalloway2G
Facebook: www.facebook.com/SweetInspirationsLLC/?ref=page_internal, www.facebook.com/renee.galloway2
LinkedIn: www.linkedin.com/in/reneemgalloway/
Podcast Episode 52 - 3 Degrees and No Debt -- by God's Grace!

Rex Gaskey

Located: Covington, Tennessee
Facebook: www.facebook.com/profile.php?id=100001552254361
LinkedIn: www.linkedin.com/in/rex-gaskey-1597ba56/
Podcast Episode 210 – Tennessee Testimony

Keith Giles

Located: El Paso, Texas
Email: keith.giles@peacecatalyst.org
Website: www.peacecatalyst.org
Twitter: @keithgiles
Facebook: www.facebook.com/Keith-Giles-222496965100239, www.facebook.com/keithagiles
LinkedIn: www.linkedin.com/in/keithgiles-writer/
Blog: www.patheos.com/blogs/keithgiles/2020/04/the-path-of-peace-areyou-on-it/
Podcasts: Heretic Happy Hour, Subversive Radio, Second Cup with Keith, Apostates Anonymous
YouTube: www.youtube.com/user/kgilesify
Books: *Jesus Untangled*
Jesus Unbound Jesus Unveiled
Jesus Undefeated
Jesus Unexpected
Jesus Unforsaken
Courses: Square 1, Square 2, Square 3, Marketing #101, Author's Academy Parts 1 and 2
Podcast Episode 78 – Reconstruction! Episodes 318 and 320 Religious Deconstruction

Kerry Gooch

Located: Central Hawkes Bay, New Zealand

Facebook: www.facebook.com/profile.php?id=100000795678567

Podcast Episodes 270 & 272 "Free Indeed!"

Jerry (J.L.) Gray

Located: Lawrence Kansas

Email: faithscript@yahoo.com

Facebook: www.facebook.com/jlgray01

LinkedIn: www.linkedin.com/in/jerry-gray-b322a338/

Podcast Episode 18 – From Rodeo Riding to Grace Giving

John Grdina

Located: Cleveland Heights, Ohio

Twitter: @grdina_26

Facebook: www.facebook.com/john.grdina.1

LinkedIn: www.linkedin.com/in/john-grdina-078a9121/

Podcast: The John Grdina Classroom

YouTube: www.youtube.com/user/batmax26

TikTok: @jgrdina

Instagram: @jgrdina04

Books: *Freedom to Ascend*

Podcast Episodes 294 & 296 "Hearing from God and Molding Minds!"

Capree Green

Located: Keller, Texas

Email: capree.greene@gmail.com

Twitter: @CapreeGreene

Facebook: www.facebook.com/capree.greene.3

Podcast Episodes 122 & 124 – Ladder to Heaven Parts 1 & 2

Bishop Dr. Bill Hanshew

Located: Joplin, Missouri

Email: drbill.wbsu@gmail.com, billhanshewministries@gmail.com

Website: www.billhanshewministries.org

Twitter: @drbillhanshew, @WBSclasses

Facebook: www.facebook.com/wbsitc.drbill

LinkedIn: www.linkedin.com/in/bishop-dr-bill-hanshew-10b24a88/

YouTube: www.youtube.com/channel/UCJcL_75ZD93wubwpQSbARXw, www.youtube.com/c/WorldBibleSchoolInternationalTrainingCenter/

featured
Podcast Episode 74 – Spiritual "Route 66"

Dr. Faye Hanshew

Located: Joplin, Missouri
Email: DrFaye.WBSU@gmail.com, faye.faithunlimited@gmail.com, inspiredcreationspublishing@gmail.com
Website: www.inspiredcreationspublishing.com
Twitter: @fayehanshew, @WBSclasses
Facebook: www.facebook.com/faye.hanshew, www.facebook. com/InspiredCreationsPublishingCompany, www.facebook.com/ WBSUniversity, www.facebook.com/faithunlimitedemagazine
LinkedIn: www.linkedin.com/in/faye-hanshew-12720913a/
YouTube: www.youtube.com/channel/UCSN9ALVzjsVyfFxfoUiT48A
Magazine: Faith Unlimited
Books: *I Can, I Can I Know I Can!*
Podcast Episode 76 – Impacting People Around the World 24/7

Peter Hiett

Located: Denver, Colorado
Email: info@thesanctuarydowntown.org
Website: www.thesanctuarydenver.org
Facebook: www.facebook.com/peter.hiett
LinkedIn: www.linkedin.com/in/peter-hiett-97766515/
YouTube: www.youtube.com/peterhiett
Books: *The History of Time: and the Genesis of You*
God and His Body: The Romance of Adam and His Bride
All Things New: What Does the Bible Really Say About Hell?
An Adventure in Taking Scripture Literally (or How to be Accused of being a Liberal Heretic by Evangelical Christians)
Apocalypse Now: A three-volume commentary on the Revelation
Waking to Reality
The Soundtrack for All Time
The Prince, the Dragon, and the Bride
Dance Lessons for Zombies
Eternity Now
Podcast Episodes 312 & 314 - Where the hell is Hell? (A church with no

walls but Jesus!)

Joel Holc

Located: Pittsburgh Pennsylvania
Email: energyawarenesscoach@gmail.com
Website: www.eggshelleffect.com
Twitter: @joelholc_
Facebook: www.facebook.com/theeggshelleffect,
www.facebook.com/joel.holc
LinkedIn: www.linkedin.com/in/joel-holc-learning-disability-energycoach-82b88a84/
Book: *The Eggshell Effect*
Podcast Episodes 162, 164 & 166 – The Eggshell Effect Parts 1, 2 & 3

Bob Ingle

Located: Lawrence, Kansas
Email: iambingle@gmail.com
Blog: www.unheardwordz.com
Website (Music): www.bingle.bandcamp.com
Facebook: www.facebook.com/bob.ingle.3
Podcast Episodes 252 & 254 – Be Blessed!

Nicole Jansen

Located: San Diego, California
Email: hello@leadersoftransformation.com
Websites: www.leadersoftransformation.com, www.discovertheedge.com
Twitter: @DiscoverTheEdge, @LeadersPodcast
Facebook: www.facebook.com/LeadersOfTransformation,
www.facebook.com/DiscoverTheEdge,
www.facebook.com/nicolejanseninc
LinkedIn: www.linkedin.com/in/nicolejansen/
YouTube: www.youtube.com/channel/UCMy7Anlv7Xs43kSSW4GspZA
Books: *Power Up, Super Women*
Podcast Episode 34 – Unconditional Love and Grace, Where the Rubber Hits the Road

Brad Jersak

Located: Abbotsford, British Columbia, Canada
Email: bradjersak@gmail.com
Website: www.bradjersak.com
Twitter: @bradjersak

Facebook: www.facebook.com/bradley.jersak
YouTube: www.youtube.com/user/bmjersak
Books: *A More Christlike God: A More Beautiful Gospel*
Can You Hear Me? Tuning in to the God who Speaks
Her Gates Will Never Be Shut: Hope, Hell, and the New Jerusalem
A More Christlike Way: A More Beautiful Faith
IN: Incarnation & Inclusion, Abba & Lamb
Rivers from Eden: 40 Days of Intimate Conversation with God
Children, Can You Hear Me? How to hear and see God
From the Cave to the Cross: The Cruciform Theology of George P. Grant and Simone Weil
George P. Grant - Canada's Lone Wolf
Stricken by God? Nonviolent Identification and the Victory of Christ
Podcast Episodes 304 & 306 - A Different Agenda

Jonathan Jones (The Why Guy)

Located: Deer Park, Washington
Website: Thatwhyguy.com
Facebook: www.facebook.com/profile.php?id=100010222951552
The Why Guy Facebook Group:
www.facebook.com/groups/781987748583111
Patreon Link: www.patreon.com/TheWhyGuy
ko-fi link (buy a coffee for The Why Guy) @www.ko-fi.com/thewhyguy
Books: *Know Love No Fear— No Love Know Fear In Defense of God's Love*
Is God Bipolar?
Podcast Episode 20 – Paul and The Why Guy

Dr. Don Keathley

Located: Fulshear, Texas
Email: jdnzf@msn.com
Websites: www.donkeathley.org, www.globalgraceseminary.net
Twitter: @DonKeathley
Facebook: www.facebook.com/don.keathley
The Digital Cathedral Sundays 10 a.m. CST at www.facebook.com/groups/492234930955878
LinkedIn: www.linkedin.com/in/don-keathley-74267512/
YouTube: www.youtube.com/channel/UC3t1NGXYI91VCJwJEERDX_g
Books: *Hell's Illusion*
Religion Busters
Podcast Episodes 100 – From Religion to Revelation! Episode 102 –

Manifesting as Sons and Daughters of God! Episodes 167 & 169 – Hell's Illusion Parts 1 & 2. Episodes 324 & 325 World Wide Grace Explosion

Ross Knowlton

Located: Colorado Springs, Colorado
Facebook: www.facebook.com/ross.knowlton
Podcast Episode 58 - Inclusion, Inclusion, Inclusion!

Steve Koschella

Located: Adelaide, South Australia
Email: kosch2@adam.com.au
Facebook: www.facebook.com/steve.koschella
Twitter: @koschella_steve
LinkedIn: www.linkedin.com/in/steve-koschella-8736a2179/ YouTube Channel: www.youtube.com/channel/UCJRirOr6s4oz4YsdSQk6cA
Podcast Episode 38 – Grace from Down Under

C. Baxter Kruger

Located: Prentiss, Mississippi
Email: info@perichoresis.org
Website: www.perichoresis.org
Twitter: @perichoresismin
Facebook: www.facebook.com/PerichoresisConnection/, www.facebook. com/cbaxter.kruger
YouTube: www.youtube.com/channel/UC92MnUilbLA5KmPgPlf93tA/
Books: *Across All Worlds*
God is For Us
Jesus and the Undoing of Adam
Patmos
The Great Dance
The Parable of the Dancing God
The Shack Revisited
You Tube interview with Paul Gray: The Current Great World Wide Awakening
Podcast Episode 70 – Seeing Christ in Everyone! Episode 72 – Calm Insides

Cindy Lazor

Located: Latrobe, Pennsylvania
Email: cindylazor1@gmail.com
Website: www.linktr.ee/cindylazor, www.cindylazor.isagenix.com

Twitter: @CindyLazor
Facebook: www.facebook.com/cindy.masseylazor,
www.facebook.com/ believeinwellnesswithcindylazor
LinkedIn: www.linkedin.com/in/cindylazor/
YouTube: www.youtube.com/user/thelazorteam
Podcast Episode 92 – Jesus Bumps!

Brian Longridge
Located: India, Philippines, Egypt, and other countries
www.healingriversinternational-brianlongridge.com
Facebook: www.facebook.com/BrianLongridge88
LinkedIn: www.linkedin.com/in/brian-longridge-1494a0b6/
Podcast: Episodes 112 & 114 – Seeing Christ in those in prison and in leprosy camps

Ronel Lonzer
Located: Bremen, Germany
Email: hello@quantumyou.com
Website: www.quantumyou.com
Facebook: www.facebook.com/QuantumyouasDivine,
www.facebook. com/rlonzer
LinkedIn: www.linkedin.com/in/ronel-lonzer-a73585218/
YouTube: www.youtube.com/channel/UCp51YaI_
Cga6QO4SCvIYvGg?app=desktop
Podcast: www.open.spotify.com/show/25VK5ue7u1EfYxht0LqUhW?si=
0dac4e9e0feb41b4
Podcast Episode 112 - Seeing Christ in those in prison and in leprosy camps" and Episodes 206 & 207 – Spiritual Manifesting Parts 1 & 2

Trina L. Martin
Located: Houston, Texas
Email: inspirerspeaker@gmail.com
Website: www.trinalmartin.com
Twitter: @TrinaLMartin
Facebook: www.facebook.com/trinalmartin,
www.facebook.com/TrinaTalk
LinkedIn: www.linkedin.com/in/trina-l-martin/
Podcast: www.bit.ly/trinatalk
YouTube: www.youtube.com/channel/UCU5t4pKAl-22ykSgcjOXfFQ
Books: *From a Mess to Amazing*
Make it Happen
Podcast Episode 82 - From A Mess to Amazing

Gary Matthews

Located: Stockton, California

Email: newhair60@gmail.com

Facebook: www.facebook.com/gary.matthews.758737

Podcast Episode 56 - Surprised in Retirement!

Judi McCall

Located: Houston, Texas

Email: www.graceandbeyond.com/contact

Website: www.graceandbeyond.com

Facebook: www.facebook.com/profile.php?id=100007165565946, www.facebook.com/groups/gisforgracewithjudimccall

Books: *G is for Grace*

Podcast Episode 222 – G is for Grace

Wayne McDaniel

Located: Lawrence, Kansas

Email: wayne@mcdanielknutson.com

Website: www.mcdanielknutson.com, www.generousvision.com

Twitter: @McDanielKnutson

Facebook: www.facebook.com/mcdanielknutson

LinkedIn: www.linkedin.com/in/waynemcdaniel/, www.linkedin.com/ company/generous-vision/, www.linkedin.com/company/mcdanielknutson-financial-partners/

YouTube: www.youtube.com/channel/UCJOtu--jFeYAiQNpHHL22mg

Podcast Episodes 88, 90 – Significant Matters with Tom & Wayne McDaniel Parts 1 & 2

Michael McElyea

Located: North East, Maryland

Facebook: www.facebook.com/we.are.rising.up, www.facebook.com/ michael.mcelyea.3

Podcast Episodes 150 & 152 – Seeing Christ in EVERYONE Parts 1 & 2

Eamon McMullan

Located: London, England

Website: puregraceworld.com

Twitter: @EamonMCMullan

Facebook: www.facebook.com/eamon.mcmullan.9

YouTube: www.youtube.com/c/EamonMcMullan7/featured
LinkedIn: www.linkedin.com/in/eamon-mcmullan-b94b35b1/
Podcast Episodes 216 & 218 – Letters of Grace Parts 1 & 2

Dr. Steve McVey

Located: St. Petersburg, Florida
Email: info@gracewalk.org
Websites: www.stevemcvey.com, www.gracewalk.org, www. quantumlifewithstevemcvey.com
Twitter: @drstevemcvey
Facebook: www.facebook.com/drstevemcvey
Facebook Group: Quantum Life with Steve McVey - www.facebook.com/groups/2230455630299429
LinkedIn: www.linkedin.com/in/steve-mcvey-a115a410/
YouTube Channel: www.youtube.com/user/SteveMcVey
Books: *Grace Walk*
Grace Walk Moments
The Grace Walk Devotional
52 Lies Heard in Church Every Sunday
Helping Others Overcome Addictions
A Divine Invitation
Beyond an Angry God
Getting Past the Hurt
The Secret of Grace
When Wives Walk in Grace
Walking in the Will of God
Unlock Your Bible
The Grace Walk Experience Workbook Journey Into Intimacy Workbook
Podcast Episodes: Episode 84 – Grace in Life Experiences & Episode 86 – Inclusion Changes Everything! Episodes 329 & 330 - Rest, Relief and Peace

Evan Money

Located: Rancho Palos Verdes, California
Email: evan@evanmoney.com
Twitter: @EvanMoney
Website: www.evanmoney.com, www.evanlovessusan.com, www.takeactionproductions.com

Facebook: www.facebook.com/evan.money
LinkedIn: www.linkedin.com/in/evan-money-25508519/
YouTube: www.youtube.com/channel/UCdqvL9P8L0vW8qAP-jpAV4A/
Vimeo: www.vimeo.com/user5670036
Feature Films: Words of Art, Miracles in Action
Books: *The One Day Diet*
Take Action Now
Money Talks Negativity Walks
Happily Ever After
Podcast Episode 60 - High Energy Money!

Richard Murray

Located: Dalton, Georgia
Email: liftupjawbone@gmail.com
Website: www.thegoodnessofgod.com
Facebook: www.facebook.com/goodnessgod,
www.facebook.com/richard.murray.1840
Podcast Episodes: Episode 22 – No Hatefulness Here & Episode 24 – Lawyer Has New View of Judgment. Episodes 323 & 324 - God is good, always good, only good!

Brett Neil

Located: Bixby, Oklahoma
Email: admin@sparksbixby.com
Website: www.sparksbixby.com
Facebook: www.facebook.com/brett.neil.56,
www.facebook.com/SparksBixby
LinkedIn: www.linkedin.com/in/brett-neil-a4836a8b/
Books: Have a Grand and Glorious Day
Podcast Episodes 298 & 300 - Have a Grand and Glorious Day!

Mike Popovich

Located: Colorado Springs, Colorado
Email: info@freedomministries.org
Website: www.freedomministries.org
Facebook: www.facebook.com/mike.popovich.33, www.facebook.com/FreedomMinistriesCO
YouTube: www.youtube.com/user/freedomministriestv
Podcast Episodes: Episodes 194 & 196 – Seeing the Impossible Manifest Parts 1 & 2 and Episodes 262 & 264—Simple Spirituality That Actually

Works Parts 1 & 2

Dr. Darrel D. Proffitt

Located: Lawrence, Kansas

Currently Interim Rector at Holy Comforter Episcopal Church Spring, TX

Email: www.darrelproffitt.com/contact-me/

Website: www.darrelproffitt.com

Twitter: @Holy_Apostles

Facebook: www.facebook.com/dprofit

LinkedIn: www.linkedin.com/in/darrel-proffitt-7a371b10/

Podcast Episodes 147 & 148 – It's All About Love Parts 1 & 2

Boyd C. Purcell, Ph.D.

Located: Dunbar, West Virginia

Website: www.christianitywithoutinsanity.com

Facebook: www.facebook.com/boyd.purcell1

LinkedIn: www.linkedin.com/in/boyd-purcell-ph-d-1701026a/

Podcast Episodes 242, 244 & 246 – Spiritual Insanity Parts 1, 2 & 3

The "elephant in the choir and the gorilla in the pulpit:" Christianity's sacredcow pagan doctrine of "HELL" (eternal conscious torment).

Dr. Sharon Baker Putt

Located: Mechanicsburg, Pennsylvania

Professor of Theology and Religion

Email: slputt@messiah.edu

Books: *Razing Hell*

Executing God

A Nonviolent Theology of Love

Podcast Episode 120 - Razing Hell!

Fred Quartlebaum

Located: Lawrence, Kansas

Instagram: Coach Q

Facebook: www.facebook.com/fred.quartlebaumjr

Assistant Basketball Coach: The University of Kansas

Books: *The Positivity Tribe in the Locker Room*

Podcast Episode 274 - Positivity in the Locker Room

Dr. Roy Richmond

Located: Oklahoma City, OK

Email: DrRoyERichmond@cox.net

Website: www.treeoflifeok.com
Professor at www.GlobalGraceSeminary.org
Facebook: www.facebook.com/royerichmond
YouTube: www.youtube.com/channel/UC4Pglv_WlKe-VHZbBsXsiXA
Books: *Living Out of Your Spiritual Resources, Volumes 1 & 2*
No Penal Substitution, Books 1, 2 & 3
You Are the Light of the World
Living As Holy Spirit
The Unforced Rhythm of Life
Simple Answers to What Seem to be Difficult Questions
The Wisdom of the Single Eye; Tree of Life Bible Translations
A Mystical View of Romans; The Wisdom of Spiritually Mindful Counsel
How Esther Became a Star
The Spiritual Code and Symbology of The Living Word, Books 1 & 2
The Woman Within
Podcast Episode 8 – Tree of Life!

Mike Rough

Located: Incline Village, Nevada
Email: mikerough@comcast.net, mikerough@sbcglobal.net
Facebook: www.facebook.com/lawlessgracefellowship,
www.facebook.com/mikerough
LinkedIn: www.linkedin.com/in/mike-rough-40646811/
Bible Class: Law-less Grace Fellowship, Zooming Wednesday evenings at 6 pm PDT.
Radio program: Conversations in Christ, airs 8:30 PDT, Sunday mornings. Available for anytime listening at the
www. conversationsinchrist.com.
Podcast Episodes 229, 231, 233 - Law-less Grace Fellowship

Rasheed Sami

Located: Chicago, Illinois
Email: themotivator4u2@gmail.com
www.facebook.com/rasheed.sami.5,
www.facebook.com/infinitymomentsproductions
Podcast Episode 54 - Giving Grace in the Inner City

George W. Sarris

Located: New York City, New York
Email: worldsgreateststories@gmail.com, George@HeavensDoors.net
Website: www.heavensdoors.net, www.worldsgreateststories.com

Facebook: www.facebook.com/GeorgeWSarris
Blog: www.georgesarris.blogspot.com
YouTube: www.youtube.com/channel/UC1cbeuqovPFhuDS09quUh8g
Book: *Heaven's Doors*
Podcast Episode 66 – Heaven's Doors...Wider Than You Ever Believed!

Charles Slagle

Located: Tucson, Arizona
Email: charlesslagle@hotmail.com
Facebook: www.facebook.com/charles.slagle.3, www.facebook.com/groups/478339185903768
Books: *An Invitation to Friendship*
Abba Calling
From the Father's Hear
Power to Soar
Podcast Episode 14 – From Despair to Joy

Robin Smit

Located: Southern California
Email: robinsmit7@gmail.com, itisfinished.blog@gmail.com
Website: www.robinsmit.com
Blog: www.robinsmit.com/blog
Facebook: www.facebook.com/itisfinished.blog
Books: *It Is Finished*
Awakened
Course: www.iocc.us entitled Full Redemption Practitioner Podcast
Episode 186 – It Is Finished! & Episode 188 – Awakened!

Carolyn Smith

Located: Michigan
Facebook: www.facebook.com/carolyn.smith.9847867,
New Covenant Grace Family: www.facebook.com/groups/236426860185745
Podcast Episode 42 – Grace Changes Lives

Jennifer Smith

Located: Topeka, Kansas
Founder "Grace For Single Parents" Free Affirmations: www.view.flodesk.com/ pages/5fb9884d7f165bdeaa669270
Free Single Mom Survival Kit: www.view.flodesk.com/pages/5fb954dd1cb5fe78f3a2e136

Overwhelmed No More Single Mom Resource Vault $9 (digital): www.graceforsingleparents.com/resource-vault/
Single Mom Prayer Journal: www.graceforsingleparents.com/6-weekprayer-journal/

Malcolm Smith

Located: Bandera, Texas
Email: malcolmsmith.org@gmail.com
Website: www.malcolmsmith.org
Twitter: @malcolmsmith22
Facebook: www.facebook.com/bpmalcolm
LinkedIn: www.linkedin.com/in/malcolm-smith-845731124/
YouTube Channel: www.youtube.com/user/MalcolmSmithWebinars
Podcasts: www.podcasts.apple.com/us/podcast/unconditional-loveinternational-ministry-malcolm-smith/id510973441
Books: *This Son of Mine*
Fear Not Study Guide
The Lost Secret of the NEW COVENANT
Podcast Episode 50 – God IS (not "has") Unconditional Love

Harry Spaight

Located: Miami, Florida
Email: harry@harryspaight.com
Website: www.harryspaight.com, www.sellingwithdignity.com
Facebook: www.facebook.com/harry.spaight
LinkedIn: www.linkedin.com/in/harryspaight/
YouTube: www.youtube.com/channel/UCQsEo5Irz-prm_keMn-QWXQ
Books: *Selling with Dignity*
Podcast Episodes 282 & 284 - Selling with Dignity!

Keith Stanton

Located: Clearwater, Florida
Mission: The Refuge of Clearwater, Inc.
Email: therefuge16@yahoo.com
Facebook: www.facebook.com/therefugeinclearwater, www.facebook.com/kei.ton.18
Podcast Episode 48 – Being Ministered TO by Those Who Are Homeless and Episode 115 – The Refuge!

Brian P. Swift

Located: Burbank, Illinois

Email: bswift62@comcast.net, soar@soarnonprofit.com
Website: www.brianpswift.com, www.soarnonprofit.com
Twitter: @S_O_A_R_nonprof
Facebook: www.facebook.com/SOARnonprofit
LinkedIn: www.linkedin.com/in/brian-p-s-7b2a8010/
Books: *Up: Getting Up is the Key to Life*
Rising Up
The Quadfather
Godly Men Make Godly Fathers
Go Ask Your Dad
Developing True Grit
Podcast Episode 46 – The Quadfather

Wes Tarpley
Located: Richmond, Texas
Twitter: @AddaTman
Facebook: www.facebook.com/wesley.tarpley
LinkedIn: www.linkedin.com/in/wes-tarpley-580b3082/
Podcast Episodes 276, 278, 280 - Poetic Justice Outreach

Mo Thomas
Located: Detroit, Michigan
Facebook: www.facebook.com/mo.thomas.77
LinkedIn: www.linkedin.comin/mo-thomas-354613/
Books: *Into the Abyss*
Online Publication: Elisha's Riddle (contributing author) - www.elishasriddle.com
YouTube: www.youtube.com/channel/UCTGX5CixHtW1WwmtCvHdHg
Podcast: Episodes 176 & 178 A Garden in the Abyss

Bill Thrasher
Located: Atlanta, Georgia
Facebook: www.facebook.com/bthrasherv2.0
LinkedIn: www.linkedin.com/in/bill-thrasher-62980870/
Books: *The Jesus Purpose: Born to Die, Created to Live*
Podcast Episodes 116 & 118 – U.S. Marines, Billy Graham Crusades & Grace and Episodes 333 & 334 - The Jesus Purpose Revisited

Catherine Toon
Located: Colorado Springs, Colorado

Email: info@catherinetoon.com
Website: www.catherinetoon.com
Twitter: @CatherineToonMD
Facebook: www.facebook.com/CatherineToonMD, www.facebook.com/groups/139324283414672
LinkedIn: www.linkedin.com/in/catherine-toon-7a924340/
YouTube: www.youtube.com/channel/UCCqjtcC6dkLRBP-8-6T8EQA
Books: *Marked by Love*
Course: Marked by Love Course www.mbl.catherinetoon.com/saleslanding
Podcast Episodes– Marked by Love! Episodes 321 and 322 Connecting with the God whose love is UNCONDITIONAL!

Stan Tyra

Located: Lancaster, Pennsylvania
Email: styra2157@gmail.com
Facebook: www.facebook.com/stan.tyra
LinkedIn: linkedin.com/in/stan-tyra-b3a810196
Books: *Awakened to Love; The Journey from Beliefs to Awareness* Podcase
Episode 142 – You Can Know the Bible But Not Know God!
Episode 144 – No Room at the Inn of Familiarity

Mark Venable

Located: Murfreesboro, Tennessee
Facebook: www.facebook.com/mark.venable.71
Podcast Episodes 172 & 174 - From Legalism to Grace Parts 1 & 2

Debra Westbrook

Located: Pleasant Hill, California
Website: www.debra-westbrook.ck.page/
Facebook: www.facebook.com/debra.westbrook.1
YouTube: www.youtube.com/channel/UCgzci9qWQrA-dp8jfIeXryw
Podcast Episode 202 – Interview & 204 – Leaving the Echo Chamber of the Mundane Episodes 212 & 214 – Hearing the Sound of God Parts 1&2

Chris Wirth

Located: Greenwich, Connecticut
Email: chris@noquitliving.com
Website: www.noquitliving.com
Twitter: @noquitliving
Facebook: www.facebook.com/cjwirth, www.facebook.com/

NoQuitLiving
LinkedIn: www.linkedin.com/in/christopher-wirth-0071a3198/
YouTube: www.youtube.com/channel/UCMPPrI72nGxtG5cmba7cWjA
Books: *The Positivity Tribe*
The Positivity Tribe in the Locker Room
Podcast Episodes 158 & 160 - The Positivity Tribe

Ron Wright

Located: Exeter, Ontario, Canada
Email: soulwind@live.ca
Facebook: www.facebook.com/soulwind12,
www.facebook.com/SoulwindCreations/
Podcast Episodes 104 & 106 – Ontological Mysticism Parts 1 & 2 and Episodes 327 & 328 - An ocean of ontological light!

Tracey S. Yang

Located: Birmingham, Alabama
Email: www.traceysyang.com/contact/ (Contact submission form on website)
Website: www.traceysyang.com
Twitter: @traceysyang
Facebook: www.facebook.com/profile.php?id=100001865143378
LinkedIn: www.linkedin.com/in/tracey-s-yang-2b9073110/
Books: *Power Up, Super Women* (Co-author)
Podcast Episode 36 — Mercy From Alabama to Japan

Fred Young

Located: Independence, Missouri
Email: fred.young@eschurch.com
Website: www.eschurch.com
Twitter: @PastorFredYoung, @es_church
Facebook: www.facebook.com/fred.young.161446,
www.facebook.com/ eschurch87
YouTube: www.youtube.com/channel/UCvuHmUOlwxzedxAB3qp-j-g
Podcast Episodes 126 & 128 - Recovering Legalistic Pastor!

Wm. Paul Young

Located: Washington
Email: wmpaulyoung@gmail.com
Website: www.wmpaulyoung.com
Blog: www.wmpaulyoung.com/paul-young-blog/

Twitter: @wmpaulyoung

Facebook: www.facebook.com/wmpaulyoung

LinkedIn: linkedin.com/in/wm-paul-young-5497946

Books: *The Shack*

The Shack: Reflections for Every Day of the Year

Crossroads

Crossroads: Reflections

Eve

Lies We Believe About God

The Pastor: A Crisis (With Brad Jersak)

Podcast Episode 64 – Being Yourself is Easy!

Mike Zenker

Located: Waterloo, Ontario, Canada

Sr. Pastor of Hope Fellowship, in Waterloo, Ontario, Canada Hope Fellowship, Your Community Church:

www.hopefellowshipycc.com

Twitter: @mikezenker7

YouTube: www.youtube.com/c/MichaelZenker

Still Growing in Grace - YouTube Playlist: www.bit.ly/2u6pLE8

Weekly Blog: www.mikezenker.blog/

LinkedIn: www.linkedin.com/in/michael-zenker-95b2a917b Podcast

Podcast Episode 16 – Still Growing in Grace!

Anissa Zucker

Located: New Hartford, Connecticut

Email: nissbliss777@gmail.com

Website: kainoseducation.com

Twitter: @nissa360

Facebook: facebook.com/groups/kainoseducation

LinkedIn: www.linkedin.com/in/anissa-zucker-m-ed-94b05123/

YouTube: youtube.com/c/AnissaZuckerKainosEducation777,

youtu.be/tGO5IpVrNgE

Book: *The True Story of Santa Claus*

Podcast Episodes 190 & 192 – Demystifying Mystics Parts 1 & 2

About the Author

Paul Gray is the developer of PURE LIGHT WALKER, an eight-module personal and group mentoring experience. He is the author of two novels (Amazon Best-seller *Convertible Conversations* and *The Fish Net Experience*), the daily inspirational book *Notes From Papa* and *Grace Is ...* He is co-author of *Godly Men Make Godly Fathers*.

Paul Gray is a contemporary mystic who, for many years, has been helping people attain insight into spiritual mysteries transcending ordinary human knowledge. Paul is grounded in Trinitarian Inclusion and focuses on helping people experience direct communication with The Trinity.

He and his wife of fifty-three years, Kitsy, live in Lawrence, Kansas, where they continue to facilitate growing in grace with the group they founded in 1991, New Life in Christ. They have three wonderful grown children and 6 amazing grandchildren!

Paul's career began with his studies at Kansas University in 1965, where he formed his band, the Gaslite Gang, which made several national television performances and recorded five albums. They performed full-time from coast to coast for many years, doing educational concerts and clinics, as well as performing at a variety of venues. He was inducted into the Kansas Music Hall of Fame in 2013 as a member of the Junkyard Jazz Band. Paul owned a variety of businesses, ranging from five retail music stores to a long-distance telephone company, as well as Paul Gray's Jazz Place, a popular Lawrence, Kansas, jazz venue where he performed with his group. Concurrently, he served in the United States Army National Guard and Army Reserves for twenty-four years as a bandmaster.

In 1999, his group started a medical clinic for homeless individuals, The Heartland Medical Clinic, where he was CEO for seven years. It continues to serve the medical needs of thousands of patients each year.

He is the founder and administrator of The Grace Restoration Team, which provides financial and spiritual resources to single parents and their children.

Paul's message "Grace Is UNCONDITIONAL Love In Action"

focuses on helping people experience and enjoy God's love WITHOUT CONDITIONS for all people. He has found that knowing God personally leads to enjoying and experiencing life at a much higher level!

Paul Gray holds an education degree from the University of Kansas and a degree in Grace Theology from Global Grace Seminary.

Paul posts often on Facebook at "Grace to ALL." He hosts a twice-weekly podcast, "Grace to ALL" (with Paul Gray) at www.gracetoall.net, which has over 300 episodes. His musical recordings, spiritual articles, and videos can be found at www.gracewithpaulgray.com

Paul's eight-week online interactive course can be previewed at www.gracewithpaulgray.com/pure-light-walker-8-week-course/.

Contact Information for Paul Gray

Phone: 785.766.3624

Website: www.gracewithpaulgray.com

Twitter: @chiefpaulgray

Facebook: www.facebook.com/paul.gray.37201901

www.facebook. com/groups/gracetoallwithpaulgray

LinkedIn: www.linkedin.com/in/paul-gray-51a99144/

YouTube: www.youtube.com/c/PaulGrayGraceToALL

To donate to The Grace Restoration Team's ministry to single parents and their children, use PayPal and the email gracerestorationteam@gmail.com.

Paul's books are available on Amazon. For signed copies and bulk rates, go to www.gracewithpaulgray.com/books/.

Other Books by Paul Gray

Grace Is ...

In *Grace Is ...*, Paul Gray employs succinct one-page-a-day nuggets about the positive joy experienced by those who 'dance with God' as they go through life's ups and downs, including tragedies like Hurricane Harvey. *Grace Is ...* explains how for the first 300 years after Jesus' death the church believed in the Eternal Conscious Unconditional Love of God for everyone. Gray is part of a rapidly expanding network of people reclaiming that teaching of joy, peace, acceptance, and inclusion and rejecting the distorted religious belief of fearing Eternal Conscious Torment from a fictitious 'angry god.'

Notes From Papa

What do you do when you hear about yet another school shooting, get a bad report from the doctor, or read about hate crimes? We may not be able to stop those things from happening, but there is hope and grace to help and sustain us! You are about to embark on an amazing life-long journey of hearing from God. That's really good news because what you're going to hear is how much God loves you unconditionally; how God delights in you; how much God loves being with you; how proud God is of you, how much God likes you and likes being with you; how God has already included you in His family; how God's amazing grace is continually working in you to empower you to be the wonderful you He created you to be; how you have never been separated from God; how God is into restoration, not punishment; how God's grace has already taken care of everything for your relationship with Him; how God does 'putback,' never 'payback'; how God's good news doesn't contain any bad news; how God is totally good, and there is nothing bad about Him! In *Notes From Papa*, each day you'll enjoy learning how to hear God's voice yourself, and you'll delight in seeing that God is even better than you thought the day before! Join multitudes of people in becoming awakened to who God really is, who they really are, and who all others really are! Hear for yourself via *Notes From Papa!*

Convertible Conversations

Suspense. Intrigue. Hope. Motivation. Inspiration. Romance. Encouragement. 1000-year Hurricane Harvey took the lives of eleven-year-old Jack Miller's parents, moving him from Texas to live with his aging grandparents, who introduced him to love without conditions. In addition to the heart-wrenching grief of suddenly losing both parents, Jack witnesses the horrific murder of a classmate's mother's boyfriend and subsequent chaos. He also experiences fear of losing his grandfather/mentor from a heart attack. There is reason to hope, and God's love is unconditional, meaning there are NO conditions!

Godly Men Make Godly Fathers

A collection of fathers from across the globe sharing and implementing lessons learned through their Christian faith to encourage fathers, children, and families. In this book, several men share their Christian stewardship and values in hopes of spreading the message of love, joy, and family that transcends religion, culture, and generation. *Godly Men Make Godly Fathers* has been the making for decades, and its powerful message will impact and change you.

The Fish Net Experience

An autobiographical novel which takes twenty years of a jazz musician's life and spiritual journey and condenses it into the senior year of a college student/bandleader. It moves from self-centeredness (typical of entertainers) to being grace-centered.

ACKNOWLEDGEMENTS

My very deep thanks and appreciation go to all of the podcast guests on "Grace to ALL" who are featured in this book. They are not only a tremendously important part of the Grace Restoration Team, but they are also heroes of mine, wonderful inspirers and super encouragers. I can't wait for you to connect with them!

Special thanks to those who have partnered with the Grace Restoration Team financially and prayerfully to make it possible to write, compile, edit, and publish *Grace to ALL*!

Special thanks to my friend and publisher Dominick Domasky and his team at Motivation Champs, who are not only first-class publishers but also delightful to work with and great champions of providing inspiration to an ever-growing worldwide audience!

Special thanks to Lisa Wentworth Couture and Melissa Kaye Jarrett, who have contributed their writing and organizational talents and gifts to bring *Grace to ALL* to fruition!

Special thanks to Gene Fritzel, who initially encouraged me to question what I believed and continually reminded me, "Christ is in you, the Hope of Glory." It took me a little over a decade, but Jesus and Gene were very patient with me!

VERY special thanks to Kitsy, my wife of 53+ years, who partners with me in ministry to our family and friends, and who is beautiful in every way. Like her mom, Marie Waggoner, Kitsy truly manifests 'Grace to ALL!'

Words can never convey my thanks and gratitude to Papa, Jesus, and Grace—who have given me (and you) all things for life! I love the Mirror translation of 2 Peter 1:3, "By His divine engineering he gifted us with all that it takes to live life to the full, where our ordinary day to day lives mirror our devotion and romance with our Maker. His intimate knowledge of us introduces us to ourselves again and elevates us to a position where his original intention is clearly perceived!"

Made in the USA
Middletown, DE
13 June 2022

67022449R00186